BOATS
UNLIMITED

Harold Wilson

THE BOSTON MILLS PRESS

Canadian Cataloguing in Publication Data

Wilson, Harold, 1913–
  Boats unlimited

ISBN 0-919783-98-8

1. Wilson, Harold, 1913–   . 2. Motorboat racing – Canada –
Biography. I. Title.

GV835.9.W5A3 1990   797.1'4'092   C90-093885-4

©Harold Wilson, 1990

Published by:
THE BOSTON MILLS PRESS
132 Main Street
Erin, Ontario N0B 1T0
Tel.: (519) 833-2407
Fax: (519) 833-2195

American Association
for State and Local History
Award of Merit

Winners of the
Heritage Canada
Communications Award

Design by John Denison
Cover painting by Kelley Aitken
Cover Design by Gill Stead, Guelph
Edited by Noel Hudson, Guelph
Typography by Lexigraf, Tottenham
Printed by Ampersand, Guelph

The publishers wish to acknowledge the financial assistance and
encouragement of The Canada Council, the Ontario Arts Council and the Office of the Secretary of State.

Contents

The Author – today.

Foreword

I think boats, generally, have more appeal for men than they have for women. The ladies, I fear, are too practical to appreciate men's love for things that float. My wife — a perfect first mate — brought this to my attention by posting the following on the bulkhead of my sloop *Lorna M.*

The difference between men and boys is the cost of their toys.

A boat is a hole in the water surrounded by wood, into which one pours money.   Anonymous

I am the captain of this ship, and I have my wife's permission to say so.   Anonymous

I countered by tacking up this little gem:

The Cardinal Laws of the Sea:
Law No. 1 — The Captain is always right!
Law No. 2 — In the unlikely event of the Captain being proven wrong, Law No. 1 shall apply!

And that, gentlemen, to my mind, sums up the matter.

I dedicate this book to my wife — my racing mechanic, first mate, and navigator — and to the rest of my family, at whose instigation it was written. The writing afforded me great pleasure. I am uncertain as to which part of my boating career, racing or sailing, afforded me the greatest satisfaction. The first is definitely over. The sailing continues and will continue as long as the Good Lord gives me the health and time to go down to the sea in ships.

Harold Wilson

Skipper of the team – Ernie Wilson.

Chapter 1

Beginnings

All boat races start at the drop of a white flag. My first race, and longest, began when the nurse dropped the first diaper on me back on October 14, 1911, in the city of St. Catharines. I haven't finished that one yet. I am counting on doing quite a few more laps before I get the checkered flag.

My father was an Englishman, Ernest Albert Wilson (Erniè to all his friends), a self-taught, self-made mechanical engineer. He was also a very successful businessman. After trying various lines of endeavour in his early years, he settled in the small inland Ontario town of Ingersoll. There he started a manufacturing concern, Wilson & Short, which soon became Ingersoll Machine & Tool Co., Ltd. This company was a large supplier of parts, particularly steering gears, to the rapidly growing automobile industry. After a few years he also gained control of a much older Ingersoll firm, the Morrow Screw & Nut Co. This company was a huge supplier of nuts and bolts, and fasteners of all descriptions, to the automotive industry and to all manufacturing concerns generally. He ran these companies until his retirement, when I took over and did the same until it was my turn to hand the reins over to my first son, Ernie Wilson II.

My mother, Sarah Maude (Walsh), was Canadian born of mixed English and Irish blood. While my father was at all times a very practical person, my mother was anything but. From my father I inherited my great interest in all the mechanical marvels that were being brought into being so rapidly during the early days of the twentieth century. At school in Ingersoll, and later at Ridley College, in my old home town of St. Catharines, my interest increased, so it seemed only natural that I should finish my formal education by training to become a mechanical engineer at the University of Toronto's famous old engineering faculty, the Little Red School House.

Quite early in life I developed an abiding passion for things that float and my lifelong hobby has been the study of all aspects of the design, building, development and operation of boats. My father's pet hobby was cars. He loved driving fast cars and watching others race them. For years he attended the Indy 500 without fail. From him I developed a great interest in the application of the marvels of engineering ingenuity to my own hobby, boats. But at the same time I discovered that something more than pure engineering skill was necessary in the building of successful boats. Besides being an engineer, I also had to be a bit of a dreamer, an artist, and a romanticist. From my father I got the hard facts of life, from my mother I inherited this very necessary something else.

My first love of things nautical was not, in truth, directed at a boat, but rather at a yellow celluloid fish. It may not have been a true boat, but it did float. I have a treasured photograph of myself clad in my all-together, lying prone on the grass beside my little bathtub and playing with the thing. That picture, to me at least, indicates the very beginning of my boating hobby. Another photograph taken just months later, showing me sitting proudly at the wheel of Barney Oldfield's racing car at Indianapolis, provides evidence of my early interest in the internal combustion engine.

Shortly after these pictures were taken, my father, who had been superintendent of the Crocker-Wheeler Co. in St. Catharines, decided to go into business for himself and moved the whole family to Detroit. There he set up a small manufacturing plant on the second floor of a building — only to be put out of business a short while later when the owner of the building, for reasons best known to himself, decided to burn the place down! Leaving Detroit and heading back to his home port of Montreal, my father passed through the small inland Ontario town of Ingersoll. He discovered a small, unused factory building, bought it and established the Ingersoll Machine & Tool Company. That was the beginning of my association with Ingersoll, one that would last without interruption until my retirement from business in 1972.

As I said, Ingersoll is an inland town, the nearest large body of navigable water being Lake Erie, some 30 miles to the south. But the town is not without water. It is situated on the banks of the Thames River, a quite impressive stream to my young eyes. In those early days there was even a steamer that plied certain stretches of the Thames (it sank one day, after hitting a sand bar, I believe). Besides the river, Ingersoll also had three sizable ponds. These were Smith's Pond, Carroll's Pond and Memorial Park Pond. So although our connection with the Great Lakes System was 30 miles away, there was enough of the wet stuff around to make a person think of boats and man's way with them.

In 1919 our family spent a winter vacation at St. Petersburg, Florida. There I rode in my first real motorboat. Granted it only had a one-lunger engine and it didn't go very fast, but it did take our party out into the Gulf of Mexico, where during that well-remembered day we caught 300 pounds of fish! Although I caught a few of those 300 pounds, the real thrill for me was having my father explain how that big, noisy hunk of iron in the centre of the boat propelled us all day and got us home safely that night. This experience really whetted my appetite for boats and engines — I was hooked!

Our winter holiday in Florida brought me into contact with yet another user of engines, the aeroplane. My father found out that even in 1919-20, there was a flying service there, so one day we contacted Johnny Jones, the owner, and arranged to be taken up in his two-place, open cockpit, sea-going biplane. When my turn came, it was decided that I should go up with my father, sitting on his knee. An open cockpit and no seat belt for me? A great way to take my first aeroplane ride! Off we went. Being a seaplane, until it left the water, it was just a boat ride, but a very fast one. Soon, with a shake like a dog shedding water, the old pusher biplane got itself off the water and up into its natural element. What a thrill that was! There was the whole of St. Petersburg laid out below me, just like a big map. The flight was short, 15 minutes, but I enjoyed all of it. Boats were still tops in my estimation, but these flying boats were something else!

We had driven all the way from Ingersoll to St. Pete in our sporty Cadillac tourer. It was an open, eight-passenger car with a convertible-type rag top. And it was fast, about the fastest production car of its day. It was a great trip, but dusty, as most of the roads were not yet paved. To avoid all the dust on the return, my father loaded us and the car onto an ocean liner headed for New York. Great, I thought, more boats! About all I remember from that trip — apart from my numberless rush trips for the rail, "Always to windward," cried Father — was the time my mother tried to use her 110-volt travelling iron on the ship's 32-volt system and blew out the cabin fuses, luckily located in our cabin. My father, not wanting to incur the captain's wrath, and fearing a possible sojourn in the brig, quickly made a fuse out of several strips of metal-foil gum wrappers and shoved it in. It worked! Perhaps it didn't live up to marine safety codes, but it worked.

Back home in Ingersoll after an exciting winter, I was ready for more watery experiences. An early spring brought the first one. As soon as the Thames was free of ice, a friend and I launched our homemade raft on the icy waters and took off on a journey of adventure. It didn't amount to much in distance or time. In fact, somehow our engineering failed. The raft wouldn't bear our weight, turned over rapidly, and we had to jump for safety on the river bank. We landed in a bed of stinging nettles! Undaunted, I next tried a canoe ride on Smith's Pond with another friend. This was better. We had a reasonably good, slightly crab-wise trip halfway across the pond before we upset and had to swim for shore. Luckily I had learned to swim during my stay in the sunny south that winter. We found out that, although a very fine craft in the hands of an expert, a canoe can be pretty tricky transportation for a couple of tyros!

Our church in Ingersoll had a quite large, and good, boys' choir, which I joined at the age of eight (I finally retired from active choir work in 1984). One of the privileges of singing in the choir was the chance to attend choir camp at Port Burwell, a small fishing village on the shores of Lake Erie. Open water at last! Port Burwell was the Canadian terminus for a large transport ship which made twice-daily trips across the lake, carrying loaded railway coal cars from the mines of Pennsylvania to Canada. It was also the home for a fleet of about eight steam-powered fishing tugs. Our campsite, being near the harbour, provided me with many opportunities to witness at close hand the daily comings and goings of the coal transport, *Astabula*, and the more spasmodic operations of the fishing fleet. The *Astabula* was viewed from a distance, mostly, as the captain took a very dim view of young lads running all over his ship. But I did wangle an invitation to go aboard one day, and, believe me, I took it! For a coal transport, the *Astabula* had very pleasing lines. The hull, some 200 feet or more in length, was jet black with snowy-white upper works. I was shown the engine room with its large twin steam engines, and the bridge with its rows of gleaming, and to me incomprehensible, instruments. The loaded coal cars were run in on rails through the stern, which opened up to allow entry to the bowels of the ship. I spent several happy hours watching the skilful manner in which the captain handled his ship in harbour. He would steam headfirst into the harbour and back into the railway unloading dock. If the wind was strong and adverse, this operation was sometimes done with the aid of a steel cable fastened between the ship and a bollard on dockside.

This operation was responsible for a very nasty accident that happened while I was there. A shore hand had just made fast the steel cable to the bollard when a sudden swing of the ship caused by the wind tightened the cable like a bowstring, and it snapped! The released cable whipped about like an angry cobra, and the poor shore hand was swept off his feet. He was terribly mangled and later lost a leg.

To recover from this sad and unsettling experience, I spent many hours down at the fishery docks. The eight tugs were all pretty much of a size, about 80 feet long, but varied considerably in design. My favourite was *The Winner*, a rather sleek-looking white ship trimmed with red and with quite a gaudy stack. As Lake Erie can be very rough at times, all of these fishing boats had foredecks that were at least partially protected from the seas. One of them was completely decked in from the cabin roof, which ran right out to the bow, to a point about halfway to the stern. While perhaps effective, this feature was far from pretty. I believe that it was a minor form of the whaleback freighters that were used on the Great Lakes at that time. The fishing fleet made three trips a week and sold their catch both locally and in nearby towns and cities. There was lots to see: the boats getting up steam for the trip, the excitement of bringing in a big catch, and the smelly but interesting process of cleaning the catch for market. Then there were nets to be dried, repaired, and stored for the next trip.

One day, the captain of *The Winner*, having seen me hanging around for days on end, invited me to go for a day's fishing with them. What a thrill! We left at sun-up the next morning and sailed for quite a distance before reaching the first fishing ground. The whole day was work, work, work: casting and pulling in nets, storing the fish on ice in large tanks, and grabbing a sandwich (well flavoured with fish) and a beer. I had lots of new experiences that day, including the beer. I didn't think much of it then, and I still don't. The men were equipped for rough weather, with rubber boots and oilskins. I had on shorts and running shoes. The real thrill for me was when the engineer invited me to come down to the engine room to see what made the ship tick. The power plant was a four-cylinder vertical steam engine. It was giving off a delicious aroma of hot oil, hissing steam and burning coal. It made a lot of noise also, boxed in as it was in the very small engine room. I was goggle-eyed as the engineer tended his charge's every need to keep it working at maximum efficiency. I guess my hero worship was showing, and the engineer, with a sly grin, put on a show for my benefit. The engine was an open-crankcase job; the cylinder head, with its pistons and steam chest, was connected to the crankshaft (mounted in the lower engine frame containing the main bearings) by six long struts. The rest of the engine was wide open, so one could see all the innards working like mad. The four connecting rods flashed up and down and around, and were matched by other rods which operated steam valves and pumps and all sorts of interesting things. The engineer, with the remark "Well, I must see if the old girl is not getting too hot," plunged his hand and arm right into the middle of those flashing steel things and grabbed hold of one of the connecting rods! His arm flashed madly up and down until I thought that it would be torn off. But no, he knew what he was doing, both with the engine and the ten-year-old lad watching him. "Fine," he said, "just about the right temperature." He eased his arm out to safety, and I breathed again. The captain even let me steer *The Winner* for a while on the way back to Port Burwell. By late afternoon, when we got in, I had had enough fishing for one day, so I skipped the fish-gutting, wash-down period and headed back to camp. Boy, did the baked beans and weiners taste good that night!

Two years later, I had graduated from choir camp to the Boy Scout camp near Port Dover, also on Lake Erie. Here I learned quite a bit about the fine craft that the Indians had invented and passed on to us. Up until then my canoe experience had been confined to light 14-footers. Now, at Fisher's Glen Camp, I was given a paddle and assigned a seat in one of the camp's 14-passenger war canoes. There were also monster 20-man canoes for the experienced paddlers. I spent a few days learning how to paddle, and how to do it in rhythm with the other paddlers and the shouted orders of the coxswain. That under my belt, the day came when I was moved up to the big boats. It was a real thrill to be aboard one of these canoes as it sped through the water in a race with three other similar craft. I still had lots to learn about canoes, but this Fisher's Glen experience went a long way in making me aware of the possibilities of the canoe.

Jumping ahead nearly half a century, it was in far-off New Zealand that I saw the largest war canoe ever built. It was a ceremonial war canoe 120 feet long! It was beautifully carved out of one tree trunk and it carried 150 men (80 warriors and 70 paddlers). It must have been quite a sight to see that long canoe flash across the waters of the bay.

I guess the excitement over the boats and the tremendous amount of sunshine that I absorbed while out on the water were just a bit too much for me. I came down sick and was sent to hospital with a bad dose of sunstroke. This was a bad time to have this problem, as I was slated to become a boarder student at Ridley College, a famous Canadian boys' boarding school located in my old home town of St. Catharines. I was entered all right, but I spent my first two weeks there in the school's "pest house" trying to get the sun out of my eyes.

Ridley is located on the banks of the first Welland Canal, the important waterway built by Canada to allow passage of ocean-going ships from the St. Lawrence River and Lake Ontario to the upper Great Lakes, and thence right into the middle of the North American continent. The first canal was no longer in use at the time that I attended Ridley. It had been replaced by the new Welland Canal, much larger and located just a couple of miles east of the school. The old canal carried no boat traffic whatsoever, but I was able to make several trips to the new one and spent many happy hours at one or other of the huge locks, watching the tremendous lake freighters as they passed on their way to the lakehead or to the Atlantic Ocean. I wasn't able to board one of these freighters or the occasional passenger ships that used the canal, but it was fun and a great way of adding to my knowledge, just to see them, learn from which countries they hailed, and dream of the day when I would be able to travel around the world in one of them.

16

Chapter 2

My First Boat

The summer of 1925 started out tragically for the Wilson family. My younger brother, Ernie, just turned four, while riding his tricycle one evening, shot unexpectedly and unseen up our driveway, right under the wheels of our own car, and was killed. A deep and gloomy sense of loss hit the household. Hoping to lighten this load, my father suggested an extended holiday for the whole family. We headed for a place we hadn't visited before, the Muskoka Lakes, probably Canada's greatest vacation-land. This area of numberless clear, cold lakes, thousands of islands, rivers and streams, and dark green pine forests is located about 125 miles north of Toronto. We went to the largest lake of all, Lake Muskoka, to the little village of Beaumaris, and settled in for a month's stay at the Beaumaris Hotel. Well, we ate breakfast and dinner there, and slept there, but the rest of each day was spent at nearby Keewaydin Island.

This island was inhabited by a fair number of Ingersoll families, amongst them the Hargans. Ed Hargan was superintendent of the Morrow Screw & Nut Co., in Ingersoll, and my father was its manager. Ed had three lovely daughters and a son. But far more important, he owned three boats! The largest of these, a family launch named *Weyburn*, was reserved entirely for the adults. The other two, a rowing skiff and an unusual motorboat called a Disappearing Propeller Boat, were available to the Hargan children. As son Al and I were already bosom pals, this meant that I too had access to a real motorboat for the first time.

I'll describe the Disappearing Propeller Boat for the benefit of younger readers. You may be lucky enough to see one of these fine craft chugging its way across the lake. You may even be very lucky and wangle a ride in one. The Disappearing Propeller Boat, D.P., or as it was affectionately known to all admirers, the Dippy, was a most satisfactory all-purpose boat. First of all, it was safe. The inventor, Billy Johnston of Port Carling, advertised it as "the safest boat ever built." To prove his statement he published a picture of a standard 16-footer putting along serenely with a crew of 19 fully grown men! Leg room was in short supply, but there still was a bit of freeboard. The Dippy was easily handled and, being slow, could not be considered dangerous. The standard hull was 16 feet long, pointed both ends, and of lapstrake construction. The engine was a single-cylinder, two-stroke, water-cooled type boasting 5 to 7 horse-power. To drive the boat, the engine was connected to a thing which the inventor called a "device," which was in turn connected to the shaft, which had at its outer end, under water, a propeller to do the shoving. Now this device was just that. It was a long metal housing which allowed the shaft to pass through — the shaft being in two pieces joined in the middle by a universal joint. This universal meant that the second half of the shaft, plus the propeller, did not have to stay in line with the first half. The outer end of the shaft passed through a hole in a skeg, which protected the propeller. When this skeg hit anything, it promptly pushed the propeller up into a waterproof metal box at the tail end of the device. As the propeller was then above the bottom of the hull, it had disappeared, hence the name "disappearing propeller boat." This was first of all a very important safety precaution, but it also had other purposes — or perhaps I should say attributes, as I am almost sure that Billy Johnston didn't really design them into his invention. As the engine and propeller were direct-connected without the use of clutch or reverse gear, this meant that all the time the engine was running, the boat was in forward motion. Or it would be, unless the operator made use of a hand lever which, if raised, did exactly the same thing as hitting a rock: the propeller came up into that magic box at the end of the device and all motion ceased. Well, almost. Although this acted as a neutral gear for a short time, soon the operator would find his craft drifting astern with a slight bit of crabbing to port. Well, this was good too, in a way. Given patience and control, one could bring the D.P. to a reasonably controlled stop, even reverse, just a bit. In the hands of an expert a sudden stopping of forward motion and a full-power reverse could be effected. This was done by cutting the ignition switch off and just before the engine stopped, turning the switch on again. A peculiarity of the two-stroke engine is that it will run forwards or backwards. So if the operator was adroit enough, the D.P. was suddenly in reverse, and full power if need be. The resultant stop was sudden and satisfactory. But it could be tricky. Running in reverse tended to unscrew the packing gland of the shaft log, which allowed just enough of Lake Muskoka into the boat to sink it!

Recently, and probably due in great measure to the public's interest in antique and classic boats, the Dippy has once again become very popular. Most of the D.P.s appearing at antique boat shows have been lovingly and superbly restored to their original pristine condition. They afford the boating enthusiasts of the present generation a real opportunity to become acquainted with this wonderful little boat.

The Hargan D.P. was affectionately known as *Flaming Youth* — not that there was much youth about her, nor was she hot enough to flame. But she was a boat, she had a motor that worked, and she was ours to use. Al and I used her as much as possible (consistent with his three sisters' partial rights) and we explored as much of Lake Muskoka as we could.

Later that summer came a wonderful day. My father, up from his work in Ingersoll for a weekend with the family, said, "Well, Harold, let's go up to Port Carling and have a look at some of the new boats." Port Carling was the home of the Dippy, so naturally I felt that we were headed for the Disappearing Propeller Boat factory. On the way Father said, "I think we will buy a boat for ourselves." I was thrilled no end, but confused when we walked right by the D.P. factory without even stopping. Why, I thought we would be getting a new standard 16-footer at least, maybe even one of the super-deluxe 18-footers with striped mahogany deck and the great big 10-horsepower twin-cylinder engine. If not a D.P., just what new boat could my father be thinking about?

We went into Port Carling Boat Works on the Lake Rosseau side of the locks and had a ride in one of their brand-new Sea-Birds. What a boat! It was an 18-footer, lapstrake, with glistening mahogany decks. For power it had a four-cylinder Universal Flexifour engine which would cough out 15-horse-power. It had upholstered seats, one in the stern, one in the middle where the driver sat, and a bow cockpit. These three seats could hold eight people at a squeeze. After a short ride we went back to the factory, talked a bit, my father produced his chequebook, and we were the proud possessors of a new Port Carling SeaBird. D.P.'s? What were they?

I was ready to jump right in and drive it home — but not so. First of all there were some finishing details to be completed. The boat would be ready on Monday, and this was only Saturday, Also, it seemed that I had to take a course of instruction before I would be allowed to take the boat out by myself.

I was up there early on Monday morning. First I was taught how to operate the boat. Then I was drilled on the rules of the road. Then came a lecture on the care of the boat, the engine, and all the other bits and pieces. Then came instruction in knotting and splicing of ropes. All this took hours — or so it seemed. But finally I was told to take the boat out by myself, drive it around the bay, and bring it back and land it. Easy! Well, that is what I thought, but the landing bit almost did it. After three tries I got her tied up properly to the dock, and I was given my papers.

Very carefully, and slowly, I took my new boat through the lock and into the Indian River on my way to Lake Muskoka. My boat? Well, of course the rest of the family can ride in it, but it's mine, isn't it? Finally I got back to Keewaydin and was welcomed by my family, Al Hargan, and all the rest of the Ingersoll people there. I certainly was a very lucky and very proud boy that day. The new boat made our daily trips between Beaumaris and Keewaydin faster, more enjoyable and cheaper. After all, we didn't have to pay for a water taxi ride every day. The cost of the boat? Well.

Al Hargan and I drove the SeaBird as much as possible. I found out everything I could about the performance of the Sea-Bird, in good conditions and foul. I also found out that a careful driver keeps his eyes open all of the time. I hit a large deadhead floating almost submerged, and bounced over it. Luckily the only real damage was to my pride. I covered many, many miles, explored the Muskoka Lakes, and used up a great deal of gasoline. But all good things come to an end, and Labour Day was that end. Back to Ridley College I went, and the SeaBird went back to Port Carling to be stored for the winter months.

That winter at Ridley seemed endless — not that I didn't enjoy school, but what were we going to do next summer? We had a boat but no place to live where the boat was located, unless we went back to the hotel at Beaumaris. My father had ideas. One of the houses on Keewaydin, owned by an old Ingersoll widower, Ed Hugill, was vacant, and my father rented it for the whole summer. So as soon as I was finished at Ridley, and my two sisters were finished public school for the summer, we moved up to Muskoka and into Mr. Hugill's house. The very day that we arrived there, so did our boat. It certainly was great to get behind the wheel once again.

Along with the obtaining of a cottage for the summer, we also acquired two new boats. The first was a 14-foot skiff, or rowboat. The second was a fine 14-foot, canvas-covered canoe. Both of these were excellent craft and afforded a means of learning much about the basics of water travel. Both were excellent, but I certainly leaned towards the canoe. The skiff was all right, but I always felt that I wanted to see where I was going, and after all, you do row a skiff backwards. So I concentrated on the canoe and left the skiff to my two sisters.

That summer, good things came aplenty. No sooner had I begun to accustom myself to the new boats, and brushed up on the operation of our motorboat, when my father announced that we were going to get a new, faster motorboat! Less than a year ago I had been wondering if I would ever have the chance to have a boat of my very own, and now I was about to get my second one! So up to Port Carling again with my father to see the new models. The one that we liked best was the new SeaBird — smooth-skin hull (rather than lapstrake, or clinker-built, like our present boat), with brilliant mahogany decks and a windshield. The seating arrangement was similar to our last-year's model, but it had a larger engine, a full 25 horsepower. The demonstration run proved that this was a considerably faster boat, carried a load better, and was much more easily handled. As it was quite obvious that I was more than pleased, my father got out his handy chequebook once again, and a few minutes later we were on the way home in our new boat, which I promptly named *Ridley*.

To make the family's enjoyment even more complete, we acquired an aquaplane. To modern-day water-ski addicts, the old-fashioned aquaplane is tame and antique. Be that as it may, I can tell you that all of Keewaydin's young people had a ball that summer riding our aquaplane behind *Ridley*. And being towed at better than 20 miles per hour occasioned many hard and long-remembered spills, chills and thrills. (I firmly believe that at the end of a 50-foot tow rope, and negotiating a full-speed, full-rudder turn, the terminal speed attained by a skilful aquaplane operator is higher than that attained on skis under the same conditions.)

With the help of the new boat, Al Hargan and I established and ran a business that summer. It was known as the Keewaydin Supply Company. Three days a week we travelled to Port Carling to purchase supplies to fill orders that we had been given by the cottagers the night before. We got a 10-percent discount from all the local merchants and charged our customers a further 5 percent for prompt and courteous delivery. This may not sound like much to present-day vacation workers, but remember this: we had no overhead, we used my boat for pick-up and delivery, and my father supplied all the gasoline. Every penny was clear profit — except for the losses due to dropping a few things into the lake once in a while. Even that wasn't all loss; we passed off most of the dunked stuff, sans labels of course, on our long-suffering mothers. We made enough profit in the first month of operation to buy ourselves a sailboat.

This was a partnership deal. The boat was an old 20-foot catboat with one big lug sail carried on a mast mounted well forward on the deck. The man that sold her to us, Tom Wroe, God bless his soul, said, "She is sound, but may leak a little." A little? She took on water faster than we could bail it out! After having done all the normal things to eliminate this problem, without success, Al and I gave her a heavy bottom coating of tar below the waterline and christened her *Black Bottom*. Al and I knew absolutely nothing about the fine art of sailing, but we were anxious to learn. So, in between canoeing and motor-boating, we spent quite a bit of time learning all possible about *Black Bottom* and how sailboats operate. We found out, for instance, that you don't jibe (we broke our mast off at the deck trying it) and you don't run over reefs (we got our heavy steel centreboard caught firmly between rocks when we tried it). When we finally did get out of that mess, we found that we couldn't raise the centreboard. It was bent into an "L" shape. We cut quite a picture that afternoon, trying to sail home like a crab! But we also learned a lot about the proper things to do when sailing. We got this experience partly from friendly sailors like Art Fry (also a Keewaydin man), but mainly from the school of hard knocks.

Naturally, that summer I also spent a lot of time learning all that I could about *Ridley*. I learned how to tune up and adjust the big Buchanan Bulldog engine to give absolutely maximum speed. Having found out how fast I could go, I now went around looking for other boats to race. I found that my boat was faster than quite a few, could hold its own with others, but could be severely trounced by many of the bigger craft. Hearing that some boat races were to be staged at the Muskoka Lakes Regatta in

Lake Rosseau, I decided to go and see if I could get into a race. As I wasn't sure what the family would think of this idea, I said nothing. I grabbed Al as my racing mechanic, and we found our way up through the Port Carling locks and on to the Muskoka Lakes Country Club, where the regatta was to be held. And, yes, there was a race for 25-horsepower boats. There were quite a few races listed for many sizes of boats, from the lowly D.P.'s up to monsters like Fred Burgess' *Mowitza*, a 200-horsepower Ditchburn. I watched several races, trying to understand what the drivers did to keep ahead, how they handled the turns, when somebody yelled, "Hey, Ridley, you are in the next race." Boy, did I get the five-minute-gun jitters!

Then Al and I were out at the starting line with about eight other entrants. This was a standing-start race. Funny how hard it is to keep a boat motionless and in place while you wait hours (it seems) for that starting gun to be fired. But finally it did boom out, and we were off. The course was an oval one and went around a couple of small islands. We had to do three laps. Right away I found that my boat had a bit of an edge on the others. Great stuff, isn't it, Al? We were enjoying it so much that I made a miscue at one turn and dropped back to fifth place. That would never do! Halfway around the third and last lap, I had recovered the lost ground and moved back into the lead on the home stretch. The next thing we knew, they were waving a big checkered flag at us as we crossed the finish line. What a thrill that was — my first race and I came home a winner!

In retrospect, I wonder what might have happened if I had come last that time? Might I have quit the racing game there and then and saved myself and many others a great deal of worry and expense? I don't think so.

When we got back to Keewaydin we met frowning faces. "Well, where have you been all day?" This changed in a moment when they saw our grinning faces and the beautiful trophy lying on the cockpit seat. We received congratulations when we told our story — especially from my father. He had been a bicycle racer in Montreal in his youth, so he knew all about the racing game. I was just starting out on a racing career that would last for many years, and I certainly valued the encouragement that I received from my father that day.

Chapter 3

Racing Days

That first win changed my whole outlook. For the first time I began to take a serious look at boat racing. I guess I didn't appreciate all the hard work, disappointment and tremendous expense that faced me, and my backer, if I was to make a success of this new hobby. If I had been told just what was in store, I might have picked something less demanding.

The three main lakes, Muskoka, Joseph and Rosseau, with their clear, deep and expansive areas, their hundreds of islands, the absence of dangerous shoals and rocks, and the shelter from high winds provided by the rocky, pine-rimmed shores, are in my opinion the best boating waters this world has to offer. The sheer beauty of its water, trees and rocks makes Muskoka absolutely breathtaking, And the best way to see all this beauty is at the wheel of a good boat. With all this beauty waiting to be seen, is it any wonder that this same Muskoka area saw the creation of literally thousands of the most beautiful boats in the world? Clever boat designers and builders became synonymous with Muskoka, men like Herb Ditchburn, Bryson Shields and his partner Bill Minnett, Tom Greavette, and Doug Van Patten. And there was a host of others — Billy Johnston of Dippy fame, Barnes, Purdy, Milner, McCulley, Duke, Skinner . . . .

The summer of 1927 was another banner period for us Wilsons. My father bought the old cottage that we had rented from Ed Hugill — Uncle Ed, or Mister Muskoka, as he was sometimes called — and had it torn down and replaced by a new, modern one. It was ready for us when we moved up to Muskoka on the first of July. My father liked my little SeaBird all right but felt that the new house demanded something a bit more impressive in the way of a boat, so that summer we also acquired a 28-foot Ditchburn Viking powered with a large 200-horsepower Kermath engine. This was a hydroplane — that is, there was a transverse step in the running bottom which tended to lift the boat out of the water, reduced the wetted area and thus increased the speed. It was capable of about 45 miles per hour. But being a very heavy hull, the speed was not great enough to make it a serious contender in races with other similar-powered craft. Although I did race the *Miss Canada* once that summer, I stuck with my little old *Ridley*, winning the 25-horsepower class at both the Muskoka Lakes Regatta and one held at Bala on Lake Muskoka.

I was now becoming familiar with the many sizes and types of boats that were being built in Muskoka, and elsewhere, of course. But as I always claimed the best were built right here at home, I concentrated on the home products. The choice was large and quite catholic. At the bottom of the list — but definitely not to be sneezed at — was the lowly Dippy. Round-bottomed utility boats and hard chine or planing hulls were in the same category. All of these were powered by various sized inboard engines, or even by the new light outboards now making their appearance. One could move up to small, medium, and large family runabouts. These could be round-bottomed (if so, they usually were very long and slender, and cut through the waters with very little fuss, though their speed capability was limited) or they could be built as hard-chined planing hulls with much more interesting performances. The ultimate in pleasure craft was the cruiser. This could be a day cruiser, meaning that it would provide everything needed for day-long pleasure cruising, or it could have all the facilities of home and be used for day, overnight, weekly, or as-long-as-one-liked cruising. And there was one more class: the out-and-out racer. This was my cup of tea!

The racers were of several different classifications. The first was the racing runabout, a light, ultra-fast version of the popular "gentleman's runabout." It was almost always of very flat vee-bottom construction (there were early round-bottom hulls of course, built before the vee-bottom became popular) and was built and powered for top performance. These were generally inboard powered, but there were some outboards in this category also. Then came the hydroplanes, the ultimate in high-speed water travel. Essentially, a hydroplane, or hydro, as it is known today, is a very shallow vee-bottomed hull with a step in the bottom transversely across and about midships. As I mentioned when describing *Miss Canada*, the reason for this step is to reduce the wetted area, the area of the bottom which is supporting the boat as it travels at speed. The more the wetted area can be thus reduced, the higher the speed possible. The step itself can take a multitude of forms. The first and simplest step is the transverse amidship type. There can also be two or more steps spaced more or less evenly from bow to stern. Two or three steps would be called two- or three-step hydros, but if more steps are used, the hull is said to be shingle-bottomed. There were quite a few of these built.

From here on all sorts of things happened to the step. An early one, not really a step hull, although it did accomplish the same desired effect of reducing wetted area and thus drag, was the Higgins Sea Sled. In effect this was a displacement hull which was split end to end down the keel line, and then the two halves put together the wrong way round! This produced a vee-bottom with the vee contained between the two vertical sides (the hull was now rectangular in shape with no curvature of the sides fore or aft). The wetted area was reduced because the vee shape forced water, and air, under pressure into this vee-shaped hull-length tunnel, thus forcing the boat out of the water. The modern-day, popular sports racing hull, the tunnel boat, is an adaptation of the Sea Sled design. Another was the Hydrodome, developed by Alexander Graham Bell and his partner, Casey Baldwin. This was a stepped hull with a difference. The hull itself could actually be a round-bottom type or a modified vee-bottom, but the step was where the difference came in. Actually there were two steps, one about a third of the hull length from the bow, the other right at the stern. The front step was cut in two, each half mounted on strong streamlined struts and rigidly fastened, one on each side of the hull. The second step (usually in one piece, but it could be split like the bow step) was mounted right at the transom, either in the centre (if it was one piece) or one on each corner of the transom (if it had been split in two). Now these steps were mounted quite some distance below the hull. As the hydrodome moved forward, it was at first supported entirely by the bottom of the hull, but as speed increased, the planing action of the submerged steps, fore and aft, lifted the whole boat completely off the water, thus reducing the wetted area dramatically. This brought about a great increase in speed. Back when Casey Baldwin was testing the Hydrodome, he attained the then staggering speed of 62 mph with, I believe, just a 200-horsepower engine. The present-day hydrofoil — now jet propelled to further reduce drag by doing away with the underwater propeller — is to be seen in operation all over the world.

Another interesting invention was the original Ventnor bottom. Although there were no transverse steps, this hull did have a series of longitudinal steps. As speed increased, the hull rose out of the water, from one step to another. Naturally this reduced drag and increased the speed, but as the running surface presented to the water got narrower every time the boat climbed onto another step, I would think that the boat would have become less and less stable.

The later Ventnor hydro, the three-pointer, then came along. It was a very popular and very successful racing machine. Again the step was cut in two (as with the Hydrodome) and one half fastened to each side and well forward of amidships. But unlike the Hydrodome, and more like the original transverse-step hydro, the step was just a few inches lower than the bottom of the hull. At high speed the boat was supported by the two steps, or sponsons, as they were called, and the stern at the transom. This is where the name "three-pointer" came from.

In the late forties, the present type of hydroplane racing hull was invented. This was really just a further development of the three-pointer. The longitudinal balance of the hull around the sponsons, as the balance point, was carefully calculated so that, although the transom did offer some support at low speed, very quickly, and as speed increased, the stern lifted completely off the water, the shaft line came up to the surface, thereby making available for forward motion the full power of the engine and propeller. The boat became what is now known as a "prop-rider." This is because the stern of the boat is now supported by the propeller — actually only half the propeller, as the shaft lies on the surface while the upper half of the propeller rotates in air. This would seem to indicate a great loss in propulsive effort. It does increase the percentage of slip, a measure of the efficiency of the propeller (the higher the slip, the lower the efficiency) but actually something very different takes place. It has been proven that more forward motion is produced by the bottom half of the rotation of the propeller than by the top half. So it was reasoned that with half the propeller out of water, the engine should be able to turn a propeller twice as large as one that would be fully submerged. And as the bottom half is better, so is the speed. There is a great deal more to it, but that is the basic principle.

Both the three-pointer and the prop-rider channel great volumes of air down between the sponsons. Being under considerable pressure, this air lifts the boat even further off the water, and it is said to be partially airborne. This, of course, reduces the drag further still, with a consequent further increase of speed. One unfortunate characteristic of the prop-rider is that it can be quite unstable. In effect, the bottom between the sponsons is like the underside of the wing of a fast-moving aeroplane. In normal condition the bottom is almost parallel to the water surface, but let something throw the bow up considerably, and suddenly the air pressure on the surface of the boat's bottom, now pointing towards the sky, can, and often does, cause the boat to leap clean out of the water, even do a back somersault.

So the calculated design, while making the prop-rider the fastest racing boat in the world today, also makes it a very dangerous one.

Chapter 4

Early Race Boats

I had heard that a couple of very fast outboard hydros, called (in Canada only) "Sea Fleas," had made their appearance on our Muskoka Lakes. I hadn't seen them and really wasn't very interested, but one day I heard the loud roars of two powerful, high-revving engines, and they seemed to be approaching Keewaydin. Sure enough, when I ran out onto the dock, I could see two tiny specks flying across the water at incredible speed — and headed right for where I was standing. A minute later two tiny cockle-shells pulled up at our dock and stopped. The boats were named *PDQ* and *Applesauce*. The two drivers climbed up onto the dock and introduced themselves. Fred Hauserman, from Ohio owned *PDQ*, and *Applesauce* was piloted by a Canadian, Bill Freyling. Seems that they had come with the express purpose of trying to get me interested in outboard racing and in the purchase of one of these very fast boats, so the two started to give me a thorough indoctrination. The hulls were the same, Hurricane model, made in Peterborough. They were 9 feet long, about 4½ feet beam and weighed in at around 120 pounds. They had quite large cockpits for such a small craft — in fact, except for the fragile but very light deck, they were all cockpit. This meant that a passenger could be carried along with the pilot; a squeeze, certainly, but possible. Present racing craft of this type have very narrow cockpits, just sufficient for a slim pilot driving in the kneeling position.

The Hurricane was a hydroplane, and, as such, my first introduction to this type of boat, a type that would be my choice for practically all of my racing days. It was of the original transverse-step configuration. The stern, or transom, was quite broad, actually as wide as any part of the hull. This provided the necessary bottom area to keep the boat from sinking stern-first when at rest and when the heavy engine was fastened onto the transom. One had to be very careful to keep one's weight well forward when starting the engine. The engine itself was a dream, the mighty Johnson four-cylinder, which boasted the highest horse-power available in an outboard motor at that time, 32 raring horses!

Fred Hauserman then asked me if I would like to go for a ride. Silly question: I thought he would never ask! Quickly donning the proffered life jacket, I stepped very gingerly into *PDQ*. I lay on one hip and hung onto the rear end of the deck to allow enough room for Fred to fit in beside me. He stood up, cranked the engine, and like a bullet out of a gun, we were off. Boy, could that boat go! No wonder he called it *PDQ*: it certainly was Pretty Damn Quick! It seemed no time at all until we were pulling up at our dock after having gone all the way round Keewaydin.

After he and Freyling had answered my many questions, I put forword one more. Would they let me take one of the hydros out for a spin by myself? Fred said, "Sure, go ahead." When I stepped into the cockpit this time, it seemed vastly different. Standing up and facing the engine, I discovered that water was just begin-ning to come over the transom. "Lean back or you'll sink," yelled Fred. Getting myself properly positioned — near enough to the engine to start it and far enough forward to keep *PDQ* from becoming the first outboard-powered submarine — I listened carefully to the detailed instructions for starting. First, open the release charger. This was a lever that opened two of the cylinders to the air and which, by thus killing the compression in these two cylinders, made it possible to pull the long starting cord wound round the flywheel. Next, advance spark lever to half position and set hand throttle to one-third open. The engine, being hot, would not need choking this time. Then, get a good hold on the starter rope and pull like hell! Wow! It started first pull! Very quickly I turned around, flopped down onto my side, and grabbed the steering wheel. That was when I discovered that you had to be an accomplished one-arm driver! It was a case of left hand on the squeeze throttle and right hand on the wheel. What a ride I had! It was a strange feeling, rather like riding on a shingle being pulled through the water at high speed, and just about out of control. The steering was very quick indeed. Until I got the hang of it, my wake looked like the passage of a very big and very lively snake. When I felt that I was more or less in control of this lively little Sea Flea, I squeezed the throttle wide open. Holy smoke! *PDQ* shot ahead — this time out of control, for sure. But this experience was what I wanted, so hang on, Wilson! In no time at all I had made a couple of very quick laps around Keewaydin and was being waved in by Hauserman and Freyling. As I slowed down, more frantic waving on their part reminded me of their last-minute slowing-down instructions. "Don't shut the throttle right off, as the boat comes off plane and starts to sink, stern first. Keep jogging the throttle in short bursts until you are safely at dead slow speed, without sinking." I did this, and although some water did spill over the transom into *PDQ*, I got to the dock on top of the water and shut off the 32. What a thrill that was!

Then I found out the real reason for the visit by these two Sea Flea enthusiasts. Freyling and Hauserman wanted competition in the summer's racing. They owned the only two 32's in Muskoka. Also, Freyling was the agent for the Peterborough builder of the Hurricane. As it was quite obvious that I had been badly bitten by a Sea Flea, these two then went after my father. And he, being just as interested in speed as I was, gave them an order for one.

About a week later the Muskoka Lakes Navigation Company steamer, *Cherokee*, landed a brand-new Peterborough Hurricane and an equally new Johnson 32 racing engine on our dock. So here it was, my first real out-and-out racer. I spent a couple of days uncrating both and reading all the instructions. The engine, of course, had never been mounted on the transom, so there was quite a bit of installation work required. Then the throttle had to be mounted on the left-hand side of the cockpit in such a location as to allow easy operation and still provide a means for my left hand to do its share of the job of holding me in the cockpit. Actually, at first I used the wheel centre throttle control supplied with the boat, but realizing that just staying in the boat with both hands on the wheel was going to be very difficult, I changed right then to the aircraft-type squeeze throttle supplied with the engine. Finally, after three days of tiring but very interesting work, I had my new outfit ready for the water.

With the help and free advice of all my envious friends on Keewaydin, I got the boat into the water and the engine mounted on the transom. There sure wasn't very much freeboard at the stern (about 2 inches). Any quick movement astern caused a flood to come into the boat and a fast forward movement was required to avert disaster. I was so anxious to try it out, I decided to make a run steering only by the steering handle on the engine (I'd leave the pesky rigging of the steering ropes until later). So I started to crank and crank — and crank. I took quite a long time to get spark and mixture controls set, and the engine refused to do anything more than grunt a couple of times until these adjustments were made. But then the 32 burst into song and away I went. It was next to impossible to control the boat with the steering handle, try to keep the throttle where I wanted it, see where I was going, and stay in the boat, all at the same time. I very quickly admitted defeat, shut off the engine and signalled for my eager pit crew to come out in *Ridley* and rescue me. That was all for that day: it took a long time to put those steering cables in place. This was the first time that I had ever rigged steering cables, and I will admit to quite a bit of indecision as to just how it should be done. But next morning I was ready for another trial. Headed straight out from the dock (always a good precaution with racing boats) I cranked up and took off first crack. That's better, I thought. Well, so it was — as long as I continued straight out from the dock. But when I started a cautious turn: disaster! I turned to starboard and the boat went to port! What was wrong? A very gentle nudge to port with a consequent swing to starboard confirmed my suspicions. I hadn't done that cable-rigging job properly after all. After another rescue by my pit crew — now laughing their heads off at my mistakes — I went to work and soon found the trouble. The cables had been wound around the steering wheel drum the wrong way. That didn't take too long to correct, but it sure hurt my ego. On the next go, everything went perfectly. Being brand-new and quite stiff, the engine needed a bit of a run-in period. But how much? And how long could I restrain myself from squeezing that throttle wide open? After two or three laps around the island, I squeezed as hard as I could for just a very short run. But that was enough to see my tachometer rev over 5000 rpm. Boy, could that thing go! Back at the dock I did some calculating of rpm, prop pitch, and slippage, and came up with a thrilling 52 miles per hour!

I now had a real race boat and I knew what it could do. The next thing was to dream up a name for it. Something short and snappy. And a bit boastful, maybe? How about SCRAM? Sounded terrific. I got a brush and some black paint and put the name on both sides in letters as high as the boat's side, about 6 inches. Then, to leave no doubt as to the meaning of the name, I added a big black arrow pointed towards the stern, the proper place for all of SCRAM's rivals!

Right away I learned that there was a tremendous difference in handling an outboard racing hydro as compared with a big inboard-powered runabout. First there was the problem of getting the boat up on plane, or on the step as we called it. This called for shifting as much of the driver's weight as far forward as possible, while the engine was gunned wide open. After 20 seconds (that sometimes seemed like an eternity), the bow came down and the stern jumped up, and SCRAM took off like an arrow. The turning was fast and furious — that is, the wheel-turning part of it was. But SCRAM sometimes took the bit in her teeth and decided not to go where I wanted. Oh, she started to turn all right, but then she began to slide crabwise at an alarming rate and usually headed for disaster, which was only avoided by cutting the throttle. Talking with Hauserman, I learned that both he and Freyling had fastened a fin, somewhat like a shark's fin, on the bottom, amidships. This, plus very judicious shifting of the driver's weight to the inside of the turn, helped to get one around a corner in much better form. I stuck one on *SCRAM* and found the handling considerably improved.

Then the engine presented problems. I was fairly used to the Buchanan in *Ridley*, but this first outboard was something else. It took a lot of effort and time to learn all about mixing the proper amount of oil with the gas, the best setting for the ignition, and the proper tune-up of the carburetor. But it was a good training period for *SCRAM*, the 32 and me.

Around the end of July the regatta season in Muskoka got under way. The first was the MLA races at the country club on Lake Rosseau. And this year I had two boats to race: *Ridley* and *SCRAM*. Again Al Hargan raced with me in the 25-horsepower class, and again we won. The thrill was just as great as the previous year. *Ridley* did us proud again. But that race over, I had to rush to get ready for my first hydro race. I was green as grass. Also, much to my consternation, besides Hauserman and Freyling, I had competition from afar. This was no less than Lou Marsh, probably Canada's best-loved sports-column writer of all time. Lou wrote his "Pick and Shovel" column for the Toronto *Star*. Besides being the best sportswriter of his day, he was a fine hockey referee in the NHL and champion of the out-of-luck guys. He was a great supporter of good sport, but he could use his pick to devastating effect on what he considered poor sportsmanship. So here was I, a greenhorn, up against Lou Marsh, who had been in the Sea Flea game ever since its inception. His boat was naturally called *Pick & Shovel*, and it was powered with another of the fearsome Johnson 32's.

Well, as it turned out, I didn't have to race him that day, after all. Just before the race was to be called, Lou decided to go for a short trial run. Deep down in a slip between two long wooden docks, Lou stepped into *Pick & Shovel* and prepared to start his engine. A large crowd was gathered watching him. Some smart character shouted, "Be sure to give yourself a good write-up, Lou." To which Lou replied, "That's more than you will get, my friend," and then gave the starter rope a mighty yank. The 32 started with a terrific roar, and with the throttle wide open the startled boat leapt completely out of the water, headed for the sky, then settled back stern-first, and sank — boat, engine, and Lou! That finished Lou Marsh's racing for that day and it sure quietened him down quite a bit. He didn't even have a quick comeback for the smart aleck.

Right away, long before Lou could have hoped to get his engine dried out and running again, the race was called. It was a flying start, something new to me, as all my starts in *Ridley* had been dead-on-the-starting-line variety. There were three boats in the race — *PDQ*, *Applesauce*, and *SCRAM* — and I started in third place. I maintained my position for the whole race. Not so good for a starter in hydro racing, a last on the first try. I found out very quickly that afternoon that I still had lots to learn about handling a Flea as it skipped across the surface of the water.

Other regattas were presented at Bala, Foote's Bay, Woodington, Orillia, and Gravenhurst, all in or very close to Muskoka. As these craft were easy to tow behind a car on a light two-wheeled trailer, it was quite common to have racing boats from other areas compete in our Muskoka races. But over the years that I raced *SCRAM*, my main competition came from Fred Hauserman and Bill Freyling. We appeared at almost all of the races, had loads of fun, and, as I remember, almost broke even on wins, spins, and spills.

My first upset took place at the Port Carling Regatta. Trying to jump *PDQ*'s wash in an abortive attempt to pass, I buried *SCRAM*'s bow! Travelling at better than 50 per, I shot skyward while *SCRAM* did a most beautifully executed somersault. Or so they told me. I was fully absorbed in my new experience of having become an instant amphibian. One second I was flying with the birds, the next I was down chasing the black bass! In those early days, we scoffed at safety equipment. Fools! We did wear life jackets, simply because we were not allowed to start without them, but crash helmets, kneepads? We were racers not sissies! It wasn't until much later in my racing career that I realized just how important these things can be. My two sons, racing today, a full half century later, take all these safety precautions for granted.

Well, that took care of me. Luckily I was uninjured in this first upset. But what about the boat and engine? My faithful pit crew, Al Hargan and Don Gibson, came out in *Ridley* and pulled all of us — boat, engine and me — out of the water. Back home we found that *SCRAM* had not suffered, but the engine cylinders were full of water, as was the carb and the gas tank, which in those days was mounted on top of the engine and around the flywheel. We cleaned all this mess up and tried to start the engine. No dice. I finally discovered that the magneto was not delivering any spark to the spark plugs. That meant a soaked magneto. And that meant a dismantling job and a slow, low-heat drying out of the mag in my mother's oven. It took two full days to get my outfit back in operation. (I mentioned that my two sons, Ernie and Harry, are racing today. They are outboard hydro buffs. Although my outboard racing days are something of the dim and distant past, I have kept my hand in by acting as grease monkey and spiritual adviser for the two of them. Just to show how equipment and technique have improved in half a century, I have often witnessed the frantic efforts put forth by a trained pit crew in getting a drowned engine back into operation: plugs out, clear cylinders of water, drain carb, install new plugs, give the carb a quick spray of ether, back into the water, one pull of the starter as the stern of the boat, prop and all are held in the air by the pit crew's strong arms, and away goes the drowned boat in time for the next race. The time required for all this? Five minutes! That is progress.)

During the four years that I owned *SCRAM*, I had a great deal of pleasure out of the boat, and not all from pure racing. I took great pleasure out of squeezing people into the tiny cockpit and taking them out for a hair-raising ride. I guess the most hair-raising ride of all was the time I raced to Port Carling to find a doctor for my suddenly very sick mother. I located Dr. Joyce, who said that he would come right down to our island with me in my boat. Little did he know! When he saw what he had to ride in, he almost quit on me. But when I said that mother was very sick indeed, he took a deep breath and shoe-horned himself into SCRAM's tiny cockpit! To make things even worse, a good east wind had come up, and when I reached the open lake at the mouth of the Indian River, I also met some pretty respectable rollers. Old SCRAM put on a crazy exhibition. We leapt out of the water, then tried to do a submarine act. By the time we reached Keewaydin, the Doc and I looked like a couple of drowned rats, and felt worse. But Dr. Joyce, being a Muskoka-ite, a good sort, and remembering his Hippocratic oath, trudged upstairs, dripping water as he went, to minister to my mother. It was well that he did, for he diagnosed a very bad appendix, on the point of rupture, and told me to get her to the Bracebridge Hospital as quickly as possible. I said, "Okay. While my sisters are getting Mother ready, I'll run you back to Port Carling." To which the long-suffering Doc replied, "You will if you have something safe, sane, and slow to take me in. Otherwise I shall live here!" So I loaded him into *Miss Canada* and took him home in style. Back at Keewaydin a few minutes later, I picked up Mother and rushed her by water to Bracebridge, where an emergency operation fixed things up.

Although I wouldn't let just any person put a hand on SCRAM, particularly the engine, I did let my pit crew, Al Hargan and Don Gibson, take trial spins by themselves. They both drove well and enjoyed the experience. But not so Don's father. Ever since the day that I first ran SCRAM, Will Gibson had been dead set against me and my search for speed. Poor Don! He had just come in from a very fast and enjoyable ride, only to meet his irate father at dockside, shouting, "Get out of that damned floating coffin and get home. You are grounded!"

I mentioned Al's sisters earlier. Norah was a blond, my life-long failing. Kate and Norah slept in the upper level of their family's boathouse, which had a small balcony overhanging the water. Quite often the best water conditions for running SCRAM occurred in the early morning. So I, being an early riser, quite often took advantage of this opportunity. It was quite a sight, as I roared past the Hargan menage, to see blond Norah in her nightgown, standing on that balcony and screaming (I guess), "Damn you, Harold Wilson!"

My outboard days were good ones. There were lots of races, and I guess I won my fair share of them. There were upsets, sink-ings, lost propellers, and an engine that seemed to need almost constant overhauling, but all this was part of the game, all enjoy-able. I even got the urge to acquire a larger, four-place runabout hull to be powered by the same 32 as I used for SCRAM. As it was quite apparent that this boat was not forthcoming from the usual source, my father, I decided to build one myself. Not just build it, I was also going to design it. So, setting out to become the first self-taught naval architect in the Wilson clan, I made all sorts of weird and wonderful plans on a homemade drawing board. I spent a whole winter on the design, and the following spring on the building of the boat. My boat was loaded aboard the Ingersoll Machine Co. truck and carted up to Muskoka on July 1. It was proudly launched at Beaumaris and given a very speedy tow to Port Keewaydin. And well that it was speedy! My creation made it to the dock all right, but after its auspicious start at Beaumaris as a first-off outboard runabout, it ended this initial — and as it turned out its only — run as a submarine! I don't think that anything could take on water as fast as that boat did. After quite a bit of hard labour, and absolutely no luck, I burned the darn thing. It would be a long time before the next Wilson-built boat would hit the water.

That ended my active outboard hydro racing days. SCRAM was aging, and the new Johnson 50-horsepower engine had made its appearance. I could no longer make a good showing at the regattas. I realized that my real desire was to stick with the inboards, so I sold my complete outboard race outfit to another beginner. I was ready to move on to the big stuff.

Early Muskoka wins.

Chapter 5

The 100-Horsepower Class

With *SCRAM* and her 50-plus performance a thing of the past as far as I was concerned, the only thing I had to race was old *Ridley*. And although she had done me proud in many a race, her 25-horsepower Buchanan, struggling hard to produce one mile per hour for each of those horsepowers, didn't exactly look like it would provide much thrilling racing experience. A new racing outfit seemed indicated, but they don't grow on trees, and I didn't have the necessary funds. I needed a sponsor.

As my aspirations were boundless — I wanted, eventually, to drive the fastest thing afloat — this sponsor was going to have to be awfully well heeled. To date, my father had been acting in a sponsor capacity. He had already provided me with three motor-boats, two of which I had raced quite successfully. But now I was talking about racing on a different scale.

He didn't have to be persuaded. As far as he was concerned he already was my sponsor. He was possessed of enough of this world's goods to be able to meet the high costs of racing boat construction, and he shared my passionate love for speed. What more could an aspiring young boat racer ask for? Well, in getting my father as my sponsor, I got a great deal more. Dad was a great lover of sport. He was also a most indulgent father, a keen businessman, and a fine engineer. With all of these things going for me, I just had to succeed. Thus was born the Wilson Racing Team: Ernie Wilson, driving force and mentor, and Harold Wilson, driver. The association was to last for a long time, not just for the 24 active racing years, but right up until the day that Dad got the checkered flag for the last time.

Although we had serious talks about where to go next, and what boat and engine to get, really it went like this. One of us, or maybe both, would come up with a new field to be considered, and conquered if possible. If we agreed, then it just seemed natural that we would get right into the nitty gritty of the matter: what is this new class, who will be the competition, what boat should we get, what engine, what speed must we have? Based on all of this we would then pick the naval architect who would design the new racer and lay the rest of the problems on his doorstep. When the preliminary planning was settled, the next step was to find a builder. To date, of course, all of this had been unnecessary, as both *Ridley* and *SCRAM*, and their engines, were all stock production models. But now that we were going to enter all sorts of racing classes, it seemed obvious that production boats would no longer be the answer.

At this time, a new boatbuilding concern was born in Gravenhurst. It was the brainchild of a small group of boating enthusiasts who wanted to have available a source of motorboats far superior to the general run of production boats currently on the market. It was headed by Tom Greavette, a man who had been in the boating game nearly all of his life. For many years he had been sales manager for Canada's premier builder of fine watercraft, Herb Ditchburn, also of Gravenhurst. Tom, a super salesman, was now to become a manufacturer, and his new company was to be known as Rainbow Craft. In the company's formative stage, my father became the first president, with Tom Greavette as general manager. Very soon, after initial capital problems were settled, the company was reorganized. Tom Greavette became president, my father became a board member, and the company was renamed Greavette Boats.

It was felt that the new company should have a line of well-tested, successful, runabout hulls of good appearance available for presentation to the boating public. With this in mind, the company made an arrangement with an American concern, Dart Boats, to produce that maker's line of boats in Canada.

All this took place during the winter of 1928-29, while I was still at Ridley. No mention had been made of new racing boats, so I assumed that old *Ridley* would be my steed for the next summer's racing. Early in May — the ice only went out of Lake Muskoka in late April — Dad took me up to Gravenhurst to see the testing of the first Dart Ensign produced at Greavette's. This was an 18-foot hard-chine hull with a Chrysler Crown engine of 85 horsepower, and her speed was in the mid-thirties! Boy, would that be wonderful for the 100-horsepower class in the Muskoka regatta. But nothing was said, and the test over, back I went to Ridley College.

On the 1st of July we made our trek up to Muskoka for the summer. Passing Greavette's in Gravenhurst, Dad said, "Let's go in and see what they are doing." Did I get the surprise of my life? Sitting in the plant, ready for the water, was another brand-new Ensign, and Dad said, "Well, how do you like your new racer?" He sure jumped the gun on me that time! (Not for the last time, either, as you will learn.)

I had a good chance to examine my new race boat, sitting there out of water on the production bay floor. She was a hard-chine vee-bottom design and would be fast, flat riding, and easily handled. She had a tiny rudder, which rather amazed me, but Tom Greavette assured me that at the speed she would travel it was all the rudder needed. The whole hull was made of African mahogany and varnished so beautifully that when the boat was pushed out into the sunlight on the launch car, it made me realize that old *Ridley*'s white-painted hull looked just a bit dowdy in comparison. Terrible to forsake a faithful old friend so quickly, but there it was, off with the old, on with the new. "What are you going to name the new boat?" asked my father. Well, that called for a bit of thought. I didn't feel that the name *Ridley* had been too proper a name. Perhaps something a bit more meaningful. I really like Dad's choice of *Miss Canada* for the big Ditchburn. But this boat was so small. "How about *Little Miss Canada*?" Dad agreed, and *Little Miss Canada I* she was named, then and there. Standing there in the sun, she sure looked pretty. There were just two cockpits, one fore and one aft, with the engine between. The fore cockpit was the business end of the boat, where I would be doing my driving for all the racing to come. I mentioned the 100-horsepower class, and my father agreed that it was a good field to try to conquer. Both cockpits had well-upholstered seats, not just the padded cushions and hard wooden seat backs that we had thought just perfect in *Ridley*. There was a streamlined windshield to protect the driver and the front-seat passenger. And the steering! No more of those darn steering cables that can cause so much trouble. This boat had one of the new positive-drag link-type steerers that my father had developed at the Ingersoll Machine Company from parts filched from the Ford steering gears that we manufactured there. He had developed the prototype at the Port Carling Boat Works and it had been installed in *Ridley*. During the course of the next few years, practically all Canadian boat manufacturers would use this type of steering gear.

The launch car with *Little Miss Canada I* was pushed on the tracks down to the ramp leading into the waters of Gravenhurst Bay. I climbed aboard. I was going to be a part of that boat from the very start. Down the ways we went, and a couple of minutes later the boat was tied up at the dock awaiting the Greavette mechanic who was to give everything a last-minute checkover before she was started for the first time.

Finally, he said, "Okay," and I got behind the wheel. For sure, nobody but me was going to handle *Little Miss Canada I* on her first voyage. With the mechanic along, we did a lengthy test run in Gravenhurst Bay. When he was satisfied with the boat, and me, the mechanic said, "Okay, she's yours!" I thought that moment would never come. I set out to drive all the way up Lake Muskoka to our home in Keewaydin. This was a first time ever for me, so I guess I wandered all over the lake before I finally pulled up at the dock and received an enthusiastic welcome from all of the Keewaydin gang. Of course all of them had to be taken out for a test run — not that I minded in the least.

Little Miss Canada I certainly was quick, not only in top, straightaway speed, but in acceleration and flashing response to control. Speedwise, she could do a bit over 35 mph — and that was *real* miles, not Muskoka miles used by so many enthusiastic boat owners when boasting of their boat's performance. She also was quite quick away from the mark. When the throttle was opened, she jumped! But the most staggering of my new boat's characteristics was her response to control. This was my first vee-bottom boat, and although it did not ride flat on the water like SCRAM, it was much more up on the surface than the round-bottomed *Ridley*, which ploughed. The fact that she was almost on the surface at full speed was responsible in part for her rapid response to the helm.

During the first week or so I tried out all the tricks that this new craft of mine had to offer, and the last was the worst, or best, depending on the point of view. This was the boat's response to a sudden, hard over turn at top speed. To my terror, and then my delight, I found out that when the wheel was put hard over at full throttle the fastest 180-degree turn imaginable took place. The boat literally turned on its nose. The bow went down, the transom flew up, spinning wildly in the air. And that wasn't all! At the end of this turn the momentum caused the boat to continue in the same direction as just before the turn began, only backwards, sliding along on its nose, submerged almost to the deck line! This lasted until gravity took over, and the flying stern dropped into the water, the 85-horsepower engine took over, and the boat shot forward again. Startling? I'll say so! The great wonder was that this astounding turn had been made safely. Well, almost. When I first tried this stunt — by myself, naturally — I had the steering wheel to keep me in place, so nothing happened. But the first time I took a passenger along, the sudden backward movement threw him right over the windshield and out onto the dripping deck. Not hurt, mind you, but scared and very wet. Another time, while demonstrating to my girlfriend, Inez Butler, the boat stalled out just as the stern dropped back into the water. I checked things over and found the battery sitting demurely on top of the cylinder head. All the connecting wires were ripped off, which accounted for the sudden stop. Not too difficult to fix. Inez? Oh, yes. She did a most beautiful half-gainer, combined with a shattering bellyflop, and landed in the briny! As I said, this was a relatively safe manoeuvre only to be used under certain conditions.

This new product of the Greavette Boat Company, this fine new addition to the Wilson fleet, was undoubtedly a good boat, and as she had a good turn of speed, I began thinking of racing. The regatta season was approaching and all the community notice boards were covered with posters advertising the coming races. The most popular of the classes offered at all the Muskoka regattas was the 100-horsepower runabout class. So right away I began making trips to Gravenhurst to see what the mechanics there could do to help me get the absolute maximum out of *Little Miss Canada*. They tuned the boat, and me, so well that by the end of the summer's racing we had won the 100-horsepower class at all the regattas staged!

The next summer we did quite well again, although the appearance of some fine 100-horsepower engines made the going pretty tough, and we had to settle for winning just our fair share of the races. When the shouting and tumult was all over, I was faced with the same old question: what was I going to do to stay in competition next year? More particularly, what was I going to use for a boat?

I had a long talk with my father, and we agreed that to have a reasonable chance of success the next summer, a completely new racing outfit would be needed. So the two of us, plus Tom Greavette, went to see a very famous naval architect, John Hacker, an American. He was doing some designing for a new line of runabouts to be built by Greavette, so it didn't take too much persuasion to get him at his drawing board to design a new racer for us. While I was working for a year — I had graduated from Ridley that summer — the design of *Little Miss Canada II* was finished, and the building of the boat itself was begun at Greavette's.

50

When spring came around I went up to Gravenhurst to have my first look at the new boat. The hull itself was almost complete, and a very smooth-looking outfit it was. It was 18 feet long and had a very low freeboard. The driver's seat, for two people, was at the stern. There was a small cockpit forward of the engine, which was amidships. The deck was quite curved, giving the boat a streamlined appearance. John Hacker, who was with us, said that she was a monoplane. Isn't that an aeroplane? Well, John said, the special bottom was designed to make this boat plane almost like a hydroplane, hence the name "monoplane" because it was a planing hull with only one plane and no step. Drawing a pretty fine line, I guess, but it was different to any other vee-bottom job I had seen. It was designed to ride as flat as a pancake. Because of this, Hacker said that it would be extremely fast but also quite tricky. It might even be dangerous at times.

There was still quite a bit of finishing up to do before she would be ready for the water, and there was an engine to get. My sponsor/father had been at work on that also. After quite a study of all the available engines, he had settled on a Gray 100-horse-power six, and there was this sparkling blue-painted powerhouse sitting in its shipping crate right near the boat. As the hull was about ready for varnish, I settled all the colour and finish details with the master painter, Fred Purdie, and his up-and-coming son, Oscar. Although the whole boat was built of the best African mahogany, I decided that it should be finished in walnut. This caused a minor riot at Greavette's, but I held out. Not only that, I insisted that the covering board, the outer deck plank which meets the gunwhales all around, should be painted black. That settled, I went back to work in Ingersoll, leaving Greavette's to finish the hull and install the engine, shaft, rudder, skeg, prop, gas tanks and the maze of wiring and plumbing required to bring that 100-horsepower engine to life. It was a big job and there wasn't much time, but somehow they made it. There was *Little Miss Canada II* sitting on the launch

Little Miss Canada II.

car and ready for business when I reached Gravenhurst that July 1st.

Well, this time no mechanic was going to tell me what to do. As soon as the launch car was wheeled across the road from the Greavette factory, I climbed up into the boat and down the ways she went for her first taste of water. When I had paddled her into the dock, I had my first look at my new racer in her natural element. She certainly was a pretty sight. Streamlined to the *nth*, low in the water, and fast-looking even when at rest. With my special deck finish, black covering board outlining the whole shape of the boat, it looked terrific. The walnut-finished mahogany deck was just what was needed to make the whole boat look truly interesting. The black covering board was incorporated in the finish of many later Greavette runabouts.

I took *Little Miss Canada II* for her first spin, but this was vastly different to the jump-in-and-open-her-wide test I gave her predecessor. Literally everything was checked — hull, engine, electrics, fuel system, rudder, shaft and prop. Finally satisfied that all was well, I started the Gray engine, threw in the clutch, and off we went. Even then there were many more checks to be made while moving: hull leaks, fuel and stuffing box leaks. There were many tests. Even when I was finally ready to open 'er up, I had to remember that this Gray racing engine had to be carefully broken in. This was done slowly and spread over several days. Endless days, it seemed. But finally the time came to try full throttle, if just for a short burst. She could go all right! And the Gray engine seemed to have lots of stuff, even if it was more of a general-purpose unit than an out-and-out racing machine. A few days later we timed the boat over the measured mile that Greavette's had laid out in Gravenhurst Bay. A couple of fast runs proved that the new boat could reach 40 miles per hour. *Little Miss Canada I* had excelled in the 100-horsepower class until just the last couple of races, when her 35 mph had been bettered just a little bit by some of the new full 100-horsepower engines that had appeared. It looked like her kid sister was going to have just enough extra to put to shame those boats that had beaten us last year.

All this was fine, but just as I was beginning to feel that I was on top of the world, along came some news that brought me right back to sea level. It seemed that the competition hadn't been asleep all winter. New boats had been built for two of my toughest rivals, Charlie Wheaton of Toronto and Jack McGinnis of Quebec. These two boats, *Shadow* and *Miss Quebec,* were so like my *Little Miss Canada II* that it made me wonder if John Hacker had been designing boats for Canadian companies other than Greavette's. I never did find out the truth, but the three of them sure looked like peas in a pod.

I practised all of July, learning all there was to learn about the new boat, and when the first race came along at the MLA regatta, I felt pretty confident that we would show a clean pair of heels to everyone. Well, that race was an eye-opener. Right away, I found that *Shadow, Miss Quebec* and *Little Miss Canada II* were not only look-alikes, they also had the same top speed. It was the first race in my experience where driver ability seemed to be more important than top speed. I used a little trick that I had developed, called my "power turn," and I used it at every turning buoy. That little trick, coupled with all that I had learned during the previous month's practice, helped me to pull off a very close win in that race. As it later turned out, further tuning of my Gray increased top speed by enough to ensure that we could stay ahead of the competition.

Perhaps I should say a bit about this power turn. I had noticed that it was possible by proper and combined use of helm and throttle to make the stern of my boat skid sideways on the surface as the boat was negotiating a tight turn. I had also noticed with *Little Miss Canada I* and *II* that there was a considerable lowering of speed in a tight turn, with consequent loss of time. Considerable practice produced the following technique. I would shave a buoy as closely as possible, and at the instant that my bow came level with the marker, I would slack off on the throttle just for a fraction of a second. At exactly the same time

I would turn hard and kick the throttle wide open again. As I had learned in practice, the stern of my boat would start a wide sweeping skid with the stern trying to get ahead of the bow! Then came the tricky part, to ease off a bit on the helm, as the skidding stern was now making my turn too tight, and by very careful throttle control, to keep the boat in a controlled skidding turn around the three buoys before the next straightaway. As all of this was done at full throttle, there was no loss of top speed or acceleration when coming out of the turn and into the straight-away. This was much faster than the old system of steering through the turn with helm only. (I guess you could liken my power turn to the four-wheel drift used by all race car drivers in getting their fast-moving cars through difficult corners.)

As I said, we won the MLA race, but it was a very near thing. And so it turned out to be for the whole racing season. In that first year of her life, *Little Miss Canada II* was undefeated. It was a good year, but from the looks of things, it was going to be awfully tough the next summer.

And so it was. Again, as with the Greavette Ensign, *Little Miss Canada I*, this year's races brought out some new engines which, although technically rated as 100-horsepower, nevertheless, by dint of much careful tuning, could be goaded into putting out quite a few more wild horses. The result of this was that at the end of the summer, the best that I could boast was that I had about broken even, wins against losses. Still, a fine season and lots of fun, but something was telling me that if I was to continue in the 100-horsepower class again in 1932, it was back to the drafting board for the Wilson Racing Team.

By this time I had graduated from Ridley, had worked at my father's plant for a year's practical experience, and was now a student in Mechanical Engineering at the University of Toronto's famed "Little Red School House." At the university I met — when I offered her a ride during a cloudburst — a cute little blond by the name of Lorna Reid. That was a red-letter day. Our friendship grew from acquaintance, to friendship, to love, and later to marriage and the raising of a fine family. After

55

half a century we are still at the same game. Well, at least our five children are still adding names to the Wilson family roster. Lorna's participation was a big change for the Wilson Racing Team. Up until this time Al Hargan had been my faithful, and very helpful, racing mechanic. Lorna changed places with Al, taking over all the duties not only as racing partner but also as grease monkey — and she stayed right on the job until our son Ernie made his appearance.

Lorna came up to Muskoka early in the summer of 1932, giving us time to get in a lot of very necessary racing practice together. By regatta time the new Wilson Racing Team was ready for business. It was a busy summer indeed. Not only did we compete in all the 100-horsepower races, we also climbed up and entered a few races for boats with considerably more powerful engines. Again we took away more than our fair share of our own class races, and didn't do too badly against the bigger boats either.

Earlier I told you that John Hacker warned that *Little Miss Canada II* could be tricky or even dangerous at times. How right he was! In a race at Muskoka Lakes we came as close to disaster as possible without actually experiencing it. Just as I threw the boat into the power turn, I hit some rather large swells. The bow shot straight skywards, and the boat did a 360-degree spin on its transom! She sank stern-first and water rushed into the back of our crew cockpit, which was in the stern. Then — and why it happened I know not — the bow flopped back down onto the water, right side up and pointed in the right direction! The engine was still running, and although we had lost a couple of places due to this unexpected fan dance, we were still in the race. Yes, we won that one too, but it was tough.

A week later, when we were returning home after the conclusion of the day's racing at Bala, Lorna had quite an exciting experience. We had taken my father's big *Miss Canada* to carry a few guests. I was driving it home, and Lorna was elected to drive the race boat. Remember what I said about it riding flat on the water like a skipping stone and that it could easily slice into a wave instead of jumping over it? Well, as Lorna jumped over the heavy wake set up by *Miss Canada*, it did just that. There was an almighty splash and *Little Miss Canada II* almost disappeared from view. She came up all right, the engine stalled and she appeared to be sitting very low in the water. When we got to Lorna we found the race boat about a third full of water! Lorna drove home carefully at idle speed to get the boat pumped out. She heartily agreed with John Hacker's remark that this boat would be beautiful, fast and tricky.

Chapter 6
The International 225-Cubic-Inch Class

My father had the ability to think beyond and ahead of me, and he acted on those thoughts even before discussing them with me. He realized that I had about exhausted Muskoka racing, and in particular the 100-horsepower class. This class was being replaced by larger-engined craft. To continue we would have to build a new, somewhat larger and higher-powered boat. He was interested in speed, as much as possible, and he was sure that I felt the same way. So, hearing something about a new class of racing boats just becoming popular in the United States, he began to investigate. This new class was called the 225-cubic-inch hydroplane class.

Before I had heard even a word about the 225s, my father had decided that this class would be the next target for the Wilson Racing Team. That decided, he got right after John Hacker to design a new racer for us, and as soon as the first plans came from Hacker, he had the new boat started at Greavette's. All this before I had any ideas of racing beyond the Muskoka neighbourhood races.

The 225s were very new and becoming popular in the United States but were not yet known in Canada. The Canadian National Exhibition in Toronto, sensing something interesting for their popular waterfront sports presentation, set up a series of races in co-operation with the Canadian and United States boating authorities for the "First World Championship for the 225-Cubic-Inch Class." Besides having a new boat designed and built for these races, my father had also put my name down as the first challenger.

What a shocker that was! I guess that I had begun to consider myself pretty hot in this boat-racing game, but up to this point it had been pretty much friendly competition. Now I was being tossed head-first into a sport overflowing with fast boats, experienced drivers, fine mechanics, and all sorts of expensive equipment — spare propellers, shafts, rudders, even spare engines. It was enough to give me a bad dose of the five-minute jitters. If that wasn't enough, the new boat, *Little Miss Canada III* was to be a hydro — my first experience with an inboard-powered craft of this type. And somehow Lorna and I and *Little Miss Canada III* had to be ready to meet the challengers from south of the border by the end of August.

That was a busy summer. About half my time was spent at the Greavette plant in Gravenhurst watching the development of the new boat. The other half went into keeping alive my interest in the Muskoka racing circuit. Then came an exciting day: the new Ford V8 engine for *Little Miss Canada III* arrived. It was a standard Ford converted for marine use by St. Lawrence Engines. A lot of thought had gone into choosing this standard Ford over several more exotic-sounding makes. We felt that absolute dependability was more important than rather wild claims for higher power. Also, we learned that all of the other challenging boats would be Ford powered — better go along with the crowd. If all the boats were equal, it would be a tight series of races.

This boat seemed to be taking a lot longer to build than had *Little Miss Canada II* or was I just getting anxious? Just two and a half weeks before the CNE races, she hit the water for first trials. This left very little time to overcome teething troubles, and even less for Lorna and me to become familiar with all the quirks of the new hydro. It turned out to be a very easily handled, stable and fast boat. Being a hydroplane, and riding perfectly flat on top of the water, she quite naturally was somewhat rough riding. We sat side by side, and the cockpit was so roomy that it was difficult to stay in place. In any sort of chop we bounced all over. This tended not only to shake our back teeth loose, it also made us almost part company with our stomachs. To overcome the latter discomfort, we acquired two wide kidney belts, the kind favoured by motorcycle racers, and these, cinched up good and tight like girdles, kept everything in its proper place. By the time it was necessary to pack up and head for the CNE, we felt that our new racer had been whipped into shape and we were reasonably satisfied, in spite of not having handled *Little Miss Canada III* in competition.

We didn't have to wait very long for that. The CNE World Championship Races were to start the first week in September, and already we were at out pits at the foot of John Street in Toronto, right on the waters of Toronto Harbour. When Lorna and I arrived, we found the boat, Tom Greavette and a couple of his men already on hand. There was also a man we did not know. He turned out to be Bill Doherty, a top-notch mechanic with the Ford Motor Company. Realizing that there could be great advertising value attached to these races, and wanting a Canadian Ford-powered boat to do well, Ford had sent Bill to be our engine mechanic for the duration of the races. (Thank you very much, Ford. It was much appreciated, then and for years after.)

Bill was immediately at work on our engine. In no time he had the ignition and gas line bits and pieces off and spread all over the dock. I'll never forget Tom Greavette's face, or his words, when he saw this: "I thought we were coming here to win races, not destroy engines!" Bill went over the whole engine, checking valve and ignition timing, everything that could have an effect on the efficiency and speed of our engine. He proved his ability and the worth of his labours. When he had the engine all buttoned up and ready for a trial run, he predicted considerable improvement. A quick run around the harbour showed 200 rpm's more than ever before, and with a lot more feeling of go. We were ready!

The CNE 225-Class World Championship Race was actually to be a series of three races, one each day on three successive days. The course was a three-mile oval in Lake Ontario and outside the sea wall. The races were to be five laps, 15 miles long total. I found that there was quite an entry list, all either Canadian or American. The American competitors were as follows: *Emancipator*, owned and driven by Atlantic City millionaire Mortimer Auerbach; *Riptide*, driven by its owner, the celebrated eye specialist Dr. Cecil Bagley; another boat, entered and driven by New York lawyer Al Swartzler; and one driven by Florence Burnham from Baltimore, Maryland, with her husband as racing mechanic. Doc Bagley was particularly celebrated at that time, as he had very recently completed a most delicate eye operation on the King of Siam. The Canadian challengers were: *Popeye*, driven by young Herb Ditchburn, the son of Canada's premier small-boat builder; *Atom*, driven by the well-known radio sports announcer Harry "Red" Foster; and us, a couple of greenhorns driving a new and untried boat with a name as long as its hull. Here we were, ready to start our first international race, and a World Championship at that.

Just a minute or so before starting time we left the National Yacht Club and went out through the western gap into Lake Ontario, which we found was quite rough. We all got away pretty well; there were no extra laps or disqualifications. But when we were coming around on the second lap, we saw *Popeye*, the Ditchburn boat, upside down on the water. Ditchburn's teammate, Red Foster, developed problems with his engine, which caused *Atom*'s retirement. While all this was going on, Lorna and I had our hands full trying to keep *Little Miss Canada III* on top of the water, topside up, and in first place. We had been first across the starting line and, by dint of a lot of hard driving, had been able to maintain this position. *Emancipator* was right on our tail for the whole five laps, and was still there when we slid across the finish line just ahead of him and

LMC III – mechanic Lorna Reid.

received the coveted checkered flag. Al Swartzler was third, Doc Bagley fourth, and Florence Burnham fifth. Florence was the only woman driver, and Lorna the only woman mechanic — to the best of my knowledge, the only woman mechanic ever in the boat-racing game. We certainly were proud of ourselves that evening as we headed back to our Life Saving Station pits at the foot of John Street, Our first international race and already we were in the lead. Maybe only by a few feet, but still in the lead!

The next morning we awoke to find that we had become an overnight sensation. The newspapers gave us wonderful coverage, front-page pictures and fine write-ups. The Toronto *Star* put the lid on with their banner page-one headline: "Romance Rides the Waves." Lou Marsh, my old race rival of *SCRAM* days, gave me a bit of a rough time in his "Pick & Shovel" column, when he said of our win, "even a blind hog can find one acorn." Well, maybe it was true. Certainly luck was with us greenhorns and our untried boat, enabling us to turn back all that the U.S.A. had to offer, but the next two days would tell the story.

We spent the whole next day going over our boat with a fine-tooth comb. Everything had to be in perfect order for the next two races. Bill Doherty put his hand on our Ford engine after he finished his inspection and said, "She's ready to do the same thing again." But it wasn't to be. After leading for over half the race, and after a particularly bad bump which seemed to cause a heavy thump under our feet, our engine slowed down a bit, *Emancipator* passed us, and we finished that way: Auerbach first, Lorna and I second.

Now we really had a job on our hands, everything all tied up between *Emancipator* and *Little Miss Canada III*, and us with a sick engine. Back at our pits we hauled the boat out of the water and started in to find our problem. It didn't take long. One look at the propeller gave us the answer: a bent blade, the result of hitting something, probably when we heard that loud thump. This would certainly put undue strain on the engine and would be responsible for the apparent loss of power. This prop, the best we had, was also the only one in our possession with the proper size and pitch. Again my father came up with a quick and correct action. He phoned the Stannus Company in Detroit, found that they had a duplicate prop in stock, and ordered it to be flown to us the next morning by special plane. A thorough checkup by Bill Doherty turned up no other problems, so we closed up shop and went off to get a good night's rest.

The next morning we got all the previous night's papers. The 225s were plastered everywhere and much was being made of the "feud" between Mortimer Auerbach and me. Feud, indeed. We were just having a good, healthy war, and may the best man win. When we reached our pits, there was a small group of enthusiasts there, anxious to see just what was going on. In the crowd was a young man with a brown paper parcel under his arm. It was our competitor Al Swartzler, the New York lawyer.

I should tell you a bit more about the other boats in the race. I have mentioned that all of them were powered by Ford engines. The two other Canadian boats, *Popeye* and *Atom*, were Ditchburn designed and built. I cannot remember the designer of Florence Burnham's craft, but the other three, my boat and those driven by Doc Bagley and Al Swartzler, were identical. All were designed by John Hacker and similarly powered, so they had the same characteristics, same speed, and same propellers.

Al Swartzler was standing out with the other fans, so I brought him into our pit area. He talked for a while, then said, "Harold, I understand from the papers that you had prop problems yesterday?" when I said that this was true, he said, "I also heard that you do not have a spare prop. Now, you beat me fair and square in the first two races. I think that the best boat should win. And so, as yours is the best boat, I would like you to use this." And he handed me the parcel, which contained the propeller off his own boat. "Let me have your damaged one," he said. "It worked fairly well for you last night. It should be all right for me." I was overcome by this generous offer. Don't anybody ever tell me that the Yanks aren't good sports. Of course, after thanking him, I was able to tell him that our new prop was already on the way from Detroit, and that we would have it well before race time.

It arrived in plenty of time for a pre-race test that showed that our problem had been solved. The rpm's were right up there where they belonged. We hit the line right on the button. The white flag and the spurt of smoke from the starting cannon both appeared as we crossed the line. What a race that was! Again the lake was quite rough, causing us to do all sorts of spectacular leaps and dives. And although we were able to keep a slight lead on *Emancipator*, Auberbach was right there on our transom all the time. Just as we started the last lap, he made his move to pass us. Though we almost wrote our names on the first-turn buoy as we passed it, Auerbach got on the inside and started to pull up. In spite of all that I did, it seemed that he would pass us just before we reached the last turn. If he did, that would be it; nothing that I could do would overcome his advantage in the short run to the finish line. But there *was* something that I could do. Halfway between the first and last turning buoys, there was a single course marker. This could be passed on either side. I hoped that Auerbach had forgotten this. We both headed directly at the mid-course marker, and when we reached it, half of my boat was ahead of the bow of *Emancipator*. Watching each other very intensely, we both tried to come as close to the outside of the buoy as possible, without actually hitting it. Don't forget, Auerbach could legally have gone inside this buoy, passed us, and won the race. But he forgot. And just as our two boats and that marker were about to be engaged in one grand and glorious crash, he quit! Cutting his throttle a bit, he pulled in behind us, and that was it. We beat him around the last turn and crossed the finish line a good boat-length in front. But we didn't see the checkered flag. Had we won? Did we still have a lap to go? Or worse yet, had we been disqualified for some rule infraction? I kept going at full speed, and looking back I saw that Auerbach was doing the same. I guess we must have miscounted the number of laps. So the two of us raced our heads off for another full lap, and we were only prevented from doing count-

LMC III – wins at CNE 1933.

less extra laps by wild waving of two checkered flags from the start/finish line.

We had won our very first World Championship! We were called in to the officials' stand on the sea wall, along with Mortimer Auerbach, and were interviewed on a radio broadcast — the very first time, for us at least. Both Auerbach and I received all sorts of congratulations on the fine races we had run, and we were asked countless questions. I was so excited I can't remember any of those questions or the answers that I gave, but I do remember Auerbach's reply to the question "What happened at that last mid-course marker?" Mortimer said, "If I could have got my hands on Harold's neck at that moment, I would have wrung it! But now, I am very happy to shake his hand and offer my congratulations on a wonderful series of races." Again the Yanks proved their good sportsmanship.

You should have seen the papers the next morning! Our pictures were plastered over all the front pages, with stories everywhere. A half-page picture of us crossing the finish line was published in all the Toronto papers by a very happy Ford Motor Company. A while later, when I received a large box of news clippings from the CNE, I found out that Ford had run this picture ad in all the newspapers in Canada the same day. This was pretty heady stuff for Lorna and me, and did we revel in it! The next night a big dinner and presentation party was arranged at the Embassy Club. All the racing crews were to be on hand, and the general public also. After the dinner was over, we and the other place winners were called up to the stage to receive our prizes. Ours was a quite large silver punch-bowl trophy, the CNE World Championship Trophy for the 225-Cubic-Inch Class, and was to be returned at the end of one year for the next year's race. A fine replica of this trophy was also presented to us, to keep.

It had been a very exciting year for the whole Wilson Racing Team. There were press interviews by reporters such as Lou Marsh, Phil Griffith, Ted Reeves, Red Foster and many others.

There were invitations and entertainments galore. My home town of Ingersoll, at its fall fair, headed the long opening parade with a float carrying *Little Miss Canada III* and her crew. The float had been assembled by Ford and was exhibited at several other fairs that fall. The float was quite a masterpiece. The boat appeared to be speeding along with spray flying from the bow, all of this very tastefully done with painted scenery and backdrops. The big CNE trophy was displayed on a decorated stand in front of the boat. Lorna and I sat in the cockpit as a Ford truck pulled the boat along at the head of the parade. At the park we were formally congratulated by the mayor and the Ingersoll council, and a long citation was read over the public address system to the crowd, then presented to me. It was a glowing account of our deeds and bore congratulations from the whole town of Ingersoll. It was a lovely bit of expert calligraphy doubly interesting to me, as it was the creation of John Spittal, a lifetime employee of my father's. It occupies a special place in my memorabilia.

After another hard year of engineering studies at Varsity, I was back at Greavette's the next spring, 1934, itching to get ready for another crack at the 225 class. We put *Little Miss Canada III* in the water as soon as the ice was out and did some speed trials in Gravenhurst Bay, on the measured mile that Tom Greavette had laid out on the ice during the winter. The results of these tests were just a wee bit discouraging. Although she had beaten all the competition that the Yanks could offer the previous season, when her actual speed was compared with speeds now being established by new American boats, it was quite evident that *Little Miss Canada III* would be in the also-ran category in a race with the newest 225s. Now what? More talks with my father, followed by consultation with John Hacker, and soon a new racer, *Little Miss Canada IV*, was under construction at Greavette's. *Little Miss Canada III*, a racing hydroplane certainly, was in appearance more of a "gentleman's runabout," with its large, comfortable cockpit and rakish windshield, just the kind of craft that a gentleman might be expected to choose for getting about rapidly and in style. *Little Miss Canada IV* was

69

quite different. The running surface had been further refined, reducing the wetted area considerably, and thus adding, theoretically at least, to the speed. The large side-by-side cockpit had given way to two very small, kayak-type cockpits, placed one behind the other. This arrangement was the brainchild of John Hacker, who felt that the great difference in weight between my 225 pounds and Lorna's 118 pounds would cause the boat to list to starboard. I never did agree with this, and the fore-and-aft seating was inconvenient (but it did have one big redeeming feature, as I'll relate later). The deck was definitely whalebacked, streamlined to the *nth*. There was no windshield; the only protuberances above the sleek deck were the two intake manifold stacks (which faced backwards) and our bodies from the waist up. The rest of us were hidden below decks by the deck itself, which fitted us closely in the kayak-style cockpits.

Well, that was the new boat, *Little Miss Canada IV*. Now something about the engine. Remember that Ford had been quite excited about our win? When they learned that we were building a new and hopefully faster boat to defend our World Championship in September, they presented us with a new engine — two engines, in fact, just in case we needed a spare. These engines were, of course, Ford V8s, but with a difference! And what a difference. Externally they somewhat resembled our old faithful St. Lawrence conversion of 1933. These engines had been developed from standard Ford V8s by well-known racing-engine builder Harry Miller. For years his engines and cars had been the most feared racing machines at the Indianapolis 500-Mile Race. He had done all sorts of things to these Fords: special high-lift camshafts, Scintilla magneto ignition instead of the standard coil type, and a special two-carburetor, four-barrel intake system that was designed to make the engine produce more power.

Building racing hydros was getting to be old stuff for Greavette's, and it didn't take very long to get *Little Miss Canada IV* off the building ways and into the hands of the engineers, including Bill Doherty. (Ford was anxious for a repeat win in

1934, and to make sure that the new, more powerful engine did its stuff, they made Bill available to us for the whole racing season.)

We had everything ready so early, we were able to test *Little Miss Canada IV* out in one race in Muskoka before the big test at the CNE in Toronto. We found it to be very fast, easily handled, and very stable and safe under almost all conditions. We practised a lot and got used to the tandem seating, although it certainly cut down on conversation.

The end of August came and we were back at the foot of John Street in Toronto once again. We went over to the National Yacht Club to see our old racing friends of last year and to get a first-hand glimpse of the new 225-cubic-inch hydros. Most of the old gang was back, plus a few new ones. One of these was a strange-looking craft indeed. The crew sat in front of the engine, which of course was in the stern. The drive shaft, instead of going forward to a gear box and then back under the engine to the prop, was a long straight one stuck out through the transom to the prop, which was at least 4 feet behind the back of the boat. This long, highly flexible shaft was kept steady and under control by a long, sloping strut bearing. As the deck line cut down quite low as it approached the transom, there was a high, mahogany-planked hump over the engine. Lou Marsh, in his "Pick & Shovel" column, called this boat "the mahogany toothpick with the mumps"! The owner-driver, Roy Foyle of Lake Hotpatcong, New Jersey, was in high anger when he read Lou's column. This year there were only two Canadian entries, both by the Wilson Racing Team. Fred Burgess, a good friend and an excellent racing driver from the Muskoka circuit, was to drive the old boat, *Little Miss Canada III*. For a racing mechanic he had chosen his brother-in-law Jack Wellsman, also a Muskoka racer. Naturally Lorna and I would be driving the new boat. Our old friend Mortimer Auerbach was on hand with a new and reportedly much faster *Emancipator*.

The three races, on successive days, were pretty well repetitions of the last year's races. We won the first, with Auerbach in second place. The next day we reversed positions. Then came the last and deciding race, and wouldn't you know, old Lake Ontario was rough once again.

Earlier I mentioned a couple of *Little Miss Canada IV*'s features that were quite different. These were the tandem seating arrangement and the backward-facing intake stacks. Well, the first of these almost cost us the race, and the second saved it for us. We were leading *Emancipator* comfortably, provided we kept up our speed. Communication between pilot and mechanic was quite difficult because of the tandem seating coupled with the engine and wind noise. Lorna was keeping me posted by shouting instructions in my ear. We were riding the high waves at a speed that allowed us to stay on the water at all times, which meant that we were going along in a controlled series of ups and downs as we raced over each big wave. On the last straightaway before the home stretch, Lorna screamed something which ended in "gaining." Taking this to mean that *Emancipator* was making his move to pass, I opened the throttle wide just as we were shooting up the face of a wave. *Little Miss Canada IV* gave a startled leap which lifted us clear off the crest of the wave and into the trough. The whole boat became a submarine and drove right through the next wave. Spectators said that boat and crew completely disappeared underwater. We came out the other side of the wave, soaking wet but with our engine still running. This is where the backward-facing intake stacks won the race for us. Had they faced forward, the engine would have gulped a lot of water and stalled. But we had slowed down, and *Emancipator* drew even with us. Hard driving and the excellent turning ability of our boat paid off. We got around that last turn in first position and finished that way.

We were thrilled — our second World Championship in two years! Again the newspapers gave the 225 class tremendous coverage. The Ford Motor Company, very pleased that their products had been responsible for the winning of two World Championships, entertained the whole Wilson Racing Team

LMC IV repeats at 1934 CNE.

with a dinner party at which presentations were made to Lorna and me.

That wasn't the end of racing for 1934. Shortly after the end of the CNE races, we received a pressing invitation to represent Canada at a regatta being staged by the Baltimore Yacht Club. We accepted and were immediately caught up in all sorts of preparations, like finding a trailer to carry our boat, arranging with Ford to permit Bill Doherty to go with us, and, biggest of all, making arrangements for Lorna to travel. We weren't married at that time. Lorna's parents were very co-operative, and we arranged for Bill Doherty and his wife, Margaret, to act as chaperones.

It was a long haul to Baltimore towing *Little Miss Canada IV*. We arrived in the late afternoon of the day before the race. We were royally entertained by the members of the Baltimore Yacht Club, and in the evening were taken to see a fancy-dress parade of all the boats belonging to the Yacht Club. There were scads of them, all beautifully decorated with flowers of all descriptions, multitudes of flags, and thousands of coloured lights. The lead boat, a huge power yacht, was owned and driven by the commodore, the celebrated baritone of the Metropolitan Opera Company, John Charles Thomas. We were given front-row seats for this once-a-year gala celebration.

Early the next morning we were hard at it, getting our boat ready for the race that afternoon. The regatta was to be opened by John Charles Thomas singing the national anthem, accompanied by a large U.S. Navy Band. The race-boat crews were lined up in front of the bandstand. The band struck up the opening bars of the U.S. national anthem, and John Charles Thomas waved for the conductor to stop! He came down off the platform and spoke quietly to the conductor, then climbed back up again. The U.S. Navy Band accompanied Thomas as he sang "God Save the King"! It was a fine gesture to us two lonely Canadians. He then sang "The Star Spangled Banner," and the regatta was on.

The course was laid out on the Patapsco River. The starting line was a large barge anchored in mid-stream. Just a couple of hundred yards past the start was a large, high-level bridge over the river. The course led upstream under one bridge arch, around the upper-end turn, back under a second arch of the bridge, around the lower turn, and back to the start. We hit the starting line just a few feet behind the leader. Immediately we were at that awe-inspiring bridge, and realizing that there just wasn't room for the two of us abreast, I pulled in behind the flying American boat. As I did, a great wall of water hit us in the face, blinding us momentarily. Seconds later — and very luckily, as we got through that arch without hitting the bridge — we were in the open river, and in the lead! Where was that leading boat? Nowhere to be seen. We charged ahead. As we finished the first lap I saw all sorts of excited movement on the starting barge, arms being waved at us and people shouting, although they could not be heard. Lap after lap, as we crossed that line we saw the same thing. Finally, as we crossed the finish line and received the checkered flag, we realized that we were being motioned in to the barge. After all the other race boats had finished, we pulled up to the barge and shut off our engine. "Did you see what happened at the bridge on the first lap?" voices screamed at us. "Where did that lead boat go?" I asked. Well, it seemed that the first boat, just as it was about to enter the arch of the bridge, had hit a heavy cross swell, gone straight up into the air and done a back somersault! Unaware of what was happening, we had gone right under him. The people on the barge said that this flying boat had missed our heads by only inches as it slammed back, upside down, into the river!

The Americans were good sports. We received warm congratulations from all of our competitors, the regatta committee, and the general public. There was a fine dinner party for all those connected with the regatta or the races, and the prizes were presented. We received a fine silver trophy which still occupies an honoured place in our trophy room.

The next morning we started the long tow back home. This was the end of our racing for the year, and I was very pleased with the results. I felt deep appreciation for everything that the crew — Dad, Lorna, Bill Doherty, and his wife, Marge — had done to help me win these races. It had been a good year.

Back at varsity for the winter, besides trying to keep up with my engineering studies, I began to do a little sweating about the next racing season. Although I had had little or no trouble with the competition to date, I had heard somewhat disturbing rumours of a hot new 225-cubic-inch racing engine that was going to make my trusty Ford look sick. This was a Lycoming 6, built by the company that had powered the fine Auburn and Cord cars, and were now producing very good aero engines. My father and I talked about the engines, and when it became apparent that nothing new or more powerful was forthcoming from Ford, we decided that we had better join the crowd and ordered a new Lycoming for *Little Miss Canada IV*. The installation of the new engine was done during the winter and everything was ready for spring trials. These were not as successful as I would have liked. The boat was undoubtedly faster, as much as seven or eight miles per hour faster, but the new engine was nowhere near as dependable as the old Ford. As these trials indicated, so it developed in actual racing. I won a couple of races but failed miserably at Toronto defending the World Championship that Lorna and I had held for two years. We finished in the money, but pretty well down the line.

In late September we were invited to race in the 225-cubic-inch class races to be held at Washington, D.C., in conjunction with the prestigious President's Cup Regatta. Again we were to be the only Canadian competitor. By this time Bill had quit his job as head mechanic for Ford and had acquired the Ford agency in Gravenhurst. He was still acting as my mechanic, although we now had the Lycoming instead of the Ford. Bill and I towed the boat while Lorna drove with Marge, who again acted as chaperone. We were stationed at the huge Navy Yards, and felt very much like a small frog in a very large puddle. When we arrived there we found to our surprise and chagrin that the races were to be held on Saturday and Sunday. This presented a real problem. To date we had never raced on Sunday, and we had no desire to do so now. We could have said, "Sorry," and gone home, but a lot of money had been spent to get down there, so I decided that we would race, at least on Saturday. We did, and won. I had second thoughts about Sunday, so I asked my father what I should do. He said, "Use your own judgement. Whatever you decide is fine with me." So, like the Arabs of old, we packed up our tents — and our boat — and left for home. I have never regretted my decision.

That was the end of the 1935 racing season. Not a very impressive or satisfying one, but a good one nevertheless. One thing that I learned is that you only win your fair share of races, and then only if you are mighty lucky. I also learned that if you are to be popular with your racing friends and the public, you have to take whatever comes with a grin.

The prospects for the 1936 season looked pretty grim as far as the Wilson Racing Team was concerned. I had gone through one season when I definitely wasn't top dog, and as far as I could see, 1936 was going to be a repetition of 1935, and I didn't like that. My father was still a member of the board of Greavette Boat Company. A fellow board member was Andy Davis of Newmarket. He was head of the Davis Leather Company, an excellent sportsman, and a boat lover. Feeling that my racing had done a lot for the reputation of Greavette, and knowing that my father must have spent a great deal of the coin of the realm in making it possible for me to race, he offered to build *Little Miss Canada V* for me at his expense. This was a grand gesture on his part, and my father and I were delighted to accept. Of course Greavette was to build the new boat, but who designed it I never knew. It didn't look like a Hacker design. All the same, it was a beautiful hull — too beautiful, almost, for a racing boat. The seating was side by side again in a large cockpit. It fitted the description "a gentleman's runabout" even more than did *Little Miss Canada III*. The Lycoming engine from *Little*

Miss Canada IV was installed, and early in the spring I tried her out. What a disappointment that boat was! It was easy to handle, safe, and very comfortable to ride, but it just would not go. We tried all the tricks we knew, but no dice. It was just what I said above, a gentleman's runabout. Sadly, we had to say, "Thank you, Andy but we can't use it." The racing season was rapidly approaching and the Wilson stable didn't have a horse. A young man named Douglas Van Patten had been an employee of the Greavette Company for quite some time. Van Patten was a young American naval architect, and we appealed to him for help. He offered to design a new boat, to have it built in time for the CNE races, and promised that it would go. Although Doug was a dreamer at times, an artist and a person who liked to take his own good time in all things, he lived up to his promise and the new boat, *Little Miss Canada VI*, was ready for trials well ahead of the CNE Regatta.

This was a radically different racer. The cockpit was in front of the engine, which nestled in a smoothly streamlined cowling at the stern. The engine faced backwards, driving forward to a vee-drive gear box located between driver and pilot's knees, and then astern and under the engine to the propeller. The cockpit, fitted for the abreast seating, was almost directly over the step. As the step probably hits the water harder and more often than any other part of the hull, you can imagine how enjoyable was our ride. But she was a beauty, this new boat of mine. Not only were her lines pleasing and her finish like a grand piano, but she was fast! When that Lycoming chose to exert itself, it could show speeds in the very high seventies. Unfortunately, that engine didn't always want to exert itself but Bill Doherty felt sure we could make it behave. Tests over, we packed up everything and headed for the CNE again. There were a great number of new boats on hand that year, including the first three-pointer we had ever seen. There were also some different engines, including a very fancy-looking overhead-cam four owned by a chap named Fox.

Little Miss Canada VI.

In the first heat, we started well and were in the lead, shaving the turning buoys as closely as possible to keep ahead of the competition, especially that new three-pointer. We shaved one marker too closely. Shaved, did I say? We went right over top of that 6-foot-high pylon and reduced the plywood to matchsticks and the flag and fluorescent red sides to tiny rags. And our boat? Well, we ruined the propeller, chopped the rudder off and sprung a major leak in the hull. That finished us. We watched the second and third races of the year's World Championship event from the shore. That finished my racing for the year, a poor one indeed.

The next year, 1937, went a bit better. We won a couple of races in Muskoka with *Little Miss Canada VI* and made entry into a new racing circuit, at Picton, Ontario. But again the Lycoming gave us trouble and quit while we were running in the lead. We were scheduled to race at Tweed, about 80 miles from Picton, two days later, and there I was with a dud engine. This year I had a new mechanic. Bill Doherty had finally given up trying to keep up with the Wilson Racing Team. The new man was George McMurray from Ingersoll. Actually, he was my father's chauffeur, but he filled in as my mechanic whenever needed (which was quite often). George and I worked until sundown trying to get that cranky Lycoming to co-operate, but it was useless. After a very brief council-of-war, we yanked the whole engine out of the boat and managed to stuff it into the trunk of my Ford. Then we took off for the long 200-plus-mile drive to Ingersoll. There, very early in the morning, we resurrected the old Lycoming from *Little Miss Canada IV*, pulled off ignition and carburetion parts from the defunct engine, installed them on the spare, loaded this engine into the overworked Ford trunk, and took off for Picton. Arriving there, we worked until late afternoon installing the engine, and by five o'clock had had a quite successful test run. We then loaded the boat onto our trailer and set out for Tweed, arriving just before dark and in time to get the last motel unit available. Lorna had waited all day for us in Picton and of course went with us to Tweed, but we had decided that as all the other boats were now being raced with one-man crews, we had better do the same. That extra 120 pounds might just make the difference between first and second place. So for the first time Lorna would sit on shore to watch me race. And just as well, as things turned out.

The next morning I had a look at the course — a horror! The lake at Tweed was quite small, and the course was in keeping with the size of the lake. It was triangular, all sides the same length, and the three turning buoys were 120 degree turns! Well, maybe this might be an advantage. My boat had exceptional turning ability. I felt that this, plus the extra speed to be gained by reducing the crew load, might just bring me in at the head of the pack. My chief competitor was Pop Cooper from St. Louis, Missouri. His new Ventnor three-pointer, *Tops*, could show me a clean pair of heels on the straightaway, but it wasn't too good on the corners.

We fought like dogs, alternately leading or being led on each straightaway. Coming up to the last turn, with the finish line and that lovely checkered flag only an eighth of a mile further on, Pop and I were running neck and neck. But I had the inside track! If I could take *Tops* on the last turn, Pop wouldn't have an earthly chance of catching me in time. As we swept into the turn at better than 70, I shaved that marker as tight as I could, and Pop and I went around just about touching. I had him! Almost. Just at the tightest part of the turn, my chine tripped on *Top's* bow wave. A wild flurry, impossible to describe, and I came up to the surface to see the bow of my boat pointing skyward, with all the rest underwater! Air trapped in the bow kept her afloat until the crash boat arrived, pulled me out of the water, and very carefully began towing my sinking boat back to the pits. Arriving there, and with the boat safely back on its trailer, I had a chance to assess the damage. Of course the engine was drowned and would need an overhaul. The hull appeared all right, but where was the steering wheel? It — in fact the whole steering mechanism — was gone! Then I realized that I was limping and that my left knee was very sore. It seems that in

LMC VI upsets at Tweed.

being tossed out my left leg had jammed between the wheel and the deck, and this was responsible for the loss of the steering and my sore knee. Also, my shoes, tightly laced before the race, had disappeared. They were discovered two days later jammed up in the extreme apex of the bow.

This was to be my last race in the 225-cubic-inch class. It had been a wonderful experience. I had raced in Muskoka, Picton, Baltimore, Toronto, Washington, Tweed, and other places. I had won two World Championships, and many other races. On the flip side of the coin, I guess I had lost just as many races as I had won. But I was more than satisfied. I had made a host of new friends. All of my competitors had been top-notch sportsmen. All in all, the 225 class had been a wonderful introduction to the exciting world of international motorboat racing.

Chapter 7

The Gold Cup

After retirement from business my father and mother spent long winter holidays in Florida and California. While in California during the winter of 1934-35, my father attended several regattas. At these he became acquainted with a new (to him) class of racing, the Gold Cup class. He met and became friendly with the then holder of the Gold Cup, George Reis of Lake George, New York. Reis was the builder, owner and driver of the well-known *El Lagarto*. When Dad got home that spring, he was bubbling over with excitement about the Gold Cup. And when my father got excited about something, look out! I have already remarked on his propensity for jumping the gun on me. Well, he did it again. First, he led me like a lamb to the slaughter by describing the exciting races he had seen and the fine showing made by *El Lagarto*, and asking, "What would it be like to drive a boat like that?" I was thrilled with the idea, but of course it was out of reach of even the fastest of my *Little Miss Canada*'s. "Well, what if there was some way we could get a Gold Cupper? Do you think you could drive it?" Silly question! Excited as I was by then, I was sure that I could handle one of these big heavy hydros, even if they were capable of hitting speeds in the high eighties. That was when I learned all about his jumping the gun once again. Not only had I already been entered as a new Gold Cup driver, John Hacker had my new boat, *Miss Canada II*, on his drafting board, and our new engine was already under construction. George Reis had tried to interest my father in a complete, ready-to-race, built-by-George-Reis boat. Not only was George Reis a boatbuilder, and a good one, he also had designed and built the marine conversion required for the aero engine he used in *El Lagarto*. Feeling that there was no sense in being content with a run-of-the-mill production job, my father had elected to have Hacker design a boat using the very successful *Little Miss Canada IV* lines. For motive power he really went exotic. At the races he had met Harry Miller, the motor genius whose race cars had become synonymous with racing generally and the Indy 500 in particular. He persuaded Miller to build a special, one-of-a-kind racing engine to power our new racer.

So there it was: a Canadian challenge for the Gold Cup had been made by the Wilson Racing Team and the boat was to be a Greavette-built, Hacker-designed, 24-foot hydro powered by a 1,000 horsepower engine of 7-litre piston displacement. The announcement in the papers made quite a fuss and made doubly hard my struggle at Varsity with such mundane things as calculus and analytical geometry!. How was a guy supposed to study when dreams of thousand-horsepower engines and boats doing a 100 miles per hour danced in his head? That was what I was going to have to handle, 1,000 of the best, and at 6,000 rpm! We found out that Miller had actually built one of these monsters before, for the United States government, and it had been utterly destroyed while undergoing maximum power tests. I wondered if that disease might be catching!

Hacker had the boat plans in Tom Greavette's hands by early spring and an immediate start was made. I had my first look at the plans when the hull was just in the framing stage. The new boat certainly looked like a big sister of *Little Miss Canada IV* — very low in profile, sleek and with rounded decks that blended almost into the water at the transom. As with the 225 hull, Hacker figured that the great difference in my weight as compared to Lorna's would make for unsteady lateral stability, so again we were placed one behind the other, me in front as the driver and Lorna behind in the mechanic's seat. As in *Little Miss Canada IV*, these two cockpits, located aft of the engine, were quite small and almost form-fitting. Work seemed to be progressing well, and it looked like the hull would be ready for the hoped-for early summer testing. But what about the engine? Where was that Miller?

Miller's plant was in Butler, Pennsylvania. Reports from him indicated that all was well, the engine would be ready as soon as the boat. He certainly was enthusiastic, if not downright cocksure. He got the engine to Gravenhurst just as the last finishing touches were being lovingly applied to *Miss Canada II*. He got it there all right, but in pieces! There were crates of pistons and rings, some extra connecting rods, and boxes of ignition and fuel system parts. The engine itself was an imposing, shiny aluminum engine frame with twin overhead camshafts and a most complicated-looking intake manifold nuzzled down between the two camshaft housings. All this was in an open crate, and there it was on the floor beside the boat. Along with these engine parts came Harry Miller and two of his merry men, one of them a wild Russian by the name of Joe Kerchoff. It seemed that they were there to finish assembling our engine. Maybe they would make it yet. Our engine was what Miller called a link-rod engine. It was a 12-cylinder with two banks of six at 60 degrees to each other. Instead of all 12 con rods having their large ends running directly on the throws of the crankshaft, only the six cylinders on one bank were so mounted. The connecting rods on the other bank were shorter and their lower ends were pinned to the sides of the master rods in the other bank. Hence the name, "link rod." Keep this unusual type of connecting rod construction in mind. It had a profound effect on the operation of our Miller. The engine seemed to be pretty well assembled, but the sassy-looking supercharger which was to run at better than 30,000 rpm was still to be hung on, and there were boxes of stuff, such as the magnetos and wiring manifolds, still waiting to be mounted. This was late June, and that Gold Cup race in which I was entered was slated for early August. It was going to be tight.

Much of this technical stuff was pure Greek to me, but very interesting. I spent my time between the boat and the engine, either watching Greavette's men installing the engine bed, shaft, rudder and propeller, or Harry Miller and Joe Kerchoff as they lovingly assembled the supercharger and spent hours attaching it and the two magnetos to the engine. These magnetos had been made in Germany by Bosch, and they were 18-cylinder mags. How could they possibly be used on a 12-cylinder engine? Miller gave me an answer, but I am afraid it was not understood. I could write a whole book about that Miller engine. Even if it never did anything, it certainly was a work of art. The whole outside was dowel-polished aluminum. The insides of all castings were hand-scraped to remove any traces of foundry sand that might get into the engine oil and damage bearings. The maker's plate fastened to the base of the engine said, "Miller V12 Marine Engine–7 liter–1000 h.p. 6000 r.p.m." What a wild tiger I had by the tail!

Those thousand horses didn't show their heads all summer. The engine was in and out of the boat several times, and the engine accessories seemed to be in a constant state of assembly or disassembly. By mid-July we were still awaiting the first bark from the Miller's exhaust stacks. Finally, one day, Harry Miller said that we needed fuel and lubricating oil. Well, the fuel was easy. Any nearby service station could supply the fuel. Or could it? Apparently this new engine of ours had a mighty and very sensitive appetite. Nothing but aircraft-quality gasoline of 150 octane rating would do. We located a bit, enough for early tests, at the Gravenhurst airport. But the oil really threw me. Nothing but the best, said Miller, and the best was pure castor oil. The local drugstores had a few six-ounce bottles, but we needed gallons. In desperation I telephoned Drug Trading in Toronto. Could they supply castor oil in bulk? "How much?" My reply of a 40-gallon drum elicited a gasped "My God, man, you take that stuff in small doses!" But we got our 40 gallons. We were ready for our first test run, but the Miller still wasn't.

Besides getting the boat ready for its first race, we also had to find the means of getting it to the race site, Bolton Landing on Lake George in New York State. We found a two-wheel trailer and built bunks on it that would hold the boat in place during

Gold Cup *Miss Canada II.*

the long, hard tow through the hilly country leading in to Lake George. Then came the day when the boat simply had to leave for Bolton Landing. The engine still hadn't made its first revolution. It seemed silly to be packing up a racing outfit that had never been tried. Perhaps we should just phone and say, "Sorry, our boat just isn't ready yet." But Miller said, "No, the engine will be ready to run at Lake George." So everything went on that trailer and the trailer went on behind Greavette's truck, and off it all went to Lake George. Our boat was on its way, and supposedly would be ready to race, but how about the crew? Lorna and I knew absolutely nothing about Gold Cup racing, our new boat, or that 1,000-horsepower powerplant.

My good friend Fred Burgess — remember, he drove *Little Miss Canada III* for me at the CNE — and his wife, Launi, offered to drive Lorna down and to act as chaperones for us. We accepted, but decided that all four of us should travel in my car. When we were going through a fairly mountainous area of New York, down a particularly steep and twisty hill, I heard a violent and almost continuous horn blasting behind me. It was nearing us at an alarming rate. A few seconds later a spanking-new Pontiac screamed past. It was towing a wildly swaying trailer carrying *Miss Canada II*. The car must have been doing 80, and how it negotiated all those wild gradients and turns I know not. A couple of minutes later we caught up. The car and trailer were stationary at the side of the road, and the two occupants of the Pontiac were sitting down on the roadside, heads in hands. One was Harvey Doherty, treasurer of Greavette's. The other was a very badly frightened friend of his. We soon got the story. They were on the way to Lake George in Harvey's brand-new Pontiac. Earlier in the day they had come across our race boat, stuck with a very sick Greavette truck. Harvey immediately had a jury-rig tow bar installed on his car and started off to tow our heavy boat to Lake George. All had been going well until just before they passed us. It seems the Pontiac's hard-pressed brakes had given up the fight, resulting in a wild downhill slalom which had scared the daylights out of Harvey and friend, and almost wrote finis to my Gold Cup racing career before it even got started. Taking it very easily after that, Harvey and his Pontiac got the boat safely to Bolton Landing late in the afternoon of the day before the race.

The next morning there was utter confusion at the Wilson Racing Team pits. Greavette's men were doing all they could to get the boat ready to race, Harry Miller and crew were madly assembling the engine, and Lorna and I were trying on our new racing outfits and life jackets. Into the water went the boat, and Miller announced that we were at last ready for a test. What a time to have a first-ever test — half an hour before the start of the race! I must give Miller credit for keeping his word. After a few refusals, the engine roared to life, and for the first time in *my* life I was at the wheel of a Gold Cupper. But it didn't last long. After getting up to what Joe Kerchoff optimistically claimed was well over 60 miles per hour, there was a foul smell of burning rubber followed by a continuous series of very loud backfires, the Miller quit, and *Miss Canada II* was dead on the water. A quick inspection showed that the intake manifold had come loose from the two cylinder banks. The whole manifold system would have to be rebuilt, a long job. There would be no racing *Miss Canada II* for the Gold Cup that year. We watched the race from the grounds of the Sagamore Hotel, where we were staying, and saw George Reis and *El Lagarto* come in first quite handily. Afterwards, we packed up and headed for home.

We headed for home, but the engine didn't. Miller's mechanics pulled it out of the boat, loaded it onto a truck and took it back to Butler. The engine was certainly far from finished; the best place for it was back where it was born.

Ours wasn't a very good start in the Gold Cup class, but we weren't downhearted. Greavette's wood butchers got right to work as soon as we reached Gravenhurst, and I packed my bag and headed off to Butler to find out all that I could about the innards of our Miller engine. I stayed there for a week, watching everything that Miller and his men did to turn this polished hunk of aluminum into a thoroughbred racing machine. The work was done in time for the engine to be installed in the boat on its way to Washington at the end of September. I was scheduled to drive *Miss Canada II* in the President's Cup race, the same class of hydros as the Gold Cup. When I caught up with the boat at Washington, everything seemed to be in finished condition and Miller said the engine was ready to race, and to win. Just to be on the safe side he had brought along a Bosch ignition expert to put the final touches to our ignition system. The expert was a German named Lou Vollmar.

We were stationed at the Navy Yards, as were all the other racers. The next day, well ahead of starting time, we launched our boat and followed all the others out to the race course, which was laid out on the Potomac River. We started the engine all right, with Miller's help, and moved up to the start. This big boat sure seemed sluggish and difficult to handle when compared to the lithe *Little Miss Canadas*, but we started fine and ran pretty well, definitely in the money, until the third lap, when horrible burned-rubber smells and expensive sounds poured out of our engine compartment. And as at Bolton's Landing, the Miller began backfiring. The engine temperature gauge appeared normal, no overheating there, but when I tried to restart, no dice. So we sat out the President's Cup too — in the middle of the Potomac! It is sad indeed to watch a race from a dead race boat and on the infield.

That was our second attempt in the Gold Cup class; not a very impressive record so far. When we were towed back to our pits at the Navy Yards, the rest of our crew were there to find out what had happened. It didn't take long. The intake manifold, which nestled in between the two banks of cylinders, was connected to the 12 intake ports by 12 short pieces of oval tubing, 12 pieces of large radiator hose and 24 hose clamps. The extreme heat from the cylinder blocks had melted all the hose connections, and all this stuff — manifold, bits of rubber and useless hose clamps — all was bouncing around loose between the cylinder blocks! No wonder the engine was backfiring. And the smell in the engine compartment, you wouldn't believe.

1000 H.P. Miller – *Miss Canada II* power plant.

Later that night the whole team was drowning its sorrows and talking over the sad events of the day. Miller, a bit more drowned than the rest, said that a big mistake had been made in sending out "that little girl" as mechanic. To which the Bosch ignition expert responded, "Mistah Milla, if your engine had half the guts of that little girl, *Miss Canada II* would have won the race today!" That squelched Miller. Back to the drafting board again for us.

And back home for us also. But we didn't just lie down and quit. We were into this 7-litre racing for a purpose, and that was to win. After some discussion we came to the conclusion that although Miller could certainly build a beautiful engine, he couldn't make it run. My father did a lot of investigating with racing car owners, who all agreed with our thinking about Miller: let him build the engine, but someone else has to make it run. And who might that be? He got the name of a supposedly very good mechanic in the Detroit area, Bill Mueller. Mueller came to Ingersoll that fall and stayed all winter working on the Miller. A new intake manifold had come over from Miller's plant in Butler and Mueller installed this. By early spring Bill said that the engine was ready, so back to Gravenhurst. But at this point, Mueller told us that he would like to bring in another man, who had been Louis Meyer's mechanic at Indianapolis and who was a wizard on Miller engines. So our crew increased again. The new mechanic was Charlie Volker, also a Detroit man.

The two of them, Bill Mueller and Charlie Volker, went up to Gravenhurst with the engine and set about getting it installed in the boat once more. After a short time it became apparent that Charlie was a far better mechanic than Bill, so after some sort of amicable arrangement was made, Bill went off the job, leaving Charlie to make *Miss Canada II* show her stuff. Let me say right here that Charlie Volker was the best mechanic, machinist and friend that anyone could desire. But even with him on the job, our troubles were not over yet. Although the Miller was running fairly consistently, it certainly didn't feel like it was developing the thousand horsepower that Miller had spoken so glowingly about. Despite this, Charlie and I both felt that it was finally ready to race.

The next event was scheduled for Labour Day at the Detroit Yacht Club. We arrived there a few days ahead of time and established pits at a marina on the Detroit River. We had a few practice runs on the river and found it surprisingly rough. When Lorna arrived, I found that I had a new big problem. Lorna's mother absolutely refused to let her race. We had to do some rather hurried enlarging of her small cockpit to fit a man. Then, the day before the race, Lorna's father arrived. He was a 100-percent true sportsman if ever there was one. He promptly put everything right by saying, "Lorna, you race with Harold." We didn't have time to refit the enlarged cockpit to Lorna's smaller frame; she would just have to hang on a bit tighter. We were facing a truly international field of boats, from Italy, United States, France and Canada. The Italian boats were driven by Count Theo Rossi of Martini and Rossi fame, and his second driver, Guido Catanio. There were two American boats and one French, driven by Farnham.

Lorna piled into her outsize cockpit, which didn't give her the support she needed, and off we went to the starting line. We started well and ran well. We led at times and then dropped back a place or so. But was it rough! We absorbed a terrible pounding, and this was almost responsible for a very sticky end for the Wilson Racing Team. Coming out of the upper turn and headed directly for the 6-foot-high, solid-stone sea wall on the Detroit side, the steering jammed! At 100 miles per hour we were doomed to hit that wall head on. I cut the throttle and put all my weight into trying to turn that steering wheel. No luck! Then, just as we were about to crash, the boat responded and we tore along the face of that wall so close that we could have reached out and touched it. That was a mighty close call, but now we had to catch all those boats that had passed us while we were doing that wild manoeuvre. We didn't manage it. We finished, but certainly not in the lead.

As we headed back to our pits to make ready for the second heat, I realized that we had other problems besides our jammed steering gear. The boat was definitely losing speed and it appeared to be getting very sluggish in the water. As quickly as possible we lifted the boat out of the water and — what was that? Streams of water were pouring from the boat's bottom from end to end! With her lying in her cradle on the trailer a few moments later, we discovered that there were several inches of water in the hull and that this was pouring out of all the seams in the bottom. The rough waters of the Detroit River had literally pounded our boat to pieces. Hacker had used a highly unusual construction on the bottom. The planking was narrow, about $1\frac{1}{2}$ inches, and ran longitudinally from bow to stern. Three quarters of these strips were $\frac{5}{8}$ inches thick. The other quarter were double that thickness. The result of this unusual construction was that every fourth plank was a heavy stringer, supposedly adding much to the longitudinal strength. Obviously it didn't work. The pounding that we had absorbed had made every one of those long seams leak water like Niagara Falls. We went out and watched Theo Rossi drive his *Alagi* to victory.

Miss Canada's bottom wasn't the only one that got knocked about by the Detroit River that day. Lorna, sitting in that too-large cockpit, found it almost impossible to stay with the boat. She ended up lying on her back, half on her seat and half on the boat's bottom, with her feet braced against the deck over her head and her arms wrapped around the ruins of her bucket seat, which her wildly bouncing body had smashed to pieces. The stuck steering gear that had almost caused a very bad accident was due to a piece of her seat jammed between the steering cable and the rudder quadrant. Call it what you will — quicksilver thinking, woman's intuition, or pure blind luck — somehow Lorna summoned the strength, skill and nerve to stick her hand into that mess and yank out the offending piece of wood just in the nick of time. All of this took its toll on Lorna. Shortly after the race was over, when the excitement died away and her supply of adrenaline was exhausted, reaction set in. She began to stiffen up, and by noon the next day she was black and blue from the waist down and could hardly walk. But she recovered well and quickly — and just as well that she did, because just three weeks from then another big change was scheduled for the Wilson Racing Team: Lorna and I were to be married in Toronto on September 28, 1937!

We took *Miss Canada II* back to Gravenhurst for further tests and found that the hull was going to have to undergo a major rebuild to make it fit for racing. Also, the Miller was developing that nasty backfiring habit once more. We discovered that the intake manifold was again loose between the cylinder banks and that all those blessed hose connections were fried. There was lots to do the winter of '37. Greavette's would put the hull back in shape while Charlie Volker worked on the Miller in Ingersoll. As it was quite obvious that the intake manifold just was not right, Charlie set about designing a new one. This was an aluminum casting that was made almost a press fit between these cylinder banks — an almost impossible job, but Charlie did it. This eliminated all those troublesome hose and clamp connections, but what about the high heat that had caused all the problems? Charlie turned that problem over to me, and I designed a water-cooled jacket for the manifold The whole winter was spent on these important alterations. By early spring the Miller was in the best condition that it had ever been in.

The tests proved a lot of things. The engine was now working quite well and seemed to have got over the backfiring problem, but the boat itself was far from well. The strengthened bottom was better, but under the strain of many fast test runs, it began to leak once more. Even worse, as our speed increased with better engine performance, *Miss Canada II* began to show a bad tendency to gallop, or porpoise. The faster we went, the worse the gallop. My father was watching me drive at top speed over a mile course when the jumping became so bad that the stern lifted completely off the water, allowing the prop to spin in air, then the bow took a determined dive for the bottom. Test over, my father said, "Take her out of the water. You will not drive that boat again. It is altogether too dangerous!"

That seemed the end to my aspirations as a Gold Cup racer. But remember Doug Van Patten, the young American naval architect who had designed my last 225 hydro, *Little Miss Canada VI*? Well, as *Miss Canada II* came out of the water for the last time, Doug came up to my father and said, "I think I can fix that boat to ride properly, Mr. Wilson. Will you let me try?" My father gave his assent as Doug said that it would be a relatively simple matter. But the next afternoon, with nothing done on the boat and Van Patten sitting in his office daydreaming and smoking his pipe, my father said, "Let's go home. He doesn't know what he is doing!"

Well, he did. The next morning carpenters were hard at work on the forward third of the boat's running bottom. Reasoning that the porpoising was due to the fact that the boat was too evenly balanced between the two planes and that because the forward plane did not have enough load-bearing area, the boat was literally teetering on the step, Doug designed a second step which did two things when it was built onto the bottom halfway between the original step and the bow: it held the bow up because of its relatively greater area, and it made it impossible for the boat to teeter, as there were now two steps instead of one.

All of this theory stuff was very interesting, but the proof of the pudding is in the eating. Boatbuilders, mechanics, spectators and the Wilson racing crew were all anxious to see what improvements, if any, Van Patten had made. In she went for another (maybe final) run. And what a run. Cautiously, I ran up to the engine speed where the porpoising usually started to develop. No jump. Keeping an eagle eye on the tachometer, I gradually and carefully opened up the throttle. Faster and faster we went, purring as smoothly as a kitten. Finally, throwing caution to the wind, I floored it and held it there until I ran out of lake at the end of Gravenhurst Bay. Terrific! No jump, no porpoise, just the best run I had ever made. On the return run, we timed ourselves over the measured mile. In excess of 100 miles per hour! Congratulations showered on Doug Van Patten. He had definitely made a silk purse out of a sow's ear. Now we had a Gold Cup racer.

But when *Miss Canada II* was triumphantly hauled out of the water, there were those darn telltale streams of water pouring down from all those overstrained and leaking seams. Now we could beat anyone speedwise, but could we stay afloat long enough to do it? Long discussions brought agreement from all: as a race boat, *Miss Canada II* was finished.

Further talks with Greavette, Van Patten and my father finally resulted in the decision to have a new *Miss Canada* designed by Van Patten and built in the Greavette works. Feeling that we had learned a lot from our experiences with *Miss Canada II*, we decided that the running surface of the new boat should be as like the final form of the *Miss Canada II* as possible. All other details were left to Van Patten. The design of this boat would take considerable time, and the actual building would take longer. As summer was already on its way, that meant that there would be no Gold Cup racing for us in 1938. You have read earlier that I raced *Little Miss Canada VI* during that summer; not too successfully, but it helped to keep my driving hand in. My real interest, however, lay in the lines which I watched emerging on Doug Van Patten's drafting board, and much later in the actual start of construction of *Miss Canada III*. This was to take the rest of 1938 and well into the spring of '39 when, finally, Doug's drawings would become an actual creature of wood, aluminum and steel.

Just about this time there came another change that profoundly affected the Wilson Racing Team. Lorna announced the mid-December arrival of our first-born. Another dose of what she had suffered at Detroit would do her in and the next-generation race driver also. Lorna's replacement was Charlie Volker. Although I would miss the very close mental contact that Lorna and I had developed, Charlie Volker's wonderful mechanical ability would be a fine thing to have in the boat.

The second Gold Cup – *Miss Canada III*.

The Skipper at work.

The power for the new boat was to be the Miller from *Miss Canada II*. It took considerable time to install the engine and all of its appurtenances in the new boat. Although the outside running surface of the bottom of the new boat was almost identical to the Hacker design, the actual construction of the bottom was entirely different. Gone were those troublesome narrow planks and the multitude of leaky seams. The bottom was now double-planked, the inner layer herringbone style and the outer layer longitudinal. The framing of the hull was also much different. All of these things affected the engine installation, but finally, near the end of July, everything was finished and *Miss Canada III* was ready for testing.

Right from the start, luck was with us. The *Miss Canada III* was as fast as lightning and handled just like a canoe. The Miller appeared to have forgotten her bad habits and was acting like a lady. Charlie and I had about three weeks to make ourselves into a smooth operating team and to learn all we could about this very fast boat that we were going to race at Detroit on Labour Day. That was only a week off. Where had the summer gone? The race at Detroit was the Detroit Silver Cup, and it was one of a series of worldwide races that would determine the 12-litre World Championship. Besides the Detroit Race, there was the President's Cup in Washington and two races each in England, Germany and Italy. How we were going to manage those offshore races, I had no idea, but we were going to put our best foot forward in the North American events.

At Detroit, this time at Keen's Yacht Harbour on the Detroit River, we found that we would be racing against several American boats and Count Theo Rossi's *Alagi*. The race was a good one. We ran quite well but, perhaps because we didn't yet know all the fine points of our new racer, we had to be content with second place behind the very professionally driven *Alagi*. Again Theo Rossi was taking home the bacon. We weren't disappointed. After the first race toward the World Championship, we were in second place. That night at a dinner for all contestants, we helped congratulate Count Rossi on winning the

Never printed news flash!

Silver Cup and were in turn congratulated when the second-place Meighan Trophy was presented to us.

But it was a sad day nonetheless. Canada had just declared war on Germany and the Second World War was on. Charlie, a German, and me, a Canadian, at war with each other! It just didn't seem right or possible. Charlie had been living in the United States for several years and had every intention of becoming a naturalized American citizen, but he hadn't done so yet. A great deal of the thrill of the day's racing disappeared when I thought of what might lie ahead.

Although we had done well, neither Charlie nor I were completely satisfied with our boat's performance. The President's Cup was scheduled for just two weeks later, so we kept the whole outfit in Detroit, at Keen's, and did all sorts of necessary engine work at Charlie Volker's Engine Works. It was a tough period. We worked 15 hours a day or more. We quit when we dropped and went back at it again after just a few hours of shut-eye. When I wasn't at Charlie's, Lorna and I worked all night long on the boat at Keen's. Finally ready for racing again, we loaded *Miss Canada III* onto our fine new four-wheel trailer, fastened it on behind my Mercury, and set off on the long haul to Washington.

The trailer and boat were a terrible load for my Mercury, but the trailer was equipped with air brakes operated from the car, and it towed very well. The only thing it would not do was back up. We had two bad experiences on the way. At a sweeping uphill bend, finding the whole road taken up by two huge trucks, I had to run off the road. I smashed off a big highway sign, yanked on those air brakes, did a wild skidding bounce, and ended up stationary with the front axle of the Mercury straddling a cement culvert! The boat slid forward on its cradle and bashed in the rear of my car. But no one was hurt, and with help from passing truck drivers, we got back onto the road and crawled our stricken Mercury to the nearest Ford dealer for a checkup. Surprisingly, there was nothing wrong. Then, later that night, in a blinding rainstorm, our poor car just gave up the ghost. No longer could it tow that two-ton trailer load up a mountain. With Lorna holding a flashlight, Charlie and I had to disconnect the trailer and turn it around by hand so that we could go search for a less hilly route. We reached Washington early the morning of the President's Cup first heat, early enough to allow us to grab some necessary rest before we had to go to our pits at the Navy Yard for the start of Saturday's race.

When we reached the Navy Yard, I found all sorts of problems. First, as Canada was at war, the U.S. Navy wasn't very anxious to let us in. That settled, I then learned that our shipment of special racing fuel sent from Toronto by British American Oil had not arrived. The U.S. Navy wouldn't let the truck in, so it had taken off and was apparently at Baltimore. There wasn't enough time to have the fuel brought back to us before the start of the race, so although I hated to do it (BA Oil had been supplying all of our petroleum needs ever since we started in the Gold Cup), I accepted Gulf Oil's very noble and generous offer: they would supply us the fuel needed, and if we won, Gulf would allow BA Oil to take the credit.

We headed out to the Potomac and upstream to the start. We were first across, and we stayed in that position for the whole race. Our closest rival was Dan Arena in Herb Mandelssohn's boat *Notre Dame*. This had a fabulous 24-cylinder Dusenberg engine. It emitted a high, loud exhaust scream from its 24 short stacks. We could hear it right behind us the entire race. We were pleased as Punch when we returned to the pits; a win in the first heat certainly put us in the driver's seat. But again the matter of driving on Sunday came up. My father said, "We have proved that we can win. Do just what you think you should." Well, I worried about this all that night, but by morning I had made up my mind to race. My father had spent a mint of money chasing the elusive Gold Cup. Now that we had at least one hand on it, would it be fair to give up? I didn't think so. If I could win the President's Cup for my father by racing on Sunday, so be it.

Charlie, Lorna and I were at the boat early in the morning, making certain that everything about the Miller and the boat was as perfect as we could make it. Barring accidents, we felt fairly certain the *Miss Canada III* could repeat the fine performance of the previous day. We went out to the start with the rest of the boats, started in first place, and by driving just as hard as necessary to keep ahead of the roaring *Notre Dame*, we held our position, swept across the finish line and got the checkered flag. The start/finish barge was the U.S. Coast Guard cutter *Apache*, anchored midstream in the Potomac. As soon as all the boats had finished, we reported to the officials aboard the *Apache*. We had won the President's Cup. What a thrill! After four years of tremendous effort and bitter disappointment, we had finally made a major win in the Gold Cup Class.

My father and Lorna were aboard the *Apache* to congratulate us. Dad was as proud as could be. There was a national radio hookup operating from the *Apache*, and we were asked to speak on it. The announcer asked my father if he ever rode in the racing boats. "Certainly," said Dad. "I go with Harold quite often on test runs." Actually he had never been in the boat. "Well, then, Mr. Wilson," said the announcer, "I can't think of a better time than right now to go for a ride. There are a quarter million people on the river banks who have watched your son win today. They would be delighted to see you both in the boat." Then a scream: "Hey, *Miss Canada* is sinking!" Sure enough, the stern of my boat was just about to slip underwater! Charlie and I slid down a rope, grabbed a large suction pipe tossed down to us by a wide-awake Marine who also put in motion a powerful sump pump attached to it. This quickly lowered the level of water in the hull and soon *Miss Canada III* was floating properly again. What had happened? Had our new, supposedly much stronger, boat been battered to pieces like her predecessor? No, there were no leaks or cracks. It was just that in the excitement of winning we had forgotten to plug the two large bilge drain holes that we always left open to get rid of any water that might get aboard while running. No damage done, but the two of us were sort of red in the face when we climbed back up to the *Apache*'s deck. And there was that announcer

Winning 1939 Presidents Gold Cup.

again, with a life jacket in hand. "Come on, Mr. Wilson, put this on and get into that boat." What else could my father do? So, the two of us slid down the rope and settled into the cockpit. "Now, Harold," said Dad, "the people have seen you racing all afternoon. Now they want to see the two of us. So just go slowly, about thirty, and we can wave to the crowd and they can all get a good look at us." As that was what he wanted, and it was his boat, I started out to do just that. He was a bit startled when the Miller burst into life. We were up to that 30 miles per hour in a couple of seconds, but as we swung around and headed down-stream very near the shore, Dad was waving to everyone and really enjoying the ride. Then, way ahead, I saw a large cruiser dash across our route back to the Navy Yards. That cruiser would be kicking up very large swells, and this suggested something that I just could not resist. With a shouted "Hang on, Dad!" I put my foot right into it and we hit those swells at about 100 miles per hour! *Miss Canada III* soared into the air and for about 75 feet travelled like a rocket! It was a thrilling, short flight through space, and a rather violent landing. Back at the Navy Yards a few minutes later, when he had both feet firmly planted on terra firma, my father said, "You'll never get me in that damn thing again as long as I live!"

There were great celebrations that night and the next day. All of the Wilson Racing Team were invited to the White House to meet President Roosevelt and to be presented with the President's Cup. After a few minutes wait in the famous Oval Room, with its large, beautiful table made from a California redwood trunk over 20 feet in diameter, we were ushered into the President's executive office. The President was seated at his desk. Our team was arranged behind him, and all of us faced a battery of reporters and photographers. Mr. Roosevelt asked several questions about our boat, and then formally presented the $13,000 gold trophy to me. "I suppose you will now take this home to Canada, Mr. Wilson," he said. Before I could reply, one of the young reporters said, "I'm sorry, Mr. President, but he can't do that." "And why not? He just won it!" said Roosevelt.

F.D.R. presents his trophy.

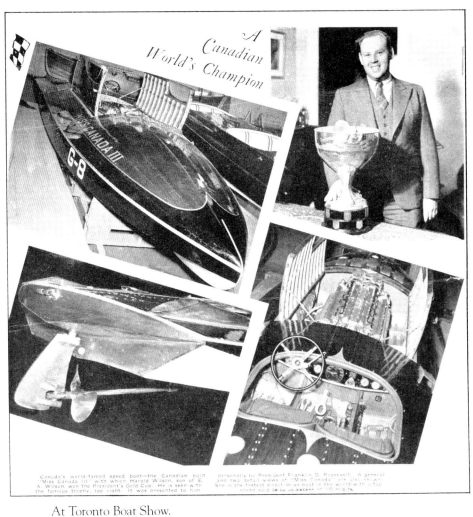

A Canadian World's Champion

Canada's world-famed speed boat—the Canadian built "Miss Canada III" with which Harold Wilson, son of E. A. Wilson, won the President's Gold Cup. He is seen with the famous trophy, top right. It was presented to him personally by President Franklin D. Roosevelt. A general and two detail views of "Miss Canada" are also shown. She is the fastest direct drive boat in the world with a top speed said to be in excess of 110 m.p.h.

At Toronto Boat Show.

"Because the deed of gift of the trophy says that, although it can be won by a foreign country, it cannot be taken to a foreign country," replied the reporter. The President looked him up and down for a couple of minutes, then said, "My dear young man, you had better realize that Canada is not a foreign country; it is a brother country. Take it home, Mr. Wilson." And so we did, for the year allowed on such challenge trophies. But we didn't dare keep it in our house. We were certain that thugs with big blow-torches would be lined up outside, three deep, waiting for a chance to put that $13,000 worth of gold into a more fluid state.

We loaded up the next day and began the long trek back home. Sadly, at Buffalo, we had to say goodbye to Charlie Volker. Being a German and not yet in possession of U.S. citizen-ship papers, it would have been most inadvisable for him to enter Canada. We were tendered a fine reception when we hauled our trailer carrying *Miss Canada III* into my home town of Ingersoll. And we were glad to be home.

Alas, no rest for the wicked! Canada was at war and everyone had a job to do. Almost immediately I was caught up in muni-tions work at the Ingersoll Machine & Tool Co., making shells for the Bofors anti-aircraft gun. All of our racing equipment was carefully oiled, protected, and put away for the duration, either in Ingersoll or Gravenhurst. And that ended my racing career in the 12-litre class, or at least suspended it until the war finished. But racing was not quite forgotten.

The United States was still at peace, so it was business as usual. First there was a big dinner in Detroit, hosted by Count Theo Rossi. All the drivers and owners were there. At that dinner, and afterwards, Count Rossi tried very hard to persuade my father and me that we should take *Miss Canada III* to Europe for the 7-litre races. It seemed that the races in England, France and Germany had already been cancelled because of the war, but Italy, still non-belligerent, was going ahead with its two sched-uled races. This was a thrilling challenge, of course, but there was a war on and we all had our bit to do, so very regretfully we turned down Count Rossi's fine offer to pay all expenses if we would just appear for the Italian events.

Just after New Year's Day, the annual New York Boat Show was presented. I was asked to attend a special Show Breakfast presented each year by the Gulf Oil Co. Awards were made to Americans who had distinguished themselves in the boat-racing world, and a very few, including me, were inducted as the year's appointees to the Gulf Marine Hall of Fame, supposedly open only to Americans. I was introduced by Gulf Oil as the winner of the President's Cup and runner-up for the Detroit Silver Cup. I was also made a member of the Gulf 100 MPH Club. Remember that I said that Gulf would not claim credit for our win with their fuel in the first heat? Well, they kept that promise, almost. All advertising in the papers from Washington north gave British American the credit. From Washington south, credit went to Gulf. This was as fair as it could be. Although we used the Gulf fuel in the first heat, the U.S. Navy kindly allowed the BA truck in with our precious gasoline just in time to refuel for the second heat. Whether or not our association with the two oil companies at that time had anything to do with future events I do not know, but the very next year Gulf joined forces with British American in Canada. The Wilson Racing Team had become marriage counsellors.

Having just finished writing about our fuel problems, I think that I should explain how British American Oil Company came to get into the act. In Gravenhurst, when Miller was insisting that we should use nothing but pure castor oil for lubrication — at great trouble to the crew's digestive systems, I assure you — along came a quiet gentleman named Bill Schorman, who persuaded Miller that a really top-quality mineral oil would be just as good as the castor oil and not nearly as debilitating. It turned out that Schorman was chief engineer for the British American Oil Company. He had come to us with an amazing offer. His company would be pleased to supply all of our fuel and lubrication needs for racing and all the necessary pre-race testing. Not only would BA do this, they would also place Bill

Gulf Hall of Fame 1940 members – Dan Arena, Horace Dodge, Harold Wilson, Lou Fageol, Wild Bill Cantrell, Guy Lombardo.

Schorman at our disposal. We were delighted to accept. No more scrounging 150-octane super gas at airports, and no more crew discomfort from breathing hot, stinky castor oil fumes! Bill Schorman, with his vast knowledge and experience with petroleum matters, and his ability to dig in and get his hands dirty with the rest of us, was a welcome addition to the Wilson Racing Team.

A few other names come to mind, men that, although not members of the team, were always ready to do whatever was asked of them. Bert Hurst, chief mechanic for Greavette Boats, was of great assistance with the engine and other equipment installation. From Greavette's also, there were the Purdies, father and son, final-finishers extraordinaire. Fred and son Oscar (known to all as Michelangelo because of his artistry with a badger-hair varnish brush) imparted such a finish to our boats as to make Tom Greavette say that if a fly landed on the deck of *Miss Canada* it would slip and break its neck. The upper works looked like a grand piano, and the graphited bottom was as slippery as ice — that alone should account for a couple more miles per hour.

A good business friend of my father's, a Britisher from Detroit named Leonard Bradley, became unofficial supplier of all the difficult-to-find exotic mechanical items which all race boats seem to need. One time he even found two 10-foot lengths of 6-inch-diameter copper pipe to serve as exhaust pipes and carried them through customs in his station wagon. On top of all this, he owned a fine power cruiser based in Detroit, and this was always at our disposal when we raced in that city.

And then there was George McMurray of Ingersoll. Besides being my father's faithful chauffeur, he doubled as mechanic's helper to Charlie and as our truck driver whenever the boat had to be taken somewhere.

I have already mentioned many of the problems that we had with the Miller. Here are a couple more. Supercharger trouble was a major problem that developed after every hard, fast run. Remember that I said this supercharger was designed to run at

International Yachting
Union award of 1939
World Championship

Ernie Wilson, Jr. in the Presidents
Cup.

30,000 rpm? Well, to get up to that speed, a six-to-one step-up gear box was required. This contained a whole mess of gears, and all of these were mounted on two ball bearings each. After every hard run we would find some, if not all, of these bearings in very bad shape. The bearing manufacturers were not at all helpful: "What do you expect? You are way over the maximum speed for ball bearings." So we just kept an adequate supply of new bearings on hand at all times.

And there were those unusual link-type connecting rod assemblies. One day, at full throttle, we broke one. The broken link slashed a big hole in the crankcase. We patched up the hole and put in one of the three spare rods that Miller had supplied. But before long we had another patched hole and were down to one spare rod. Charlie and I always felt that the Miller was not the free-running unit that it should have been and that the thousand prancing horses that Miller boasted about had not yet put in an appearance. But we still had one spare rod and hoped that it might never be needed.

Back home we put *Miss Canada III* into a long period of hibernation and the potential solutions to all these problems in cold storage. When the war was over and we could get back into the racing game, that would be the time to lick the problems. Now we had a big job to do.

Chapter 8
The 12-Litre Class

When the war was over I decided that a bit of peace from the wild tempo of racing would also be great. Having talked it over with the rest of the Wilson Racing Team, I announced that I was hanging up my spurs. My racing days were over. After all, I had been at it for quite a few years. Failure and success had been mine in almost equal parts. Speeds were getting higher and higher and the sport more and more dangerous. I had a young and growing family dependent on me. All were pretty good reasons for calling a halt while I still could. This announcement had not been made public yet, but it was an understood fact as far as the Wilson Racing Team was concerned.

One August day in 1945, I received a phone call at our cottage from my father in Ingersoll.

He said, "Harold, I have told Greavette to get the boat out of storage. Get it on the trailer and bring it down to Ingersoll. The people at Detroit have been after me to bring *Miss Canada* to Detroit for the Silver Cup race on Labour Day."

"Look, Dad," I shouted, "remember I have quit racing!"

"Yes, I know, and we won't race. It's just that I couldn't refuse. So we'll just take the boat over there and say that we didn't have enough time to get her ready for racing, and we'll let it go at that." "Well, okay," I said. "I'll send her down in a couple of days."

"Make it as fast as you can," he said.

Knowing my father, I had a funny feeling that my racing days weren't over after all. I told Lorna what had happened and that she had better be prepared for just about anything. The next day the boat, plus every bit of racing equipment I could lay hands on, left for Ingersoll. I followed in my car. When I got to Ingersoll I found out just how right I had been. At the Ingersoll Machine Company, I found Charlie Volker busy putting the Miller into racing form. The next two weeks were hectic ones, working around the clock, trying to find vital but misplaced bits and pieces. By a couple of days before Labour Day, *Miss Canada III* and the Wilson Racing Team were back in top gear and ready to face the starter's gun at Detroit.

So, willy nilly, Lorna and I were back in the racing game again. We had absolutely no chance for much-needed practice. All we could manage were a couple of laps around the course on the Detroit River the day before the race. We felt that, considering everything, we were in about as good shape as possible, and hoped that *Miss Canada III*, after her long storage period would also be ready to do her best — like the fine showing at Washington in '39.

We made a fine start and were soon in first place, but halfway through the third lap, as we were approaching the Belle Isle Bridge, there was a horrible pounding crash from our Miller. I slowed down to idle, but the crashing and banging in the engine compartment continued. I felt that we should determine the problem before shutting off the engine, as it was difficult to start under even the best conditions and it might absolutely refuse this time, so we kept on pounding down the Detroit River while Lorna crawled out over the slippery deck, unfastened the hatches at the forward end and lifted them up. As she did this a black shower of blazing-hot engine oil flew up and soaked her from head to foot. Shutting the engine off immediately, I jumped to Lorna's assistance. She was wildly trying to get all that hot oil off her face. Luckily she was not burned, but she sure was a mess. When I had wiped off all that I could with the couple of wiper rags we carried, I had a look at the Miller. It certainly wasn't hard to find the trouble. There was a big hole in the side of the crankcase, and the stub end of a broken connecting rod was dangling out of that hole. There were bits of the broken con rod and chunks of shattered aluminum crank-

118

A broken con rod gives Lorna a bath of blazing hot oil.

case lying all over the place, and the bilge was full of the engine oil — except for what Lorna had absorbed.

Of course we were towed back to our pit and we felt pretty low. This certainly was not an auspicious start for our second go at the racing game. And as it would take considerable time, effort and expense to put *Miss Canada III* back into racing condition, this spelled the end of racing for us that year. But now that we had decided to return to racing, we went at this big rebuild job hammer and tongs. Back in Ingersoll, Charlie and I repaired the gaping hole in the crankcase with a carefully bolted on sheet of aluminum, and we used the last spare rod assembly received from Miller to replace the broken one. Remember that the rods in this engine were what were known as articulated link rod/master rod assemblies? Well, it was the smaller link rod that had broken, and the flailing broken stub end was responsible for that gaping hole in the crankcase. Hoping that this last new rod would be the answer, we put the Miller on our dynamometer and set it up for a trial run. It ran, and quite well at that. Maybe our troubles were over, but it was just turning winter and of course altogether too late for testing in the boat, so we sent the boat and trailer up to Greavette's and packed and stored away all our racing gear until the next spring. Charlie Volker went back to his plant in Detroit. We had decided that we must have a new full set of connecting rods. Charlie was to make these, and felt that he could do this very easily in Detroit.

One day he phoned and asked me to take the plugs out of the Miller and put a slim, round stick of wood in one cylinder on the master bank side of the engine to act as a gauge. I was to turn the engine over very slowly by hand until the stick showed that the piston on which it was resting had reached top dead centre. I was to note the height of the stick above the head, then, slowly turning the engine over to bottom dead centre, I was again to measure the length of stick projecting. The difference of these two measurements would, naturally, be the stroke of the engine. Then I was to repeat this procedure on the link rod side of the engine. It was quite a job turning that Miller over with a wrench on the crankshaft coupling. When I had finished, I realized that somehow I had made a mistake, so I did the whole business over again. Same result. My measurements showed that the Miller had a quarter-inch longer stroke on the link rod side than on the master rod side. This couldn't be, of course, but as I couldn't make it any different, I called Charlie back and told him what I had found. He shouted, "Just what I thought!" In making the necessary drawings before starting machining the rods, Charlie had discovered what had been wrong with our engine ever since it was built. Not only that, he had discovered why none of Miller's vee-type engines ran properly until they had been rebuilt by someone else. It seems that he had made a mistake in the location of the spot where the link rod was fastened to the side of the mating master rod, and that this error was responsible for that difference in stroke in the two cylinder banks. This meant that as we always timed the engine from the master bank, the link rod bank was always out of time, causing a tremendous overload on the link rods. This problem had been responsible for that broken rod, the hole in the engine, and Lorna's baptism with engine oil.

I have suggested before that we were never completely satisfied with the performance of our Miller. It was powerful, certainly, but it always felt as if this power was produced rather grudgingly. Particularly at top end, the engine felt quite strained and acceleration was definitely lacking, so Charlie designed a completely new set of link-type connecting rods and made them at his Detroit Engine Works. We all hoped and prayed that these new rods would be much better than the original Miller rods, and that they would overcome this major problem.

This wasn't our only source of worry. Remember that I told you about the bearing and gear problems we experienced with the supercharger drive? We could never get gears or bearings that could stand up to that terrible 30,000 rpm speed for long. One day when my father was visiting Charles "Boss" Kettering at General Motors Research, he mentioned this problem. Kettering became very interested and finally said, "Ernie, ship that damn blower over here and we'll design a drive that will work." So, over it went, and while Charlie Volker was whittling connecting rods out of tough steel, Boss Kettering and all the resources of G.M. Research worked on *Miss Canada's* supercharger.

The next spring Charlie was back in Ingersoll and working hard to put the Miller back together. The new rods looked beautiful and seemed to assemble into the engine so easily. The supercharger came back from General Motors Research, and what a job they had done, at no charge! The six planet gears, all solid helical spur gears, had been replaced by highly unusual gears. In these, the rim containing the teeth was completely separate from the hub. The two were held together by a series of strong leaf springs under great load. The reasoning behind this unusual construction was this: under normal operating conditions the gear would act as a unit (hub and rim would turn together and at the same speed) forced to do so by the very heavy loading on those flat leaf springs. But let something unusual cause a sudden increase in gear load, and the rim would slip with respect to the hub, giving instant relief to both gear teeth and bearings. Strain over, the spring load would take over and the gear would drive normally. This sounded great, if just a bit exotic, but the proof would be in the testing.

Finally the Miller was ready to run once more. It was carefully set up on our dynamometer and all-important tests were begun. The engine responded with a roar that could be heard for miles, the dynamometer went crazy, and those thousand prancing horses of Harry Miller's put in an appearance for the very first time. We were all set — back up to Gravenhurst!

It didn't take long to put boat and engine together again and get everything ready for actual performance testing. These tests showed a tremendous difference in engine performance, acceleration was staggering, top end and top speed were vastly increased, and the Miller did this all so easily. Gone entirely was that feeling of strain. Even at full throttle, the Miller was raring to go. I guess we were enjoying this new experience so much that

122

we sort of overdid things. Driving wide open in the quite rough and disturbed Detroit River, we leapt out of water completely, and the engine screamed as the tachometer went wild. The revs probably went up 1,500 when we were airborne, and the supercharger impeller, running six times engine speed, jumped over 8,000 rpm's in that very short period of free flight. Things didn't sound so good, so we hauled the boat out for inspection. The engine itself appeared to be in good order, so what was the trouble? Finally Charlie took off the supercharger and dismantled it. Horrors! All those fine flat spring assemblies, and the gear rims and hubs that they held together were, sorry-looking, burned-blue, half-melted messes of steel. Those spring clutches had sure allowed for slippage when our leap into the air caused horrible gear overload, but the slippage had caused friction which in turn had caused enough heat to melt just about everything. Right back to square one again. Now we had an engine just raring to go, but the blower couldn't keep up with it. Further examination showed that the impeller speed, which must have been up to nearly 40,000 rpm momentarily, had also baked all the bearings. If General Motors Research couldn't solve our problem, who could? I've said before that Charlie Volker was the smartest mechanic and machinist going, and he proved it again. Feeling that the G.M. idea of momentary relief by allowing slippage between the gear teeth and hub was good, Charlie set out to find a way of making it work without burning up in the process. He ended up with the movement between the gear rim and the hub being controlled by a series of helical springs which allowed the desired slippage, but *only so much*. When this "so much" was reached, the contact between the gear parts became solid and no excess heat was generated. Tested in the boat and after many deliberately provoked flights into space, we found that all the parts of this extremely temperamental supercharger drive were in perfect condition.

At long last we had all of the Miller's problems licked. It had been a long, uphill and very expensive exercise, but it was over. Again, the Wilson Racing Team was ready for the races.

Yes, we thought we were ready, but would it be the old story of our mile-trial Miller not being able to stand up to the stress of long, hard races? We discussed this at great length and at last decided that the aging and somewhat battered Miller should be put in permanent storage. It was a sad decision, as the Miller was one of the undoubted masterpieces of the old racing engine maestro Harry Miller, and as such deserved to be preserved for the admiration of future generations of engine buffs. And so it was mothballed. Sad to relate that a few years later it was destroyed in a disastrous marina fire.

What would we use as a replacement? Many engines were considered, mostly of the aero type, as high-powered, light-weight marine engines were not available. There were several possibilities, but almost immediately we settled on the Rolls Royce Merlin, Hitler's downfall. The Merlin had powered the superb Spitfire, which won the Battle of Britain. When the U.S. entered WWII, they had no aero engine to equal the Merlin. Almost immediately arrangements were made to have Merlins built in the U.S. by the Packard Motor Car Company. When hostilities ended, Packard had Merlins stacked all over the place, and no buyers. Well, a few. Boat racers are always on the lookout for exotic race engines, so my father became an early purchaser. The price was right, $500, and that included a tremendous kit of the specialized tools needed to service the Merlin. He bought ten! Why ten? Well, Dad figured that it would be much easier to just swap a new engine for an ailing one, rather than to spend valuable time repairing the defective one.

There we were with the hull of *Miss Canada III* in top shape, just waiting for her new innards to be dropped aboard. Of course it wasn't as simple as all that. The Merlin, being an aero engine, would require conversion for marine use, and this called for a great deal of thought and much skilled labour.

First of all, although a liquid-cooled engine, the Merlin's cooling system had to be altered so that it would operate efficiently from the stream of lake or river water scooped up at racing speed by the boat. Then there was the matter of the relatively slow rotative speed of the Merlin, 2,750 rpm. Can you imagine the size of propeller that would be required to harness the 1,650 wild horses of the Merlin at that slow rpm? Certainly the diameter would be so great that it would be impossible to mount it on the prop shaft and still keep it under the stern of the hull where it belonged, so why not turn a smaller prop at a much higher speed?

Charlie Volker and I, armed with a set of Merlin prints, set about the tricky job of designing a step-up transmission to be attached to the business end of the Merlin crankshaft. The case was made of cast aluminum and it contained a planetary gear set comprised of a huge internal gear driven by the crankshaft, which drove six equally spaced planet gears, which in turn drove a sun gear mounted on the propeller shaft. This planetary gear train stepped up the propeller speed to $3\frac{1}{2}$ times the crankshaft speed. We decided that a clutch to handle such power would be just another big headache that we could do without, so it was arranged that the engine could be run in neutral, for testing, or, after being positively locked in gear before starting, the boat would immediately be in motion when the starter switch was pushed. At the planned propeller speed of around 10,000 rpm, the calculated size of the "square wheel" that we settled on was 18-inch diameter and 18-inch pitch. This would fit nicely under the stern of *Miss Canada III*. What about slip with such a small wheel? Well, yes, there would be lots of slip, but at 10,000 rpm, who cares? Another advantage of this step-up transmission was the fact that the gearing caused the prop to turn in the opposite direction to that of the engine and propeller torque. It is always nice to have your race boat running on an even keel — as even as possible, that is. The design of this special transmission, and its manufacture at the Ingersoll Machine and Tool Co., was entirely the work of Charlie Volker, undoubtedly the smartest engineer, designer and machinist that I ever met.

Then there was the carburetor. The Rolls Royce carburetor, as received from Packard, was of the updraft variety. The quite large Venturi horn hung down well below the bottom of the crankcase. How was that to be put in a boat and still keep the engine as low down as possible? Cut a hole in the bottom of the boat? Stumped for a minute as to where we could get a down-draft carb that would do the job, Charlie said, "Let's put the carburetor on upside down! Should work. After all, a plane can fly upside down, so why not a boat." Not really upside down, only a bit of it, that pesky carburetor. A bit of tricky ducting was made and, presto, there was our downdraft carb! "Of course, we will probably have trouble starting," said Charlie. "In this position so much fuel will pour down into the supercharger before the engine can fire, the whole thing will be flooded." Jumping ahead, I'll tell you how that problem was solved. Lorna, as mechanic, had to stand in the engine compartment alongside the supercharger, and when I yelled contact and stepped on the starter, she would pour a Coke bottle full of gasoline into the eye of the supercharger! She had to have a steady hand, not only to dispense that heady 150-octane fuel just as the Merlin needed it, but also to enable her to close and lock the hatches and crawl back over *Miss Canada III*'s slippery whaleback as the boat charged ahead at 40 mph!

All of this took much time, thought, preparation and production, but finally the day came when *Miss Canada III*, altered here and there to fit the larger Merlin, hit the water once more. Right from the word "Go" it was apparent to us that we had a winner. The Merlin performed perfectly and exhibited none of the temperamental problems that had plagued us with the Miller. The boat — always a perfect lady — took to her new power plant like a dream. After considerable preliminary testing at the Greavette plant in Gravenhurst on Lake Muskoka, we took the boat to Picton, Ontario. I had raced 225s there several times and was quite familiar with the many-mile-long stretch of well-protected water known as the Long Reach. It would be the ideal location for a mile course which could be used for record-breaking purposes. The Prince Edward Yacht Club, located there, was very helpful in making arrangements for us to run a series of tests during which we were able to establish a new

North American record for Gold Cup-class boats. Unofficially, we later exceeded this 119 mph record speed by quite a bit. Well satisfied, we packed up and headed back to Muskoka to finish our preparations for the upcoming races at Detroit.

The boat was ready, but what of the crew? For some time a big problem had been forcing itself upon Lorna and me. We already had two children, and there would be more. With these youngsters to be cared for, was it right for mother and father to go traipsing all over the country, taking their lives in their hands every time they went into a race? This was a tough question, but one that had to be answered. We decided that one of us must stay onshore, and as I was the driver, that meant that Lorna would have to give up her mechanic's seat and take care of the family. Naturally I was also quite worried about this matter, but felt that, as my father had much desire to win and a lot of money tied up in the Wilson Racing Team, I had better carry on, at least for a while longer. Never would I be as at one with another mechanic as I had been with Lorna, but when Charlie Volker consented to be my racing mechanic as well as my engine mechanic, I was well pleased. Charlie had more skill and ability with engines than had Lorna, but he certainly lacked her long experience of racing with me, which had made us such a perfect racing pair. I would miss her nerve, skill and presence of mind, and her ability to make snap decisions which were always right. Lorna remained a full member of the Wilson Racing Team, merely moved from ship to shore. She still was in on all discussions and decision-making.

Charlie and I did a lot of practice driving, more to test ourselves than the boat. Perfect starts are always hard to make; constant co-operation between driver and mechanic is vital. Charlie and I drilled ourselves as best we could. Finally, after a couple of weeks of this, we agreed that the whole Wilson Racing Team was as ready for Detroit as it was possible to be. With George McMurray at the wheel of our tractor-trailer, the outfit left for the Silver Cup races, to be held there on Labour Day, 1946. As we hoped, and prayed, the new *Miss Canada III*

New crew – Author and Charlie Volker.

Meehan Trophy Presentation.

behaved perfectly and we ended the day with a very satisfactory win. We were presented with the fine Silver Cup Trophy by Mr. O.J. Mulford.

Leaving Detroit, we went right back to Picton to have another go at the record. Strike while the iron is hot, they say! In the midst of what certainly was the highest speed ever reached by our boat — it was estimated to be about 160 mph — the propeller shaft broke clean off right behind the strut. And that surely did end our racing for that year.

There really wasn't much to do that winter. The Merlin was running to perfection, and the boat was as good as ever. Other than providing ourselves with a stronger shaft, we spent the whole winter polishing up details. Come spring, another series of tests indicated that all was well and best left alone until race time. Labour Day saw us back at Detroit again, this time competing for the Meehan Memorial Trophy. We won quite handily.

Although I was not aware of it at the time, this was to be my last race at the wheel of *Miss Canada III*. Back in my home port of Gravenhurst once more, the racing over for the year, my father gave me the news that made me realize that *Miss Canada III* was indeed finished as a race boat for our team. He said that for some time he had been feeling that while we still had the stuff we should take a crack at the biggest class of all, the Unlimited Hydros. At that time that meant competing for the prestigious Harmsworth Trophy, the British trophy given by Lord Wakefield as emblematic of absolute worldwide supremacy in the sport of powerboat racing.

Chapter 9

Harmsworth

Getting into this absolute top class of boat racing isn't easy. Joe Blow — or his distant cousin, Harold Wilson — can't just build a boat, stick an engine in it, go to a race meet and say, "All right, you unlimited guys, here I am, ready for battle. Let's go!" It just doesn't work that way. As I stated earlier, the Harmsworth Trophy, presented by Lord Wakefield, is emblematic of absolute worldwide supremacy in boat racing. No holds barred, you can use any type or size of boat and engine. The only stipulation is that the country — not the boat owner or driver — that wants to race for this prestigious trophy must first issue a challenge to the country presently in possession of the trophy. This challenge must be acceptable not only to the challenged country, but also to the Harmsworth board. When the trophy is won by a country, it stays in that country's possession until such time as another acceptable challenge is made, another Harmsworth Race held, and a winner declared.

The trophy had been in the possession of the United States for many years, every since the day that the Silver Fox of Algonac, Gar Wood, had beaten the British for their own trophy, in English waters. The British had made several attempts to retrieve the trophy. Well-known racers like Malcolm Campbell, Scott Payne, Seagrave, Betty Carstairs and Kaye Don had done their best, but to no avail. The old Silver Fox outraced or outsmarted them all. And now, after all these years and valiant attempts, here was this Canadian team anxious to get into the act. My father and I were ready to go, so we went about entering a challenge. But you don't just call up the United States and say, "We challenge you!" First of all, the challenge must carry the wholehearted approval of the official body governing all boating activities in Canada. The challenge is made by this body as a Canadian challenge. The Canadian Boating Federation was agreeable on both counts, but we found out that Canada could not challenge in her own name because of the stipulation that everything in the boat — hull, engine and equipment — must be products of the challenging country. Canada could not provide the kind of power necessary for a Harmsworth attempt. Fuel, lubricants and other supplies also had to be products of Canada. And there was one last, really tough condition: all members of the boat's actual racing crew must be Canadians.

We knew that as the very successful *Miss Canada III* was entirely a product of Canada, the production of a suitable hull for Harmsworth competition would not be a too difficult condition for us to meet, but we were strapped nevertheless. We had used a Rolls Royce Merlin in *Miss Canada III*, but the Merlin was a British engine, not a Canadian one. My father, with a great deal of help from people like Harry Greening, the dean of powerboat racing in Canada in the last generation, Gar Wood, Charles Chapman, and Lee Barrett, came up with this idea: Could our challenge be issued in such a way as to allow us to use British-built engines? After long talks, the Harmsworth board and the representatives of the American Power Boat Association finally agreed that the challenge could be made in the name of the British Commonwealth of Nations, and this would be agreeable to all parties. Immediately our challenge for a try at the Harmsworth Trophy was presented to the American Power Boat Association, and was accepted.

Now that we could use a British engine, could we actually get one? We knew that there were several engines in England that might be suitable, but the only one of which we had any knowledge was the Merlin. Would a Merlin in a new hull be any faster than *Miss Canada III*? Doubtful. How about two Merlins? Yes, but then the Americans could use two engines also. Gar Wood had used four Packards in his last boat, *Miss America X*. So that was no good.

What about a more powerful Rolls Royce? During our *Miss Canada III* days we had received all sorts of valuable assistance from Rolls Royce. Their Chief Service Engineer for Canada, Jim Hall, was in charge of the large service contract with Air Canada (or was it still TransCanada then?) for Rolls Royce use of Merlins in that airline's planes. Feeling that he might be able to offer advice as to the best method of making an approach, we contacted him. "Go right to the Old Man," he said, "the General Manager or H.S., if you like, Lord Hives." So my father did just that in a very carefully framed letter, which was replied to by an equally well-framed letter, which said, quite plainly, "No!" No engines, no Harmsworth! Jim felt that this flat refusal was due to a board ruling made just after the end of the most unfortunate attempt by Kaye Don to win the Harmsworth. Stung badly by the implied slur on the Rolls Royce name, the ruling said that no further participation in boat racing was to be undertaken by the company. The sting was still there; so was the ruling.

One day, in our almost endless discussions, my father happened to mention the name of C.D. Howe, the head of the wartime Allied Munitions and Supply Board, of which my father had been a member. Jim shouted, "Wait, we've got something here! How well do you know Howe? Well enough to twist his arm and ask for his assistance in dealing with Rolls Royce?" The answer being yes, Dad and Jim went to Ottawa to interview Mr. Howe. He listened very carefully, was heartily in favour of our plan, and promised to send a strongly worded cable to Lord Hives. Jim was ecstatic! It seems that just days before, C.D. Howe had signed a contract with Rolls Royce for the purchase of over 900 Rolls Royce Nene Jet engines to be used to power the T33 A/C planes then being built by Canadair in Montreal. This reputedly was the largest-ever dollar contract placed in the United Kingdom. Jim felt that Rolls Royce would be sorely pressed indeed to refuse a strong request from Howe.

The very next day, Jim was called to a conference in England. He was at the Derby Aero Engine works, actually with Lord

Hives, when C.D. Howe's cable arrived. H.S. read it, thought for a couple of minutes, and then tossed it across the desk saying, "What do you know about this, Hall?" Jim read the cable, which went something like this: "Lord Hives, Rolls Royce, Derby. Would appreciate any assistance Rolls Royce could give to Ernest A. Wilson of Ingersoll, Ontario, Canada, on his Canadian attempt to build a worthy Unlimited Class challenger for the eventual return of the Harmsworth Trophy from the United States. This is a serious effort on behalf of the British Commonwealth of Nations and has my full support and backing. Personal regards, C.D. Howe, Ottawa." H.S. repeated his question: "What do you know about this, Hall? You have enough to do in Canada without getting mixed up with bloody race boats!" Pressed for his opinion, Jim said that from conversations with the Wilsons he felt that this was to be a very serious effort, and as one must look on C.D. Howe's message as almost a demand, he thought that Rolls Royce should reverse that ruling and get back into the boat-racing sport by helping the Wilsons as much as possible. "You would," grunted Lord Hives, but promised to bring the matter up at the next board meeting.

A hurried transatlantic phone call brought all this good news to us in Ingersoll that night. It was immediately decided that I should travel to Derby to place our proposition before Lord Hives personally, and before that board meeting could be held. So I packed my bag and climbed into a North Star, the Merlin-powered DC4 which TransCanada was using for ocean flights. This was my first jump across the pond and I must admit to a funny feeling at the pit of my stomach when the plane started to roll. But, of course, it was powered by the same engine that had helped us win the Silver Cup, so why worry. Arriving at Derby, I was put up at Duffield Bank, the Rolls Royce guest house for visiting businessmen and V.I.P.'s. The next morning, after having been properly attired to visit "the works" by the valet, I was driven to the Aero Engine Plant. The car in which I rode was a venerable Rolls Royce, at least 15 years old, which purred like a contented kitten and ran like a dream. I was immediately ushered into the presence of Lord Hives. Although this was not a board meeting, several members of the board were with H.S. at the time. Men such as Cyril Lovesy, Fred Hinckley, Jim Pearson (he later became general manager when H.S. retired), David Huddy, Jock Burns, Jim Kendall, Jim Wood and Len Hall were on hand to listen to this crazy Canadian's story. Before being asked to state my case, H.S. again brought to my attention the still-standing board ruling about "no boat racing," but then said, "Well, young fellow, let's hear what you have to say!" So I plunged ahead. I gave a full description of our experiences with the Merlins in *Miss Canada III*. In spite of Lord Hives' referral to the board ruling, I must say that I received very close attention from all present, and it was made quite apparent that they had great interest in our determination to bring the Harmsworth Trophy back to the British Commonwealth. That was the end of it for that day. Lord Hives said that a board meeting would be held very shortly to discuss our proposition and that I would be given the Rolls Royce decision immediately afterwards. He suggested that in the interim I should present my story to several groups of engineers located at three separate plants, all of whom would be particularly interested. And this I did. Although great attention was given to everything I said, the one thing that really got them was my story about the upside-down carburetor. "Very funny, Mr. Wilson," they cried, "but of course it won't work. You know that!" To my reply that, yes, it did work, they insisted, "Oh, but it can't!" And so it went until I asked, "Have any of you ever flown a plane upside down?" Well, of course they had, but that was different! Not really, I pointed out. In their case the whole business had been upside down; in my case only the carburetor was in the inverted position. Finally they all realized, as had Charlie and I, that only the starting of the engine under this condition was impossible, and when I explained Lorna's trick with the Coke bottle, they shook their heads and said, "Bloody crazy Canadians!"

The day after all these talks were over, I was called to another meeting with H.S. After a lengthy rerun of our whole proposition, Lord Hives said, "Well, you win, Mr. Wilson. Rolls Royce is with you all the way!" Was that a relief. Then we had quite a discussion on what Rolls Royce engine, or engines, we should use. I was given the choice of anything that they produced, reciprocating or jet engines. The mere mention of jets — very new at that time —made my hair curl! All sorts of power, sure, but how do we hitch such a high-revving beast to a propeller shaft? To be eligible for the Harmsworth, our challenger must be a boat driven by a water screw, not an aeroplane without wings! Likewise I was worried about the compounded problems of multiple engine installations. So I opted for the largest reciprocating engine built by Rolls Royce, the mighty Griffon. This engine, the largest aero engine in the world at that time, was really a grown-up Merlin. It was a V12 that produced about 2,800 horsepower as against the 1,650 available from the Merlin. That settled, H.S. then said, "Of course you must have two Griffons. We don't expect problems, but you never can tell." We were to be loaned two Griffons which were to be returned to Rolls Royce as soon as our need for them was over.

The next day my father, quite unexpectedly, arrived from his Florida home — he just couldn't sit still and let me have all the fun — so while I was cleaning up a lot of details, Lord Hives took Dad under his wing and showed him everything that Rolls Royce had to offer. Going through the tool room, a supervisor came up to H.S., touched his hat, and said, "Sir, one of my men says that he knows this gentleman with you." "Not bloody likely, he is a Canadian." "Yes, that's what my man said." replied the super. So Dad went over to a chap crouched over a lathe, to find that he was a lad who had worked at the Ingersoll Machine & Tool Company for years. Small world!

But right here, up jumped another nasty problem. The Griffon, still on the secrets list, was produced only for the British government. H.S. said, "You persuaded me all right, but you will have a hell of a time persuading the government to loan you those engines." Always a quick thinker, Lord Hives said, "There must be a way. How about this idea? Pick holes in it if you can.

Why not have two engines disappear somewhere in the works? The engine numbers can show that they are still here being tested, repaired, retested, and groomed for final acceptance by the customer, the government, and they will remain disappeared until you return them to us. Meanwhile they will have been in Canada doing their bit to help *Miss Canada IV* bring the Harmsworth Trophy back home."

And so it was arranged. I guess, after eventual return by us, the engines would be tested again, cleaned up, repainted, and turned over to the government as new. Just another case of "What you don't know won't hurt you!"

"Okay, Mr. Wilson, you can be on your way home now," I was told. "Before you go, if there are any other things you might need, please name them." My first request threw everything into a cocked hat once again. For our design of necessary conversion bits and pieces, we needed a more or less complete set of blueprints for the Griffon. "Impossible!" shouted Hives. "Don't forget the secrets list! There is no way we can let you take those prints to Canada!" Again a simple solution to a knotty problem. I was shown all the prints that I considered necessary, and after a good look at them, and a professed wish that my memory was excellent, all these prints were packed into a plain, unmarked cardboard box and put aside on a table until our discussions were ended. I then said goodbye to Lord Hives, Jim Pearson and all the others who had made my stay at Rolls Royce so pleasant, and the meeting broke up. All the staff members filed out to another meeting, and I left for the airport, just managing to slip that cardboard box under my arm as I left. And that is all that I can, or will, tell you about how those secret plans left the U.K. for a couple of years and were returned with no one being the wiser.

My father and I left immediately on our return flight to Canada. And what a flight that was! Halfway between Scotland and Iceland, and in a bitter midnight snowstorm, one of our "never-fail" Merlins packed it up! Assured that all was okay, "just a bit late," we staggered on and landed at Reykjavik about an hour late. We were told that another plane would be sent out to pick us up, but when? "In the meantime, make yourselves at home." Well, home was just a collection of three Quonset huts left over from war days when the U.S. Air Force used this airport. One was a combination kitchen, dining hall, lounge, and, oh yes, the location of all the necessary facilities. The other two were dormitories, one for the girls and one for the boys. Ours was just great. A constant stream of water ran diagonally across the floor under the 40 iron army cots placed there for our comfort, and the glaring overhead lights could not be turned off without turning off the heat — and this was Iceland in early January! After a day and a half of this, we were picked up and eventually arrived in Montreal. Jim Hall was there to meet us, and he put us on our domestic flight back to London, Ontario. I can tell you that I was very happy to be back in my own trundle bed once more and to know that our engine problems for *Miss Canada IV* were over. Now all that we had to do was to get the engines to Ingersoll so that Charlie could make the necessary conversions. He spent a busy winter designing and then making the large transmission required for the Griffon, really an enlargement of the planetary set designed for the Merlin. I know of no other person who we could have trusted to do this job for us.

Come spring, the new Marine Griffon was finished and standing on the floor beside the hull of *Miss Canada IV,* rapidly nearing completion at Greavette Boats in Gravenhurst. The hull had been under construction all winter also. Realizing that the valiant but small *Miss Canada III* could not handle the power of the Griffon, Doug Van Patten had been commissioned early on to design a new boat. This was to be almost a mathematical blow-up of MC *III.* The enlargement over *Miss Canada III*'s dimensions would be in proportion to the increase in engine horsepower and the increased speed expected of the new boat. To most of us this seemed to be a fairly simple mathematical problem, but it was much more than this to Van Patten. He burned the midnight oil all winter long, and as fast as he completed a blueprint, Tom Greavette was there to grab it out of

Harmsworth Challenger *Miss Canada IV*.

3000 H.P. Rolls Royce Griffon.

his hand and take it out to the production line to have it reproduced in oak, African mahogany and Port Orford cedar. All of this hurry-scurry paid off. There was the new boat, ready for her last coats of varnish, sitting beside her engine, both of them just waiting to get married. Under the watchful eyes of Charlie Volker, Greavette's installation team, headed by Bert Hurst, made the two one. Meanwhile others were doing their level best to ensure that *Miss Canada IV* would be the best Unlimited Hydro in every way. Percy Harris coaxed fine red cowhide into two comfortable, form-fitting bucket seats, while Fred Purdy, varnisher supreme, put the final coat of spit and polish on the hull.

She was indeed a beauty. She was of 11-foot beam, and 33 feet long. Her decks were rich African mahogany in colour. The sides, although made of very special 18-ply mahogany plywood, were enamelled a shiny jet-black, and the bottom was done in a light cream colour of special low-resistance bottom racing compound. The actual running surfaces of the three planes were jet black and highly polished with pot lead to make *Miss Canada IV* as slippery as an eel. This combination of black and cream gave a "Jaws" look to our boat. That, plus the glimpse of the monstrous black-enamelled Griffon one got when the hatches were open, gave this beauty a certain nasty appearance, and the two huge 6-inch-diameter exhaust pipes sticking out of the rear deck near the almost non-existent transom did nothing to take away from this appearance of nastiness. I say almost non-existent transom because the running bottom and deck surface came almost together at the stern; the deck line was actually awash at the stern. I spoke earlier of the three planes. *Miss Canada IV*, like her predecessor, was a two-step hydroplane which gave the three planes — fore, mid, and aft. The whole boat was as streamlined, above and below, as it was possible for Van Patten and Greavette to make her. They say "a thing of beauty is a joy forever." We would have to wait and see.

Miss Canada IV was mounted on the launching car and waiting for us at water's edge. Lorna stepped forward, and as she

Lorna christens *Miss Canada IV*.

Ready for the first run.

broke a large bottle of champagne over the boat's gleaming nose, she said, "I christen thee Miss Canada IV." The proud owner, my father, Ernie Wilson, presented Lorna with a big bouquet of red roses, and down went my newest (and last) racer into her natural element, the waters of Lake Muskoka.

Then came a few days of some very necessary preparations and testing before the boat could be given her first run. During this period we had a surprise visit from one of the men who had made all this possible, Lord Hives, H.S. himself. Supposedly he was in Canada to check that Canadair order, and for a vacation, but really I think he came to see just what kind of basket he had put the Rolls Royce eggs into. He and my father were two of a kind; they got along famously. Dad took H.S. on a tour of lovely Lake Muskoka in our 29-foot Greavette Streamliner, another *Miss Canada* but not numbered, to distinguish her from the racing hydros which were numbered II, III, and IV. Lord Hives was keenly interested in every detail of the construction of our boat and expressed confidence that the combination of our boat and the Griffon engine would win the Harmsworth. As he left for the U.K. he wished us the best of luck in our endeavour.

Next came a period of testing, not only the boat for speed, but also all the bits of equipment to determine that all were doing their parts properly. There were some problems, of course, but Jim Hall and his fine mechanics, Jack Osborne, Ernie Upshall and Bill Turner, were there on loan from Rolls Royce to smooth them out. Which they did.

Finally, along came the much-awaited speed trials. Boy, did that Griffon have GO! At top speed, besides using our 150-octane fuel, we also injected a stream of a water-methanol mixture right into the eye of the supercharger. This did two things: one, it cooled the internal parts of the engine, particularly the combustion chambers, which allowed higher compression ratios and greater power output without blowing up; and two, the 60-percent water, 40-percent methanol mixture actually burned, giving a further boost in power. Ever received an unexpected kick in the seat of the pants? Well, that will give you a faint idea of what we experienced every time we turned on the electric pump that forced that "go juice" into the supercharger. To the best of our knowledge, *Miss Canada IV* was the first racing boat in North America to use this water injection. I also mentioned that this was used at high speeds only. Below a boat speed of 110 mph, we found that the water injection actually slowed the boat down, so it was only used when we needed it, and always above the 110 miles per hour mark. And we found out a funny and very worrisome thing right there. Although we could always reach the 110 mph speed, we did not always get the expected kick in the seat of the pants when we threw that magic switch to start the pump, nor did we get the usual great increase in speed. If you like, it appeared that the boat "stalled" at a speed of 110 mph. In all of our speed tests at Gravenhurst we were unable to solve this mystery. The one-mile course there had very short acceleration and deceleration runs at the ends. Thinking that this might have some effect, and wanting anyway to find out just what this new boat could do, we loaded everything on our new four-wheel trailer, with our new transport driver and part-time mechanic, Gord Paterson, at the wheel, and set off for Picton once again. When we got into a whole series of trials, we found exactly the same thing. Sometimes we did, and more often we did not, get beyond that miserable high-speed stall at 110 miles per hour.

It seemed to us that at a certain engine speed, the power requirements of the boat to go faster were just not being met by the power output of the Griffon. Could this be possible when there was still plenty of throttle to go? And, if this could be so, why did it not always happen? On several runs we knew that our speed was way beyond the 110 mph. Eventually it dawned on us that the condition of the water had something to do with this. We found that when the surface was rougher than we thought suitable for record speed attempts, it was then that *Miss Canada IV* kicked up her heels and flew! Working on this principle, we deliberately disturbed the water well before the start of the timed mile section by making several concentric circular laps on the

Wow! Was that *fast*!

approach to the timed course. Although this was not a cure-all, it did increase, materially, the number of successful high-speed runs that we were able to make. Well, this was something, but not too satisfying. We knew that several times we had exceeded the speed record we had set with *Miss Canada III*, and by quite a bit, but could we do it whenever we wanted? After all, any race committee would take a very dim view of us running a few preliminary laps just to stir up the water! And what would the other drivers think? Crazy Canadians.

Back in Gravenhurst, we had to push ourselves to get ready for that big Harmsworth race in Detroit on Labour Day 1948. Out in the open waters of Lake Muskoka, where there was lots of room, we set up a regulation Harmsworth race of our own, 30 miles at top speed. This would be a bone-jarring, hull-and-engine-straining test of crew and equipment. On the day set for this run, 14 of our friends gathered at Greavette's to see the fun. Lorna bundled them all into my father's 35-foot twin-screw cruiser and motored out to the race site. She anchored in what she thought was a safe spot and awaited our arrival in *Miss Canada IV*. When Charlie and I did come out, we realized in our first run around the course, that the *Sarah Maude* (our cruiser) was anchored too close to our course. Lorna realized this also and upped anchor to move. We were screaming towards her at 150 mph when we saw a huge ball of red flame shoot out and envelope the whole cruiser! MY GOD! An explosion, and Lorna and those 14 friends aboard!

At our speed we were at the disaster area in seconds. I cut the engine, and as we rapidly lost speed, Charlie and I threw ourselves overboard as we shot past what was left of our once-proud *Sarah Maude*. Her bow was high in the air, the boat standing vertically with the stern completely under and sinking quickly. The whole stern section of the hull had been blown off by the force of the explosion. The air trapped in the forward cabin was holding her in this position, but it wouldn't be for long. The 75 gallons of gasoline had burst out of the tanks, spread over the surface of the water, and was furiously ablaze! As

I came above water after that quick jump from the speeding race boat, I saw all of our friends — men, women and children — floating around in this inferno. Charlie and I swam around splashing water over flaming heads of hair as fast as we could. By now, rescue boats were on the scene, and the people were being pulled out of the water. But where was Lorna? Look where I would, I could not find her. Thinking that she might be trapped in the sinking hull, I managed to get into the wrecked cabin only to find her not there. Outside again, I located her — counting heads to see that everyone had been rescued! She was hurt but refused to be pulled out of the water until all were accounted for. When seemingly all but Lorna were out of the water, she said, "Try under that wreckage over there." I ducked under and got hold of something wrapped in cloth. I pulled it out with me and found that I had the unconscious body of Roger Coles, the young son of one of my oldest friends, Marjorie (Adams) Coles. He had a broken arm and leg, and was in bad shape but alive. Thank God! Satisfied now, Lorna was lifted out of the water, and, with all the rest in the rescue boats, rushed off to hospital.

Thank goodness that Lorna was a good captain and knew how many passengers she had on her ship — and that she had refused to leave the sinking *Sarah Maude* before all 14 had been sent off to the hospital. This is not intended to be a blow-by-blow description of this terrible day in the history of the Wilson Racing Team. Suffice to say that all of them, except my father's particular friend, Mrs. Richardson, recovered from the burns, breaks and shock that they suffered that day. Very sadly I must say that three days after the explosion, Mrs. Richardson died of the injury and shock that she had suffered. Charlie Volker had married an Ingersoll girl, Mabel Clark, and she was one of the *Sarah Maude* passengers that ill-fated day. Although badly burned, she eventually recovered completely. Unfortunately, as a result of the accident, she lost one of the twin babies that were born a short time later. Two close friends, both skilled pianists, Doreen Uren and Margaret Start, were also badly burned but recovered and were able to carry on with their music careers. Lorna was also pregnant again and this fact, coupled with her badly injured ankle caused by the cabin wreckage falling on her, gave us great concern, but all went well and just before Christmas our second son, Harry, made his appearance.

The *Sarah Maude* incident sure took the stuffing out of the Wilson team. All desire to race gone, for the immediate future at least, we made an appeal to the American Power Boat Association to postpone, or perhaps, even cancel, the 1948 race. But it was felt that because the American defenders of the Harmsworth Trophy had been making tremendous efforts and were now race ready, the show must go on.

Remember that I said everything about our challenger, including the crew, had to be products of Canada? Well, we had the boat completely legal now, but what of the crew? I was Canadian, but Charlie Volker was a naturalized American of German birth, so he could not fill the mechanic's seat in *Miss Canada IV*! This problem had to be solved, and quickly. Luckily we had working at our plant in Ingersoll a young man by the name of Walter Harvey. He was of English parentage (good enough), but was also a naturalized Canadian (better still), and during WWII he had served in the Canadian army as a Rolls Royce mechanic (great). But did he want to race? His immediate answer of "You bet!" solved the problem. So the team was again expanded. During that summer Walter and I worked hard to become as efficient a racing team as had Lorna and I, and later Charlie and I. It was a tough summer, trying desperately to put our act together and all the while remembering the *Sarah Maude* and praying that all of our injured friends would recover.

But everything has an end, even that terrible summer. The day came when the boat and its team moved off to Detroit. We arrived there several days ahead of race day. We had lots of things to do to accustom ourselves to the long Harmsworth course, which passed under the very low Belle Isle bridge twice on every lap. I could almost reach out and touch both sides of the narrow gaps that we had to pass through at speeds up to 150

Harold Wilson, Walter Harvey and Gord Paterson admire the mighty Griffon.

mph. We had our pits at Keen's Yacht Harbour on East Jefferson Avenue. The first time we ran *Miss Canada IV* into the dirty Detroit River, we had a crowd of several hundred American fans down to see for themselves what these crazy Canadians had to offer as a challenge to the U.S.A. Well, we gave them an eye-opener. Lying low in the water and all ready to go, Charlie said, "Oh, Harold, we forgot something! Gordon, bring that five-gallon bucket out of the truck." Bucket in hand, Charlie brushed the dirt on the surface out of the way with his hand, filled the bucket with river water, and dumped it into the gas tank! "Look at those crazy Canucks, they think engines run on water! Sure blown their tops this time!" screamed the hundreds of Yanks. Were they surprised when *Miss Canada IV* started with a mighty roar and shot out of Keen's Yacht Harbour to do two very fast laps around that three-mile course. Of course they didn't know about water-methanol injection, and that Charlie didn't pour the water in the gas tank, he put it in the water-methanol tank, into which he had earlier put the correct amount of alcohol to give a 60/40 mix with the five gallons of river water.

The committee in charge of pre-race activities staged an interesting event for the boat crews. All of us were taken to the city airport, where we boarded a chartered DC3 plane. Aboard to welcome us newcomers was the dean of Harmsworth racing, Gar Wood, the old Silver Fox of Algonac himself. Just meeting Gar was thrill enough, but there was more coming. Shortly after takeoff, we found ourselves flying down the Detroit River. Then, at almost zero altitude we were taken on three or four very fast laps of the Harmsworth course. Besides flying so close to the water that had our wheels been down they assuredly would have touched, we did everything just as the racing boats would do — except that our pilot chickened out and didn't take us under the Belle Isle Bridge.

Pre-race days were good ones, lots of fun mixed up with the hard work. Late one afternoon we discovered that some badly needed parts were back at the plant in Ingersoll, some 150 miles away. I decided to make a fast run there and return the same night. Rushing to leave Keen's, I was stopped by the two motor-cycle policemen stationed on guard duty. One officer asked, "Why the hurry, Mr. Wilson?" When I explained, they said, "Follow us if you can!" and away they went at top speed down the whole length of Jefferson Avenue, sirens screaming as they forced all traffic to give way and let us pass. I had my Mercury at 100 mph and had great difficulty keeping up with those crazy cops who were having the time of their lives. When I reached the tunnel to Canada, one cop handed me a paid tunnel ticket and said, "Too bad we can't go all the way to Ingersoll with you, Mr. Wilson. We sure would make time!"

On race day both Walter and I got bad doses of the "five-minute jitters" but still made a reasonable start. We stayed right with the Americans for two very hairy laps. I say hairy because when we had to go under that Belle Isle Bridge I felt sure that we would hit those cement side walls as we tore through at 150 mph. Then something happened, our mighty Griffon lost power, *Miss Canada* slowed down, and we finished in last place. Remember what I said about taking the bitter along with the sweet? We had to swallow a fair share of it that day.

All the noise of battle stilled, we packed up everything and headed for home. But we weren't licked, not yet. We had a long winter to find out our problems, fix them and get ready for next year's Harmsworth, because we certainly intended to issue another challenge. Early on we discovered the reason for our apparent loss of power. The propeller was badly bent out of shape. As there was no evidence of anything having struck the prop, we could only assume that the beating it had taken from engine power, high speed and rough water had caused the propeller to go out of shape. Talking with Kennedy's, in Owen Sound, the firm that had made the wheel for us, we were told that the pitch had increased so much that it had been impos-sible for the engine to turn it at top speed. It seems that when a propeller suffers this kind of damage, it always increases in pitch, never loses pitch. We needed a stronger propeller that would not bend under stress. Our prop had been made out of the very best

151

cast stainless steel available to Kennedy's — apparently not good enough. Kennedy's suggested a redesigned, much heavier sectioned one, but that, we felt, would have a bad effect on top speed.

As we deemed it only proper that someone should go over to Rolls Royce to give an explanation for our failure in the 1948 race, I took another trip to the U.K. that fall. I spent many hours in consultation with Lord Hives, Mr. Pearson and many others. Engine problems were almost brushed aside as things that occur and which just have to be fixed. But what did we intend to do about the propeller problem? Well, of course, I didn't have an answer, except to do as Kennedy's had suggested, but this was vetoed for the same reason that had come to our minds: we were adding to the engine power requirements by swinging a much heavier wheel, and "remember the problems you had getting past that 110-mile stall!" Finally Lord Hives said, "Can you get a new, never-used propeller identical to the one you felt was best?" "Yes," I said. "We have one in our Ingersoll plant right now." "Okay," said H.S., "Cable to have it sent over here by plane. Tomorrow you and two of our engineers are going to drive to Glouster to see Rotol. That is a company run jointly by Rolls Royce and Bristol, and they manufacture propellers of all kinds. We will see what they can suggest to overcome your problem."

Next day I was talking with the top engineering brains at Rotol, men like Len Fainhurst, Allan Walker and Bob Newport. After several hours of discussion they came up with this suggestion. Rotol would forge a large billet of stainless steel, to make it as dense and strong as possible. Then, using our new cast-steel prop as a master, they would cut from the solid billet, on a large Keller machine, an exact duplicate of the Kennedy wheel, the one we had found under test to be best. They felt certain that the increase in strength of the forged stainless-steel propeller over the one made from cast steel would be sufficient to ensure that this prop would not change shape under load. They started work on it immediately and it took all winter to produce. I was told that over 1,600 hours of labour went into its production! It was finished in early spring and shipped to us at Greavette's. When we opened the shipping crate we were almost dazzled by the lovely jewel lying in the deep-red plush-lined interior.

A few short practice runs at Gravenhurst convinced us that the new wheel would do the job, so we headed back to Picton again and that lovely Long Reach. This time we were record hunting. Pleased that we had chosen Picton for the attempt on the World Speed Record, the Prince Edward Yacht Club, besides assisting as they had done before with both *Miss Canada III* and *IV*, also made my father and me life members of the club. The Canadian Army sent communications experts to set up a most useful radio contact between our pits at the Yacht Club and the mile course on Long Reach. They also took care of the accurate electronic timing gear set up at both ends of the course to catch our time as we flashed between the markers. The contact man for us at the Prince Edward Yacht Club was Jack LeHeup, and no man could have worked harder to overcome our problems as they arose. The press was there in force to cover our record attempt.

At the end of the several weeks of intense effort by everyone, we made our attempt and soon had the following to show: a new official World Speed Record of 143 miles per hour; an unofficial record of 173 miles per hour, unofficial because due to conditions we were not able to make the required run over the course in both directions; a propeller that could stand the full thrust of the Griffon and the highest speed ever travelled to that date on water. Before packing up to return to Gravenhurst, I took sportswriter Al Nickleson out for a 150-mile-an-hour spin down the Long Reach as a thank you to the press for their untiring efforts on our behalf.

We realized that we still had a problem to overcome. The new prop was even harder to tease past that 110 mph "stall" than had been the former wheel. Perhaps it was just too good, almost too efficient. Charlie Volker and Jim Hall thrashed this out and finally decided that the diameter of the propeller should be reduced one half inch. Charlie took it back to the plant in Inger-

At 173 mph. *Miss Canada IV* unofficially breaks the world record.

What 3000 H.P. and 173 mph. can do – a broken prop shaft!

The maestro at work on the prop.

The Ingersoll Tribune

The Only Newspaper Published in Ingersoll   INGERSOLL, ONTARIO, THURSDAY, JULY 28, 1949   Single Copy - 5 Cents $2.00 Per Annum   U.S.A. $2.50

"BEST OF LUCK, HAROLD"
Says Premier St. Laurent

Premier Sends Hope For Success

A special message of encouragement and best wishes has been sent by Prime Minister Louis S. St. Laurent to Harold Wilson, his crew and Miss Canada IV on the eve of their big race against the pick of U.S. speedboats for the Harmsworth trophy, emblematic of world supremacy.

Prime Minister St. Laurent, holidaying at Kent Lodge near Bathurst, N.B., took time out to send the following special message to The Tribune:

"All Canadians are interested in international sporting events and will be hoping for the success of Harold Wilson and his Miss Canada IV in the forthcoming speedboat races at Detroit this week-end. On their behalf, as well as my own, I wish him the best of luck."

LOUIS S. ST. LAURENT.

TUNING UP IN DETROIT NOW

Miss Canada IV, Harold Wilson, driver and crew, are in Detroit today getting final tune-ups prior to the first heat of the famed Harmsworth race at 6 p.m. tomorrow.

Under provincial police escort all the way down, the party which today left Ingersoll yesterday... her hundreds of people from all over had inspected the sleek craft as it stood in the market square Tuesday. Gord. Patterson drove the special truck-trailer carrying the craft, which created great excitement all the way down.

Meantime, all tickets for the special Kiwanis Harmsworth excursion have long been sold and a big parade of nine buses carrying 325 enthusiasts, will pull out from McVittie and Shelton's bus depot Saturday. They will be accompanied by 14 members of the Ingersoll Pipe Band and banners reading "Miss Canada IV—Ingersoll, Ont.," will tell the world, what is going on.

All 500 seats reserved for the Kiwanis at the race course have been sold, and interest was so great many more could have been disposed of. It isn't all Ingersoll that is going, either; there are people from Norwich, Tillsonburg, London, Woodstock, Embro, Paris, Brantford—everywhere.

Those unable to go to the race, however, will be able to hear it Friday and Saturday nights, and Monday, too, if it goes to a third heat. The Tribune is sponsoring an on-the-spot broadcast at 6.30-45 each night over CKOX.

Corp. Jack Callander and his men arranged for the police escorts of both the boat and the nine-bus cavalcade. Miss Canada IV, incidentally, will be running under the colors of the Prince Edward Yacht Club, and as E. A. Wilson, owner of

(Continued on page 8)

Miss Canada IV Roars Along At "Unofficial" estimate 150 Miles An hour

Tribune To Bring Harmsworth Race To Radio Audience

The Harmsworth Trophy speedboat race at Detroit Friday, Saturday and possibly Monday will be broadcast over station CKOX, Woodstock, under the sponsorship of The Ingersoll Tribune.

The Tribune is sponsoring the broadcasts as a public service, feeling that many, many people unable to go to Detroit, would like to listen, and mentally cheer on Ingersoll's challenger in the famed race, Harold Wilson, in his new Miss Canada IV.

The broadcasts will be at 6.30-.45 p.m. Friday and Saturday, July 29 and 30, over CKOX, "Your Ontario County Radio Station," at 1340 on your dial. Dan Fairbairn of Neighborly News, will be describing the race right at the scene. If a third heat is required, it will be Monday, at the same time, same spot on the radio dial.

Here Are Facts, Figures On Harmsworth History

Here are facts and figures concerning the British International Trophy, (Harmsworth), speedboat race, and record speeds of Harmsworth boats:

First race, 1903—Won by England, 19.53 m.p.h.
Won by U.S. in 1907, held there 'til 1911.
Returned to England 1912-1913.
Won by Gar Wood in 1920, and held in U.S. ever since, this is the U.S.'s 10th defence of the trophy.
Speed which won it in 1933—86.939 m.p.h.
Fastest lap—Kaye Don, 1931—93.010, Miss England II.
Fastest heat—Kaye Don, 1931, 89.913, Miss England II.
U.S. speed record—Gar Wood, 1932, 124.9 m.p.h., Miss America 10.
Gold Cup Record—Harold Wilson, 1947—319.008, Miss Canada III.
World's speed record—Malcolm Campbell, 1949, in Bluebird II—141.74 m.p.h.

"Ham" In Africa Reads Name Writes, And Joe's The Man

A letter arrived from South Africa for Joe Wilson of amateur radio fame, here last week.

From a Johannesburg address, it read:

Dear Sir:

"I noticed your name in the call book which lists amateur radio operators the world over, and wondered if you are the same person who was in the R.C.A.F. in Egypt, (seconded to the RAF on 581 Squadron). I was on the same unit as a corporal, fell sick and subsequently arrived in South Africa where I am now living and 'hamming.'

"Would be glad of a line from you, in any case, and when the DX season opens up a will be on the watch for your call. Awaiting your reply in anticipation.

"Sincerely, Donald Bedford."

And Joe was the same man!

"Imagine," said the incredulous Joe. "It's seven years ago since we last saw each other. He was a radar operator and was posted to my unit at Alexandria April 1942. He went through the siege of Tobruk. Later in '42, he took sick and was sent to Johannesburg. That's the last I saw him.

"It's sure a small world," he said.

Union Gives $500 For Hospital

A cheque for $500 for the Alexandra Hospital building fund has been presented to John Anderson, president on behalf of the United Steelworkers of America, Local 2918, (Morrow Screw and Nut Co.), by A. R. Horton, chairman of the new building committee. The money was in recognition of the fine work being done at the hospital, and as a token of appreciation of the hospital by union members.

Ingersoll's First Television Set Operates Okay

Ingersoll's first television set has been successfully operated.

The set was built by Joe Wilson, amateur radio expert, and Bill Barnett, who works with him in Wilson's radio repair shop. For five months they labored over it, then turned it on. Signals came through from television stations in the U.S., but no pictures. They checked it over and over, raised the aerial as much as the sky, but still no pictures.

Joe finally decided to take the set to a U.S. town with a television transmitter to see if the set wasn't built right or whether it was just a question of proximity to a station or power. So he took it to Toledo, Ohio, and turned it on.

"It worked beautifully," related Joe—just like a moving picture. So I bought a booster for added power and brought the set back home. On Saturday night I turned it on at home, and in came Cleveland pictures—clear as a bell!

Joe's big boast now is that the Harmsworth races if Detroit transmits, and Saturday, will be televised—and we'll be able to get them on his television screen. "I won't bring it down to the store, though, and then people won't... tough... but I could watch it. It's nice enough though they carry on a bit, 'too busy.'"

Walter Harvey, Ingersoll To Be Miss Canada Mechanic

Walter Harvey, young Ingersoll mechanic, who until three years ago had been in nothing bigger than a rowboat, will ride as Harold Wilson's crew in the Harmsworth tomorrow and Saturday.

Walter's choice follows the heartbreaking division of the Harmsworth officials that Charlie Volker, who has worked and ridden with Harold for years and in scores of races, is not eligible to ride in Miss Canada IV in the big race under the Harmsworth rules. All the race members have to be citizens of the country which is racing. Charlie isn't a Canadian, and thus he's out. Charlie, whose barrow, Mable Clark, was among those burned in the explosion of the Sarah Maude, took the ruling philosophically.

"If the rules say I can't, then that's that," he said.

But he will go with the boat and will be working on it right up to the race. He is given most credit for a very special gear box on the engine, which is expected to give

WALTER HARVEY

(Continued on page 8)

Those Going To Race Please Read Below

1. Buses leave Ingersoll Bus Terminal, July 30, sharp at 1 o'clock noon, Eastern Daylight Saving Time.

2. Get a lunch before leaving. There is no stop for food.

3. Buses travel to Detroit by way of tunnel direct to reserved seats for race in Detroit.

4. Your ticket covers transportation to Detroit, direct to the race, and transportation back to Ingersoll. (BE SURE AND ALWAYS HOLD YOUR TICKET) except those tickets marked in red "Seating Only."

5. After the race, buses will take passengers as soon as possible, to Detroit Tunnel entrance, where they will wait and as enough passengers return to Tunnel to fill a bus, bus will leave for Ingersoll. Last bus leaves Detroit tunnel entrance at Detroit at 12 o'clock Midnight, Daylight Saving Time, without delay. You must be there or provide your own transportation home. Bus will not leave before 12 o'clock Eastern Daylight Saving Time, until all seats are filled.

6. You can take across the border only $10 in U.S. funds and $15 in Canadian funds, unless you have a special permit from the bank.

7. Have some form of identification for crossing the border. A passport or birth certificate is ideal, or wartime identification card. But have something, if only a driver's permit.

8. For those driving their own cars, here is the route upon crossing the tunnel into Detroit: Up to East Jefferson and right along that main street several miles, and then right down Parkview, to the bleachers.

KEEP THIS COPY OF THE TRIBUNE. IT CARRIES ALL THE TIPS YOU NEED FOR THE TRIP.

These Are Expected To Form U.S. Harmsworth Team

SKIPALONG—OWNED AND DRIVEN BY STANLEY DOLLAR, CALIF.

SUCH CRUST—OWNED BY JACK SCHAFER, DRIVEN BY DAN ARENA

NOTE To Advertisers!

Best wishes – St. Laurent.

soll to do this delicate job while the rest of the crew got everything else ready for our second crack at the Harmsworth, again on Labour Day at Detroit.

I wish I could tell you that, now *Miss Canada IV* had proved that she was the world's fastest boat, we went right on to prove it again by winning the Harmsworth. But it was not to be. As in the 1948 race, we made a good start and ran very well until some minor equipment malfunction slowed us down and eventually made it necessary to pull out of the race to avoid engine damage. And that was that, for another year at least.

A FAST LITTLE NUMBER !

Another news flash that never hit the street!

Al Nickleson of the Toronto Star interviews the crew.

Sixteen sports columnists host a party for *Miss Canada IV*.

It was beginning to look like the Harmsworth was not our cup of tea. All sorts of thoughts and doubts crowded my mind during the next couple of weeks. We were back home in Gravenhurst sort of licking our wounds, putting things to rights as much as possible, and doing a lot of thinking about the future of the Wilson Racing Team. Eventually, I decided that we would continue. And what better way than to go back to Picton and take a crack at that 160 mph record that Stan Sayres of Seattle had just established, and which had beaten our 143 mph record?

Walter and I packed up and started out. This time we did not have Charlie along, as he was busy in Detroit. Perhaps, as things turned out, we should have waited for him. But, anyway, there we were, back at our old stamping grounds, the Prince Edward Yacht Club and the Long Reach. We did not plan a long series of runs, we would just be sure that all was well and then go for it. If we got over that terrible 110 mph stall and started to go, it would be all or nothing. We waited for a day with just the right weather conditions, then we gave the word to the official timers that this was it.

Coming down that fairly rough Long Reach, our prop cavitated a couple of times and away we went! The boat speed rapidly climbed beyond that 110 mph figure, and long before the beginning of the measured mile, I put my foot on the floor and held it there. The hammering we got from that fairly rough water did funny things to my eyesight. I guess my eyeballs were bouncing around so much that I could not see things close at hand, like my hands on the wheel, or the instruments, but I could see my landmark beyond the end of the course, and if I could just aim for that, all would be well. The last glimpse of the tachometer that I had, just as we neared the start of the mile, was a startling 3,450 rpm! Don't forget, our absolute top engine speed allowed by Rolls Royce was 2,750, and that only for 20-second bursts. I put my foot down as hard as I could and screamed to Walter, "Away we go!" How high that figure went I don't know, but I do know that the Griffon was accelerating all the time. Screaming like a siren gone mad, the Griffon was doing its very best to give us a record. And, for sure, we were going much faster than we ever had before, way above the unofficial 173 mph speed we had previously made. Then it happened! A horrible grinding, screaming, smashing roar — and us sitting right in the midst of it! I shut off the ignition, the noise died down, and *Miss Canada IV* drifted to an ignominious stop a couple of hundred yards short of the end of the mile course and an undoubted new record.

How fast were we going when this accident occurred? I don't know, but the last number I saw on the tachometer was 3,450. I feel that it is fair to say that when that tremendous crashing roar took place, the engine must have been turning 3,600 rpm. Because our prop had a 26-inch pitch, every revolution of the prop shaft would shove *Miss Canada IV* ahead 26 inches. If you multiply 3,600 by 3½ (which was the transmission step-up ratio) and multiply that again by 26, you will find that, disregarding slip, *Miss Canada IV* would have been pushed ahead at a speed of 310 miles per hour! Well, let's trim that by an amount more or less equal to the slip percentage we had already determined. This percentage slip was about 20 percent. So if you take off 20 percent, you come up with an actual speed of 248 miles per hour!

Back at Gravenhurst we hauled the Griffon out of the boat, and feeling almost certain that our problem was in the transmission, we tore that unit off the engine and completely disassembled it. What a mess we found! Of that beautiful planetary gear set that Charlie had so lovingly made, there was not one tooth left on any of the eight gears that it comprised. This tragedy, just like our other two breakdowns, had been caused by the malfunction of a very simple part. In this case it was the stress failure of a bearing retainer that had allowed the bearings and the large internal gear mounted on, and driven by, the crankshaft to come off the splined end of the crankshaft and fall down out of position into the other gears. No wonder all those teeth got ripped out by the roots. There were bucketfuls of them lying in the bottom of the case. Why the whole mess didn't blow the transmission case to pieces, I do not know. Had it done so, Walter and I would undoubtedly have been killed. This was certainly a disastrous end to our second year of Harmsworth racing.

What about next year? Should we challenge again? My father left it entirely up to me this time, race or retire. This called for a lot of careful thought. I realized that I should not be gambling with my life when our growing family was dependent on me, and my father was making noises about retiring from business, which meant that I would have a couple of plants in Ingersoll to run. And just when these two facts were making me seriously consider quitting, along came the clincher: my insurance company said, very simply, and in so many words, "No more racing or no more insurance." That did it. One pair of well-used racing spurs was hung up to rust.

My first race was in 1927 and my last in 1949. I had raced 11 different boats, from a small 25-horsepower job to the mighty *Miss Canada IV*. I had won three World Championships and set two speed records, one North American and one a World Record. I had been made a member of the Gulf 100 Mile Per Hour Club, and also a member of the Gulf Marine Hall of Fame — the only Canadian, I believe, to be so honoured. A few years after my retirement, I was greatly honoured by being made an Honoured Member of the Canadian Sports Hall of Fame. I had won lots of races and lost a lot more. I had enjoyed every minute of my racing career, the sweet and the bitter, but now that it was over, I was completely satisfied.

Admission to Canada's Sports Hall of Fame.

Throughout this chronicle much mention has been made of the Wilson Racing Team. I want to list all of them together as a whole, so here is the group that did so much to make my racing career such a pleasure and satisfaction to me:

Ernest Wilson, my father and the owner of all the Wilson fleet.

Tom Greavette, president of Greavette Boats, the builders of the fleet.

John Hacker, naval architect, the designer of *Little Miss Canada II, III* and *IV,* and *Miss Canada II.*

Douglas Van Patten, naval architect, designer of *Little Miss Canada VI* and *Miss Canada III* and *IV.*

Lorna (Reid) Wilson, my wife and racing mechanic without peer.

Charlie Volker, engine mechanic, also without peer.

Bill Doherty, our first 225 cu in mechanic and once chosen to be my first Gold Cup mechanic.

Walter Harvey, plucky Harmsworth racing mechanic.

Jim Hall, Rolls Royce top mechanic, made available to us at all times by Rolls Royce Canada. Besides mechanical work on our Griffons, he also was very instrumental in helping us obtain the engines and in overcoming our very difficult propeller problem.

George McMurray, transport driver and mechanic.

Gordon Patterson, transport driver and mechanic.

In closing this account of the racing years, I want to take this opportunity to thank each and every one for the prominent part that he or she played. I am sure that, in spite of all the hard work and the disappointment, they also enjoyed these exciting racing years. I especially thank my father. Without him and his very handy chequebook, there would never have been a Wilson Racing Team or any boats for me to drive.

My father – the Skipper – announces our retirement from racing.

Tom Greavette – President of
Greavette Boats – builders of
all the Wilson Racing Fleet.

Douglas Van Patten –
designer of *Little Miss
Canada VI* and *Miss
Canada III & IV*.

167

Wawanaissa Island – home of the Wilson fleet.

Bill Doherty – our first 225 cu. in. mechanic tries out the Gold Cupper *Miss Canada II*.

The Author, Ernie Wilson, Jim Hall of Rolls Royce and Charlie Volker.

John Hacker (right front) – designer of *Little Miss Canada II, III & IV.*

Both *Miss Canada* drivers – Harold Mistele & Harold Wilson.

Chapter 10

Finish Line

In 1939, feeling that new, better engines were needed for the 225-cubic-inch class, Charlie Volker and I designed and built a twin overhead-cam racing engine that was very light and developed 225 horsepower at a fantastic speed of 6,000 rpm. The idea was that these engines would be built at the Ingersoll Machine & Tool Company and would be for sale to all interested boat racers. We had one highly satisfactory test run with the engine installed in *Little Miss Canada VI*, then WWII broke out and racing was suspended. After the war the rules governing the 225 class were altered, and the use of overhead cam engines was forbidden. End of project. I sold the prototype Wilson engine to a good Detroit friend, Harold Mistele, and today it has an honoured place in his private marine museum.

All of the Wilson racing equipment, ten Merlins, the old Miller engine, the tractors and trailers, and the two boats, *Miss Canada III* and *IV*, were sold to Mr. James Thompson, president of Supertest Petroleum, a London, Ontario, firm. *Miss Canada III* was immediately put aside. *Miss Canada IV* was renamed *Miss Supertest I*, and with her the two Thompsons, James Sr. and Jr., set out to learn what unlimited hydroplane racing was all about. After a year of racing, the old boat was shelved and a new three-pointer, *Miss Supertest II*, designed by son Jim, was built. With her successor, *Miss Supertest III*, they challenged for, and won, the coveted Harmsworth Trophy. My congratulations to them for bringing the trophy to Canada and the British Commonwealth — the thing that I had not been able to do. It is very sad that their skilful and daring driver, Bob Hayward, was later killed when *Miss Supertest II* capsized in a race at Detroit. *Miss*

Supertest III is now on permanent display at the Science Centre in Toronto.

Miss Canada III was sold to Bill Morgan of Silver Bay, New York. He rebuilt it to almost original specs, powered it with a Merlin and used it as a show boat at antique boat shows. On two occasions I was asked to drive it for the crowds at these shows. She was still capable of very high speed. Mr. Morgan then presented *Miss Canada III* to the Marine Museum at Clayton, New York, where it is on exhibit today.

A replica of *Miss Canada III*, authentic in every detail except power, was built by Duke Marine Services in Port Carling, Ontario, in 1986-87 to the express order of my good friend Murray Walker. It was launched at the time of the Antique and Classic Boat Show held at Port Carling in 1987, and I was honoured by being asked to drive the new boat for the filming of a short TV documentary about the fine wooden boats built by the famous Muskoka boatbuilders. The show was headlined by this new *Miss Canada III*. This beautiful racing boat is currently being used by Murray Walker as his "gentleman's runabout." Some runabout! Even with her relatively low power (a 500-horsepower Chrysler Hemi instead of the 1650 Merlin) this replica can do a very creditable 75 mph.

Miss Canada IV, damaged somewhat in a disastrous marina fire at Thompson's boatyard, was scrapped. She was rescued from this unhappy ending by my friend Harold Mistele of Detroit. He restored her to a beautiful, if not completely authentic condition. He asked me to drive her for her first public run after rebuild, at the Gar Wood Memorial Races at the Detroit Yacht Club. For several years he took her to all the antique boat shows, along with his recently rebuilt *Miss America IX*, one of Gar Wood's old racers. Mr. Mistele had always felt that *Miss Canada IV* should be back in Canada as part of Canadian heritage, so in 1986, after some complicated arrangements, *Miss Canada IV* came back home to Muskoka, the property of the Port Carling Museum. She was taken to Duke Marine Services, where she was rebuilt for the second time. This time the rebuilding was

172

Miss Canada IV runs again after rebuild by Harold Mistele.

Duke built replica of *Miss Canada III* owner Murray Walker with Harold Wilson at the wheel.

authentic in every detail. Even the original designer, Doug Van Patten, was on hand to supervise. The work was completed early in 1988. *Miss Canada IV* was exhibited at three boat shows that summer, in Gravenhurst, Orillia and Port Carling, then she was put in mothballs awaiting completion of the new Marine Hall at the Port Carling Museum, where she will be part of the permanent exhibit of fine wooden boats, all the products of the world-famous boatbuilders of Muskoka.

While attending the Orillia show, I was surprised to see an almost exact copy of my *Little Miss Canada IV*, the boat that carried Lorna and me to our second World Championship at Toronto way back in 1934! When the owner of this Seattle-built replica learned that the original crew of the original boat was on hand, nothing would do but that we take this replica out for a run to please the crowd. So we donned life jackets and gave the crowd and ourselves a great thrill by driving this fine replica at very high speed indeed. No fools like old fools, I guess.

Our five children all shared our love of driving boats at high speed, and three of them over the years followed our example and became racers in their own right. I acted as had my father and became a builder of boats, supplier of funds, part-time mechanic and grease monkey. They all raced outboards exclusively, and they all had their share of luck, good and bad. Ernie drove in the A, B, and C classes and won the C-Class Hydro Championship of Canada several years, before retiring in 1986. Harry, who specialized in B-class racing, both hydro and utility, also won the Canadian Championship in B Hydro a couple of years. Launi didn't share their good luck as much. After a couple of wins she had a very bad end-over-end upset and managed to make a forced landing, upside down and helmetless, on the screaming flywheel of her engine. And that ended her racing career right there!

The future of the Wilson Racing Team? Well, Harry, phoning us in far-off Montserrat to announce the birth of his son Tommy, yelled, "Dad, we have a new boat racer!" Who knows?

Miss Canada IV newly rebuilt to original specs, heads for her new home – The Muskoka Museum in Port Carling.

Seattle-built replica of *Little Miss Canada IV* being tested by original crew.

Ernie (Jr.) – in *Scram II*, wins Canadian C Stock Hydro Championship.

Between heats: Harry crews for Ernie at the wheel of *Scram II*.

176

Harry and *Samurai* win Canadian B Stock Hydro Championship.

Launi – last of the Wilson racers, in *Spanku*, the first of the outboard fleet.

Chapter 11

Sail Ho!

Ever since my *Black Bottom* days, sailboats have appealed to me. In my younger days, they didn't offer the thrills of speedboat racing, and because of my great passion for speed I certainly leaned heavily towards powerboats, but always there was a hankering to know more about those graceful, white-winged craft. From my years of racing experience, I had learned that with powerboats there are a great number of things that can happen that are practically beyond the power of the human being to master. But with sailboats, practically everything can be mastered by the person in control — if he or she is good enough. I think that this is the fundamental reason why sailing always interested me and why, since the end of my racing career, it has been a deep passion of mine.

Up to the end of my racing days, all my sailing experience had been with those two old "Leaky Tiki's," *Black Bottom* and *Sea Gull I.* How I ever maintained interest while almost continually patching and caulking, I don't know. But, actually, when my good caulking arm gave out and I consigned *Sea Gull I* to the sailboat's Nirvana, I was still hankering to sail, and more than ever. Another boat was what I needed, and not another old clunker. I soon found a pretty fair hull, a 16-foot, vee-bottomed Comet. It was a sloop with two sails, main and working jib. It was quite narrow in beam, making it fast, and tender, as I found out that very first day. Displaying my new toy to the first mate (Lorna) I attempted to walk along the deck. Over she went on her beam ends and I landed on my ribs on the port stay. First lesson: watch out for tender boats!

We named her *Sea Gull II*, what else? She was a heavy hull, but due to her narrow beam and vee-bottom, she had a pretty fair turn of speed. I sailed her for several years and learned a great deal. The older children, Ernie, Launi and Marion, all cut their sailing teeth on *Sea Gull II*'s hickory tiller. Ernie, with Harry along as ballast, raced *Sea Gull II* several times, with varying success. I remember a couple of wins but still blush at Ernie's remarks when the wooden rudder broke for the second time when he was in the lead. I guess the real reason for my blushes was that these rather lurid remarks were made in the presence of our new minister!

One late summer day — bright but cold and windy — Marion and her flame of the moment, one Brian, went out for a sail in *Sea Gull II*. As they had not returned after what we considered a really long time, Lorna, Harry and I went looking in our motor-boat. Nowhere could we see hide nor hair of boat or crew. Just when we were becoming truly alarmed, we came across the boat, bottom up, mast pointed directly at the bottom of Lake Muskoka! And no sign of Marion or Brian. As Harry and I were shedding our clothes to go underwater to see if they were somehow caught in the rigging, an outboard with two teenagers aboard came alongside and told us that the crew had been taken home by another boat. This was good news, so we concentrated on salvaging *Sea Gull II*. It was quite an operation. Harry and I stripped to the bare essentials, spent a long time underwater getting the heavy water-soaked sails off. Then, unable to right the boat in deep water, we towed it upside down to a nearby island, where we finally got the mast pointed skyward once more. Back home, we were delighted to find Marion and Brian thawing out in front of a fire. Harry and I promptly joined them.

The whole Wilson family learned plenty about the art of sailing from handling *Sea Gull II*, but just like her predecessors, *Black Bottom* and *Sea Gull I*, one sad day *Sea Gull II* showed unmistakable signs of old age and regretfully she was turned out to pasture. Thus far, all my sailboats had been bought at bargain prices and their qualities had certainly been in line with their purchase price. Now I was ready for a good boat. Searching the For Sale ads, I found one that looked interesting. It was a 14-foot dinghy, a Paceship made in the Maritimes. I drove to Toronto, had a good look at it on the owner's trailer, and decided that it was for me.

The Paceship turned out to be quite a pleasant craft — reasonably stable, fast before the wind and tacked fairly well. I sailed it quite a lot (still do, but of late it has been turned over to the grandchildren as a sort of marine teething ring). Feeling that the mast was not properly supported, I rigged up two running back stays that remedied that problem but produced another. If these stays were not handled properly when the boat was tacked, they fouled the mainsheet and the sail itself. (This has made my idea none too popular with the younger generation.) To the best of my knowledge the Paceship has only been upset once. But that was disastrous. Dave Korell, Marion's husband, was at the helm and he had the mainsheet sheeted down, not a good thing to do in such a small boat where things can, and generally do, happen very quickly. A sudden heavy gust flipped the boat onto its beam ends, and Dave couldn't let go the sheet fast enough to avoid the capsize. With mast and sails in the water, the boat quickly turned bottom up. There was little trouble in righting the Paceship, but where was the rudder? This was a rather unusual rudder. The top half was a standard-looking wooden blade, but pivoted to it at the bottom was a 4-foot-long aluminum blade which, when lowered, gave a great bite on the water. As well as this worked, it had one serious drawback: the aluminum blade was heavy enough to sink the whole rudder if it should come loose from the gudgeons on the transom. And that is exactly what had happened this time. The whole rudder assembly had gone down in well over 100 feet of water! When I tried to replace that rudder, I found out that the Paceship had gone out of production. Luckily, but at some considerable cost, I located and got the last of these rudders for sale in Canada. Needless to say, the rudder is now shipped so that it cannot fall free, no matter what.

In 1963 Lorna and I built and set up our winter home in Montserrat, the Emerald Isle of the Caribbean. Our house, Wilson's Folly, sits atop an 80-foot cliff, in full view of the beautiful Caribbean and the islands of St. Kitts, Nevis, and Redonda. Also in full view are the ships, motor yachts and sailboats using these fine waters. Well, it wasn't long before all this sort of got to me — I must have a sailboat! The near presence of all that sailable salt water was just irresistible. I talked about acquiring a fine seagoing yacht, but as immediate divorce proceedings were suggested should such a craft be purchased, I gave up the project. I did get a fine 14-foot dinghy, which has filled the bill as far as day sailing off the island is concerned. It is a Flying Fish, a double-hulled, unsinkable sloop with one huge lateen sail of 132 square foot area carried on a 24-foot mast. There are no stays; the mast is as flexible as a pole-vaulter's pole. It is called "the most forgiving sailboat ever built" mainly because of the action of its whippy mast, which bends with sudden wind gusts without transmitting all the shock to the boat itself. It is extremely stable, but it can pitch pole. And if you don't know what pitch pole is, try it sometime. All you need do is run directly before the wind with the sail full out. If the wind is strong enough, the pressure will drive the bow underwater and pitch pole! End over end you go, bodies of crew members fly jet-propelled in all directions, and there is your boat, upside down with the mast pointing to the bottom! In the 15 years or so that we have owned Flying Fish, we have sailed her with great enjoyment nearly every Sunday morning at the Montserrat Yacht Club. It is standing up well, and I guess will supply us with enjoyable weekend sailing for as long as I can handle a helm.

This taste of ocean sailing certainly whetted my appetite for more, but I had to remember what the Admiral said: "No ocean-sailer, or no me." There just didn't seem to be a solution. Then, out of a clear blue sky it came — literally! As part of a three-day island-hopping trip, Lorna and I were flying to a landing on the island of Saba. This is really just a huge volcanic cone, and the airport, all 1,100 feet of it, is merely a niche cut out of the side of

My "Ocean racer" – a 14 foot Flying Fish at Montserrat Yacht Club.

that cone. There is a vertical 500-foot drop into the ocean at each end. This constituted what I considered the hairiest landing spot I had ever seen. We were in a small Canadian Twin Otter and the door of the pilot's cabin being open, we had a perfect, and rather terrifying, view of the runway as we did a vertical bank combined with a sickening sideslip to line up plane and proposed landing spot. I wanted a picture of that view, but just as I was about to take it, a passenger ahead of me craned his neck and his camera out in front of me. Seeing that his camera was the same as mine, I shoved mine into his hands and said, "Please!"

Safely landed, he and I compared notes. His name was Phil Brulé, and he and his wife, Mary, both from Ottawa, were sailing their 54-foot ketch down the Caribbean from Miami to Trinidad. As Saba has no place where yachts can either dock or anchor, they had left their boat at St. Maartens for the day. I pumped him as much as possible about sailing one's own boat, and ended up giving him our address and telephone number in Montserrat. A few days later I received a phone call from Phil, who was at the nearby Vue Pointe Hotel. We dashed down to meet him and arrived just as he was about to be escorted off to jail by a very irate policeman who charged the Brulés with illegal entry to the island. It seems that they should have landed at Plymouth and presented the ship's papers to the immigration office there. Instead they had anchored in front of the Vue Pointe. It took quite a bit of talking , by me, to the Chief Minister, to persuade him that such cavalier treatment shouldn't be handed out to a man who was one of the largest government building contractors in the city of Ottawa, particularly as Canada had just installed in Montserrat a $3 million water system free of charge. Although all seemed to have been straightened out, nevertheless the next morning at about four o'clock, the Brulé's upped anchor and left for Antigua. Again Phil called, and this time he invited us to go over and join them for a few days sailing. We were on the way before you could say "Jack Robinson"! Brulé's yacht, *Star Song*, was alongside the jetty at

184

English Harbour, and we were invited aboard as soon as we arrived. The boat was a double-ender, bow and stern both pointed, and as a ketch carried four sails — mizzen, main, Yankee and jib — on two masts.

We spent two days gunkholing, moving around from one lovely white sand beach to another and anchoring in some secluded bay at night. The Brulés took delight in showing us everything about *Star Song*, and spent a couple of hours giving us sailing instructions. *Star Song* was well equipped — electric stove, deep freeze, electric anchor hoist — everything to make it easy for two people to handle this large craft by themselves. They had purchased *Star Song* in Miami, had taken a year's sabbatical from business, and were doing this comprehensive Caribbean tour. At the finish of their tour, in late spring, they planned to have a paid crew sail the boat over to Europe, where Phil and Mary and their seven children would cruise the Mediterranean all summer. The boat was to be sold at the end of their sabbatical.

The third day we set sail for Guadeloupe. We had a good wind and the sailing was excellent. Phil let both Lorna and me take a turn at the wheel. I also helped Phil handle sail — and got the bawling-out of my life in so doing! Once, after adjusting the sheet rope of the big main, I made fast to the cleat with a couple of half hitches. Phil screamed, "Get those goddamned hitches off that cleat FAST!" I then got the worst going-over imaginable; it lasted for at least five minutes. Finally, when I had taken all the abuse I could, and was about to reply in kind, Phil said, "Harold, if you would like to know why I was so rough, it was because what you just did with those two half hitches was just about the most dangerous thing that can be done aboard a sailboat. Those hitches, under a strong pull from the sheet, will tighten to the point where the only way they could be removed would be to cut the sheet rope. That takes time, and in that time the boat could easily be upside down. I want you to remember that forever. Never, never use half hitches when sheeting down. Merely put on several figure eights. They hold

185

just as well and can be released in a second." Lesson over, Phil apologized for his rudeness, but I guess I had deserved it.

Looking astern, Antigua was gone, and Guadeloupe was still hidden in the haze ahead of us. This was my very first experience of being out of sight of land. The ocean sure is a mighty big place. The whole day was great — handling ropes, steering, helping with navigation, eating the fine lunch prepared by Mary and Lorna in a galley heeling way over to starboard. We made our landfall at the northern tip of Guadeloupe, and sailing down the west coast of the island, we pulled into Deshaies Bay and anchored there for the night, our last aboard *Star Song*. Phil and Mary set out to make it a memorable one. Just before supper we were joined by a brother of Phil's and his wife. They had just flown down from Ottawa and would take our places as crew members. Mary prepared a super meal and Phil provided enough wine to wash it down, maybe even to float *Star Song*. Dinner over, Phil produced another of the boat's goodies, a small electronic chord organ. Lorna got at it and soon six loud and lusty voices were raised in song. This was great fun, and we kept it up until a concerto of yells — "SHADDAP" — came from the other boats anchored in the bay. Next morning, after having said goodbye to Phil and Mary, we boarded a local bus and travelled halfway around Basse Terre to the airport, where we caught a LIAT flight back to Antigua and then Montserrat.

That first taste of real ocean sailing was a good one, but you can't expect friendly people like the Brulés to turn up complete with boat whenever you want to go sailing. By the time that that summer was over and we were back in Montserrat for the winter, a lot of thought had been expended on this problem, and no solution arrived at. One evening the phone rang. "Hello, Harold. This is Phil. What are you doing? Whatever it is, drop it and meet us in Grenada the day after tomorrow. We're going sailing again." Ours not to reason why, we just packed our seagoing duds and took off. At St. George's Harbour in Grenada we met up with Phil and Mary and *Star Song*. I said, "What gives, Phil, I thought you sold her?" Well, it seems that one year's

186

sabbatical just wasn't long enough, so Phil had the boat sailed back across the Atlantic and down to Antigua. Now the Brulés were off on another long cruise and we were to do the first section with them, from Grenada up through the lovely Grenadines to St. Vincent.

But before we could sail, there was quite a bit of maintenance work to be done. Phil busied himself with just about everything; Mary and Lorna dove below and put everything there shipshape; I spent two full days mending all the leaks in our inflatable dinghy, which for some unknown reason was called *Leaky Tiki*.

We set out from Grenada early one morning. It is a bit dicey getting out without trying a sand bar or two for size, but we made it. Just off the northern tip of Grenada we passed Diamond Island, better known as "Kick-em-Jenny" because of the tumultuous seas that are often encountered there. That day Jenny wasn't kicking; it was fine sailing. We pulled into Tyrrel Bay on dry Cariacou Island that night and anchored. Immediately we were besieged by an armada of small cockleshell skiffs, all manned by natives, and all with things to barter — barter, mind you, not sell. Barter for what? Water! There is none on the island. All water is imported and the boat hadn't shown up. We got a mess of native oysters from one lad who claimed he got them off the roots of the mangrove bushes in the careenage on the north side of the bay. We had a great oyster stew for supper. Hearing music ashore, we landed with *Leaky Tiki* and tracked it down. It was steel band music, but with a difference. The steel drums were all played by children, quite young ones at that, and their drums, instead of being made from the tops of gasoline drums, were fashioned from canned food containers, from gallon-size down to pint. The music, though high-pitched, certainly was very good.

Before leaving the next morning we went out in *Leaky Tiki* to the careenage, pulled up a couple of long mangrove roots, and scraped off a real mess of tiny but tasty oysters. Back on board, up anchor, and away we go! If everything works. This time the anchor winch refused. Finding that there did not appear to be any electricity at the solenoid which operated the winch, Phil and I got into work clothes and went at it. It was a hot, hot day, and *Star Song* was an all-steel boat. I spent the whole day on my back lying on piles of rusty chain in the chain locker, which was right under that steel deck. Hot? I nearly melted. Finally, late in the afternoon, I found the trouble, a broken solenoid coil. And of course there wasn't a spare solenoid aboard. Rummaging around in Phil's workshop, which was under the cockpit sole, I discovered an old but unused Model-A Ford starter switch. This was from a period before we had solenoids; the foot-operated switch passed current directly via heavy wiring from battery to starter. I threw out the defective solenoid, did a complete rewire job and, *voila*, up came the anchor. Well, it was too late to set out, so we celebrated the repair job by having two sundowners that night — or was it three?

We visited many islands, all of them beautiful. Mustique, the vacation home of Princess Margaret and her jet-set friends, presented us with a very sad sight, the wreck of the French cruise ship *Antilles* sitting broken-backed and gutted by fire on a submerged rock. There was a bright spot. At the time of the accident, the *Queen Elizabeth II* was nearby and able to take all passengers and crew off without injury.

The Tobago Cays, a series of small islets, rocks, reefs and shallows, made a great place to stop for a day's snorkeling. We had a look at Palm Island with its beautiful white sand beaches and its fine hotel. Nearby are two tiny islands, Petit Martinique and Petit St. Vincent. The dividing line between the Grenadines, controlled by Grenada, and those under the jurisdiction of St. Vincent is supposed to pass through the narrow channel between these two tiny islands, but by some mistake of the cartographer who produced the maps, the northernmost 100 feet of Petit Martinique belongs to St. Vincent and the rest of the island belongs to Grenada! We visited Petit Nevis, the site of a whale-butchering station, and were unlucky enough to see the monstrous head and the entrails of one of these harmless and fast-disappearing mammals floating off the jetty. We anchored overnight at Cannuon Island, and found out to our sorrow that the wind was howling down a mountain pass right at our boat, making this night a rather uncomfortable one.

To enter the Northern Grenadines we had to clear immigration and customs at Union Island. It was a hot afternoon and Phil and I went ashore in shorts and T-shirts to find the St. Vincent immigration officials. We received a rather chilly reception: "When you come back to me, properly attired," said the very tall, black official, "I shall process your ship." When we returned, wearing black leather shoes, blue dress trousers, white shirts, ties and jackets, we were processed, without a flicker of an eyelid from the Lord High Executioner.

Early the next day we sailed into Admiralty Bay on lovely Bequia Island. This was to be our last port of call. As we had blown out our jib sail the day before in a strong gust, Phil wanted to take it ashore to a local sailmaker for repair. The large bronze grommet in the clew of the sail had ripped out and had been badly twisted. We bagged the big sail and took it to the sailmaker. "Sure," he said, "I can repair the sail, but I don't have a grommet that size." Saying that I thought I could fix the damaged grommet, we left the sail with him and went back to *Star Song*. To get down to Phil's workshop, you had to lift the cockpit sole, step down onto the deep freeze, then down again into the workshop. Well, I slipped off the deep freeze and went headfirst into the hold, landing on my chest on top of the steel machinist's vise on the bench! Phil was flying around me as I lay in agony, and he was clucking like an old hen around her chicks. He kept shouting, "Oh my God, Harold, are you all right?" Finally, getting my wind back, I said, "Phil, get the hell out of here and let me work!" After spending an hour hammering and peening the grommet back into its original form, we took it back to the sailmaker, who declared it satisfactory and proceeded to sew it into the clew of the sail.

The next morning we left *Star Song* at her anchorage in Admiralty Bay and at 6:30 a.m. we boarded the local inter-island schooner that sailed us over to St. Vincent. There we said goodbye to Mary and Phil and went out to the airport to catch our plane to — where? Montserrat? Not on your life! We had enjoyed ocean sailing so much we were ready for more. The plane we boarded that morning took us right back to Grenada to do the same over again!

At Grenada we met four good Canadian friends, all with homes in Montserrat. They were Dr. Mal Hill and his wife, Aline, and Bob and Eleanor Robarts (brother of John Robarts, at that time Premier of Ontario). The six of us had chartered a ship called *Kebir*. We found her in St. George's Harbour, and went aboard and met our captain and crew, Claude and Annie Muraz, husband and wife, the owners of *Kebir*. In fact *Kebir* was their home, and had been since the day they were married. Claude came from Monaco and Annie from France. They had stepped aboard *Kebir* on their wedding day and had lived aboard ever since. They crossed the Atlantic, liked the Caribbean, and now were earning their living by chartering. Claude and Annie were a charming couple; it certainly looked like this second Grenadine cruise was going to be an enjoyable one. *Kebir* was the same size as *Star Song*, 54 feet long, and she also was a ketch. We were all paying guests this time, which meant that we had no particular crew duties to perform. But this didn't mean that we couldn't do all the sailing we wanted. In fact, our first day out, I sailed *Kebir* all the way from Grenada to our anchorage at Cariacou. We sure were living in the lap of luxury. Annie was a gourmet cook. Her meals were wonderful. How they were managed in such a tiny galley I know not. Besides this, Annie was definitely easy on the eyes. Bob Robarts said, "The only thing wrong with *Kebir* is that when Annie serves her dream meals dressed in that bikini I can't eat!"

We spent two glorious weeks aboard *Kebir*. Our route followed very closely that which we had travelled in *Star Song*. Claude was a good sailor, a fine captain, and a very obliging man. We had just reached the Tobago Cays when someone said how nice it would be to have a lobster dinner. Donning mask, snorkel and flippers, Claude went overboard and returned half an hour later with a real mess of langoustes, the clawless lobster of the Caribbean.

We spent a day at a tiny spit of sand called Sandy Island. The coral reef which surrounds Sandy Island makes for simply wonderful snorkeling, and we spent the whole day at it. We anchored just offshore that night and after a late dinner we were treated to a most unusual natural phenomenon. The sea was a perfect flat calm, and it was a very dark night with no moon. Suddenly, for 50 yards all around *Kebir*, the water was lit up with a glowing, pulsating light. We were astounded. What could it be? Claude said it was due to the presence in the water of little glow worms. Turning a flashlight down onto the water, he pointed out the two-inch-long worms — millions of them. Claude said that he had seen these before, a few at a time, but had never seen such a display as tonight. These little fellows didn't leave their lights on all of the time, so looking across the water we were aware of millions of points of light undulating and pulsating, just like a magic carpet flying through the sky. And then suddenly, as if on an order from headquarters, nothing! Not a flicker! The little grey worms were still there in the beam of our spotlight, but the show was over. Claude sailed us right into the waters of Kingstown Harbour, no early morning schooner trip from Bequia this time, and there we said goodbye to these two fine, young French people. Over the years we have heard from them occasionally. They eventually left the Caribbean and ended up chartering in the out islands of the Tahiti group in the far-off Pacific.

My sailing wasn't quite over for the year. The commodore of our yacht club was Bill Allen, a fine gentleman if there ever was one. He had a small sloop, *Eurus*, and he invited me to go on a day's sail to Redonda Island, about 18 miles out in front of our home in Montserrat. It was a rough day and, believe me, *Eurus* made rough going of it. She rolled and corkscrewed over the waves like you wouldn't believe. That was the day that I discovered one of the lesser joys of sailing — sea sickness! What a horror that is! You feel like you want to die, and you and everyone else aboard sure hope that you do. I am afraid that my growing reputation as an up-and-coming saltwater sailor suffered a serious setback that day.

The next winter Phil and Mary came to Montserrat for a few days, then, chartering a small plane, we flew to Tortola in the British Virgin Islands. There we chartered an Olsen 38 sloop from West Indies Yachts. This boat wasn't the best, nothing like *Star Song* and *Kebir*, but it seemed wonderful to me — my first private yacht, even if it was just chartered. We sailed the scenic Virgins for ten days. We circumnavigated or visited practically all of the British Virgins and crossed over into the American Virgins also. While in American waters we landed on St. John, although we were not strictly legal in doing so. We were free to sail wherever we wished, but landing on American soil called for going through customs and immigration, and this could easily take a full day, so we just anchored well offshore and swam in. There we explored an unusual underwater nature trail. The route was laid out by easily read signs painted on large rocks. Equipped with flippers and snorkel, it was quite easy to follow this route. It led through a veritable wonderland of coral, sea ferns, shells and hordes of tropical fish in the most amazing array of forms and colours.

Back aboard we found that something in our engine gearshift had gone adrift. We had reverse only. We sailed back into British waters and anchored for the night. Getting on our ship-to-shore radio, we contacted our base at West Indies Yachts and told them our problem. Too late at night to do anything, so "just sail in here in the morning and we will fix it." This we did, but it just wasn't that simple. We hung around the marina all day expecting that the repairs would be made any minute and that we could then continue our trip. After all, we were paying a lot for that aging Olsen and we wanted to get our money's worth. When it became apparent that we would be spending the night at the marina, the management took pity on us, gave us a blank cheque, and told us to have a super dinner at the exclusive and expensive Reef Club. We had everything from soup to nuts, and it was a good thing that the cheque was a blank one! In the wee small hours we wended our way back to the marina and in complete darkness stepped aboard our boat. Lorna went below and yelled, "Hey, the boat is sinking!" It certainly was. A flashlight showed about a foot of water over the cabin sole! Frantically I rigged the big Whale bilge pump and started pumping. Some new charterers, just checking in for a hoped-for early start the next morning, pitched in and helped. When we had started to win the battle, one of these helpful men went looking for the marina mechanic and found him asleep on one of the moored yachts. He wasn't too pleased at being hauled back to work at 2 a.m., but went to work to find the problem. It turned out to be a badly leaking stuffing box connection on the prop shaft. This was way down in the bowels, in a most difficult place. Having made the repairs, the mechanic wormed his way out and, without saying one word, left us, jumped into his dinghy and paddled back out to his yacht — and his lady love, maybe? Something had sure made him angry that morning.

During this cruise, Phil taught me as much as he could about the art of sailing and how to take good care of all a sailboat's needs. One thing I remembered was that quite often it is wise to carry less sail than you think you need, and far less than other boats sailing with you may be wearing. This is particularly true when beating into the wind. I remember him saying as we were the last of six yachts to pull out of Little Harbour, Peter Island, "Now watch. We will sail today with a reefed main and just the working jib. You probably notice that all the others had full sails up when they left. And we are the last to sail. You watch and see what happens." Well, we beat our way up the Sir Francis Drake Channel and by early afternoon had overhauled and passed all six of those early starters. They were beating their heads off and getting soaking wet doing it, while we had an effortless and much faster sail. When we finished the cruise, Phil told me that I was now ready to captain a boat myself and suggested that I sail these waters again. It sure would be good practice, but the thought of it gave me butterflies. Back at Montserrat, Phil suggested that the very best way to get the practice that I needed was to get a good sloop in Canada and learn all that I could about handling it. He also said that during the summer he would help me make the best selection. Things were moving!

As soon as possible after getting Wawanaissa ready for the summer, I began looking around for a good used sloop, or a new one if I could afford it. Dinghies are fine craft — experts say that if you can sail a dinghy you can sail anything — so this time I definitely was looking for something big. Maybe a large day sailer, or even one equipped for cruising. I learned that the very popular O'Day sailboats were handled and sold at the Hamer Bay Marina on Lake Joseph. We went up and had a look at, and promptly fell in love with, their 23-foot sloop. It was a pretty boat and, to me, looked like just about everything the doctor ordered. And it was immediately available. Well, almost. We couldn't take it out for a trial sail because the mast was broken. How come? Well, it seemed that someone unknowledgeable to the way of sailboats had taken it out with the stays not properly tuned. Something told me that, tyro as I was, it would be a good idea to get the advice of an expert before making any decisions. So I talked with Phil Brulé, and two days later he, Mary, and another sailing friend from Ottawa arrived at Wawanaissa. The three men took the now rerigged O'Day out for a trial run. I was quite impressed, but not so Phil and his friend. When they deliberately made the boat weather helm in a strong wind, the O'Day did something they didn't like at all. I think I should explain a bit about weather helming. This is a case where, when driving into the wind, and the boat is forced beyond its capabilities by the man on the tiller, the boat and the wind take over from the pilot, the rudder becomes useless, and the bow of the boat comes up into the wind. This, of course, relieves the wind load on the sails, the bow falls off again, and sailing returns to normal. Well, what the O'Day did was to come up into the wind so quickly, the bow shot right through the wind, immediately putting the boat on the other tack. This calls for quite nippy action by the whole crew. It is an unsafe and uncomfortable characteristic.

The broken mast of a few days ago prompted Phil to say that the aluminum mast used on the O'Day looked pretty skimpy, considering the size and weight of the boat. He felt that the interior arrangements were much better suited for day sailing than overnighting. And, a last beef, "Lorna won't be happy aboard this boat. It is altogether too tender" — tender meaning that it tips over too far and too easily. This added the last nail in the O'Day's coffin.

Phil and his friend both suggested that we wouldn't go far wrong if we settled on a Grampian 23. This Canadian-built sloop was, in their opinion, about the most stable of all boats in this size. It was also a well-found cruising boat, and it sailed well. Back at the classified ads, I located three of these boats for sale. I inspected them all and sailed in each of them. I found that in every respect they met the specifications that had caused Phil to reject the O'Day. The best of the three, hardly a year old, was located at Port Credit. After a short sail in it I dickered with the owner and got his $10,500 figure down to my offer, which he accepted. A quick cheque and I had my first honest-to-goodness yacht! Two days later I had Bruce Hamer and his father, the agents for the O'Day, come down with their large trailer to bring our boat to her new home waters, the Muskoka Lakes. When she was lifted onto the trailer, I saw that the hull below the waterline was a mess. Good old Lake Ontario, and a summer with practically no use, had allowed the growth of a great beard of green algae. The marina there had a steam-cleaning jenny which peeled everything off to the bare fibreglass in no time at all.

Fibreglass? Up until now, with just one exception, all of my boats had been made from wood. The one exception being our work boat, *Tin Can*, so named because it is an aluminum craft. But now I had bought a large sailboat whose hull was completely made of fibreglass. It was not the first time that I had come up against this new synthetic material, but it was the first time that I had used it. I had seen it and aluminum used for race boats but had not been impressed. Granted, both of these materials are

Lorna M – our 23 foot Grampion sloop used in Muskoka waters.

strong, but they have these bad faults: under heavy pounding aluminum will bend and take a permanent set, which of course changes the running characteristics of a race boat; and fibreglass, when it does break, shatters, which means that the hull is gone. The traditional boatbuilding material, wood, on the other hand, will crack under stress but most usually with the grain, which may cause leaks (repairable) but which will not affect the running characteristics or materially weaken the structure of the boat. In spite of my feelings, I had to admit that fibreglass offered some great advantages, particularly in the building and use of sailboats. The greatest of these is the complete absence of water in the bilge. There just is nothing worse than a leaky sailboat. So we now had our first fibreglass boat.

The Grampian was launched at Hamer Bay and I motored it all the way down through the three lakes to Wawanaissa. Bruce Hamer came down and taught me how to rig the boat, and gave me my first and only lesson in sailing her. Immediately I removed her original name, *TriPartite*, and called my new boat something really lady-like: *Lorna* M. (Some people thought that I had an ulterior motive in choosing this name.) *Lorna* M is a 23-foot overall sloop. She carries two sails — a main, and either a working jib or a very large genoa — on a 26-foot mast. Below deck she is quite spacious. Forward is a good double bunk with a hatch to the foredeck. Made private by modern-fold doors fore and aft, there is the head and a hanging locker. Then comes the main salon, which has a table and seating for five people, and a galley with sink, running water and a stove. There is a very long quarter bunk aft of the galley, and the table drops down to allow the seat cushions to form a comfortable double bunk. The cockpit is large enough to handle all five of the maximum crew if necessary. Originally, when purchased, she was powered by a 6-horsepower Johnson outboard. This was mounted on the transom, on the port side, in a self-drained motor well. This arrangement was fine except that the off-centre drive caused a lot of helm when under power. The engine itself proved inade-quate to move a 2-ton boat satisfactorily in anything but a flat calm. Taken as a whole *Lorna* M was, and is, a most comfortable cruising sailboat. I was completely happy with my purchase and looked forward to many years of fine sailing with *Lorna* M — both of them!

A few sails helped me to become fairly familiar with *Lorna* M's likes and dislikes under sail. One thing became clear that irked me a bit. To sail *Lorna* M, a crew of two was a definite necessity, and I thought sometime I might want to take her out alone. Lorna and I took a trip to Ottawa and stayed with the Brulés for a couple of days. I discussed this problem with Phil and the friend that he had brought to Muskoka to help test the O'Day. They came up with the answers, and the friend, who made a business of keeping in stock all the unusual bits of marine hardware demanded by the sailing fraternity, supplied all the necessary equipment. Bruce Hamer helped me install all this stuff, and soon I could raise all sails and furl, reef the main, and adjust tension on the fore and aft mast stays all from the cockpit and without setting foot on deck. I now had a good single-hander.

By the end of the summer I felt that I had become familiar enough with our boat to permit me to attempt an overnight cruise. One late August day we packed provisions aboard, crewed up with Harry, grandsons Norman and Harold, the mate and myself, and took off. After a pleasant afternoon's sail, we anchored for the night at the very foot of East Bay, just a few miles from our island. *Lorna* M had come equipped with a supposedly ultra-safe alcohol stove — so safe, said the instructions, that the fire could be put out with just a light dash of water at any time. I fired up the stove that night for the first time. Safe! There was a great billowing flame which only the mate's quick action prevented from igniting the cabin curtains. Had this happened, *Lorna* M would immediately have followed suit. That first overnighter brought to light a few things on which to ponder. First, get a new and safer stove. Second, how do you stop the captain's snoring from shaking the ship from bow to stern? Third, how do you make the cabin mosquito-proof? There were millions of pests in East Bay that night, most of them inside our mosquito netting. We all had an early morning swim and a great breakfast, then sailed all morning and got home in time for lunch onshore.

When taking *Lorna* M to winter storage quarters at Hamer Bay, I arranged to buy from the new owner, Terry Johnson, a new, more powerful motor. It was an electric-start, alternator-equipped, 9.9-horsepower Johnson. It was a sailboat motor equipped with low-speed lower unit gearing which allowed the use of a larger propeller and which should make it possible to handle *Lorna* M under power in any direction and under any weather conditions. I gave the old 6-horsepower kicker to Marion and Dave to use with their car-top aluminum boat, which they called *Basso Profundo*.

We so enjoyed our first night aboard *Lorna* M, we decided to do it again as soon as possible. So very early the next summer — actually before the boat had been launched for the summer — we had *Lorna* M taken by trailer to Washago at the head of Lake Couchiching, part of the famous Trent–Severn Waterway. This is a navigable route of lakes, rivers, canals and locks that crosses Ontario from Georgian Bay on Lake Huron to Trenton on far-off Lake Ontario. We were in Stratford at the time, attending a performance at the Stratford Shakespearean Festival, and returned to Washago at midnight, intending to sleep aboard and start a cruise of the Trent–Severn the next morning.

We had quite a time finding our boat at the Pier II marina. We woke up a lot of rather irate sailors, but eventually found our beautiful white yacht now painted almost jet black! Hold! That wasn't paint — it was millions of shad-flies! They were horrible and squishy. We climbed into the steaming-hot cabin, left it closed up, and put in a miserable but fly-less night.

Next morning we spent two hours restoring our ship to her pristine, pre-fly beauty, then set off to see the Trent–Severn. I had purchased a great pile of large-scale maps of the whole system. They were to prove of considerable worth and interest. First, we went west from Washago to see the end of the waterway at Big Chute. (Actually *Lorna* M was a power yacht for this trip. We had left mast, sails and rigging at home, as sailing was impossible in the narrow confines of the waterway.) Almost immediately we came to our first lock, and wouldn't you know, the highest gate lock in the system. We entered the lock very slowly and carefully, not knowing the accepted procedure. We felt quite insignificant looking up at those towering 45-foot gates, and way above the lockmaster in his air-conditioned control tower. There were long, vertical plastic-covered cables snaking over the lock side every 10 feet and disappearing into the water. The lockmaster indicated that we should pass our bow and stern lines around these and hang on. I did so with my short stern line and couldn't understand what Lorna was doing. She was handling rope like mad and still wasn't secured to the cable. Then I saw the trouble. Instead of a short bow painter, I had rigged the 185-foot anchor line to the bow deck cleat! Lorna couldn't find the end! Just when panic was giving way to frenzy, the lockmaster's voice boomed out from far above: "Take it easy, lady. I haven't lost a boat, or a lady, yet this year." This was not well received by the first mate — it was the captain's fault! I continued as captain, but for the rest of the trip the mate became the admiral.

That first lock safely passed, we travelled on with no further problems. At Big Chute there is a considerable drop down to the level of Lake Huron. As we had no intention of wetting our bottom there, we decided to overnight at the jetty and have a look at the interesting marine railway that carried boats over the height of land between the Great Lakes system and the waters of the Trent–Severn Waterway. This system is now over 100 years old. The old original marine railway which did yeoman duty for many, many years had just very recently been replaced by a new railway. The old one operated on just a single pair of rails. As the boat on the car went up, everything in it crashed to the stern. Then, as it went down the other side, the avalanche of movable stuff — food, clothing and gear — rushed headlong to the bow. Only very accomplished and knowing sailors remembered to lash everything down before starting; the rest spent the next day at dockside putting things shipshape. The new car operates on two pairs of rails, one for the front wheels and one for the rear. The elevations of these rails vary with respect to each other as they all rise up over the height of land. This variation is so arranged that the car and the boat that it is carrying are kept on an even keel throughout the whole operation.

The next morning we turned about and set out to explore the Trent–Severn from west to east, and from end to end, from Big Chute on Georgian Bay to Trenton on far-off Lake Ontario. It is a great number of beauty spots strung along the waterway like pearls on a necklace. I suppose that with all this beauty around us, it was only natural that my eyes would be more on the beauty than on my navigation. At least that was my excuse for not noticing the approach, from the rear, of a very black line squall. When the first puff hit us, I turned and saw that in just moments we would be in the very centre of a storm that would blank out everything. I saw an island just off our starboard bow and headed directly for it. Bang! That storm hit us like a ton of bricks. Visibility reduced to absolute zero, it was only because of a good compass bearing taken as the island was disappearing, and a lot of luck, that we found that blessed island. Rain was pouring down in torrents, and the wind was unbelievable. We found a very convenient dock and made fast to it to ride out the storm. We battened ourselves below, protected from the fury of the elements, brewed a pot of tea on the new stove, put a good tape on the tape player, and I beat the first mate in a rousing game of cribbage. We were as snug as those old two bugs in a rug for an hour, then the sun came out once more and we set off again across Sparrow Lake. Back at Washago, we entered Lake Couchiching. This is a long, narrow, shallow and quite weedy lake, and drawing 4 feet of water as we did, we endeavoured to keep *Lorna M* well in the middle of the two lines of buoys so thoughtfully laid out by our Department of Transport.

At Orillia we passed through the narrows, under a very low railway bridge, and out into Lake Simcoe, the largest lake in the Trent–Severn. This body of water has a nasty reputation for kicking up its heels whenever a strong wind blows, and right then a real doozer was howling. Questioned about the advisability of venturing out on the lake, a marina attendant said, "Well, some boats have been running here." If they could do it, so could we, I thought. The wind was astern, and with the protection of the causeway across the narrows, the seas were not too heavy. But as we motored, the seas got higher and higher, and when we neared the south end of Simcoe, the swells were better than 10 feet high! We didn't exactly ship any water, although we got tons of spray. Every once in a while a huge roller would pass under our transom, tossing it high in the air and making our prop spin uselessly high above the water. It was beginning to get quite uncomfortable when, with the combined help of good charts, a good compass, and a very fine navigator (the mate), we found the narrow entrance to the Trent Canal on the eastern shore of Lake Simcoe. What a relief to get out of all that rough stuff! And there was our next lock, Gamebridge.

As we came alongside and sounded our horn requesting lock service, the lockmaster strolled up and said, "Well, folks, better just tie up where you are. The canal closes for the day in 15 minutes. The facilities are better here than at the next lock. Here are the keys. Make yourselves at home. Have a good night and I'll see you at eight tomorrow morning." As he was turning away, he added, "Where have you come from?" I told him Big Chute. To which he replied, "That was yesterday, where have you come from, today?" When I again answered Big Chute, he said, "But you couldn't have. The storm warnings have been up all afternoon and absolutely no boats have been across Lake Simcoe." When I assured him that we had indeed crossed that angry lake, he shook his head and walked off muttering, "Crazy kooks!"

That was really our first night to enjoy the facilities offered to travelling yachtsmen by the Trent–Severn Waterway. We found excellent washrooms, plenty of hot water, and fine barbecues for cooking ashore, all well protected from the weather. We found the same friendly reception and the same facilities at every overnight stop we made on the whole waterway. There was a minimum daily charge for the use of the canal system — three dollars, I believe, but in the case of senior citizens (that meant us) it was all free! We stayed at Fenelon Falls, Lovesick, Peterborough and others. We went through 44 locks, high and low. The highest gate lock was that first one that saw the mate promoted to admiral, but there are two even higher, at Kirkfield and Peterborough. These are of a quite different type. They consist of what are virtually two dry docks mounted on hydraulically operated rams which are drilled deep into the earth. One of these is always at the lower level and the other at the top, and the two hydraulic rams are interconnected so that as one comes down, the other goes up. If you are going uphill, as we were at Kirkfield, you enter the dry dock, gates at both ends are closed, and the next thing you know, the dry dock with your boat and you in it goes soaring up into the sky! Well, not too far, but it is a thrilling experience. The dry dock stops at the upper level, the gate ahead of you opens, and you proceed, having climbed quite a hill in the process. All this is brought about by merely pumping water into the dry dock on the upper level until its weight becomes greater than the lower dry dock with you in it. Then down it comes,, by gravity, and up you go. Just as simple as that. Pretty smart, the army engineers who laid this out way back when.

Back to ocean sailing in Caribbean waters. The commodore of the Montserrat Yacht Club, Bill Allen, had acquired a new 35-foot sloop called *Zigzag*. She had made a name as a quite successful ocean racer. Bill retired *Eurus* to his trailer and parked it behind his garage. He and Eleanor, his wife, invited us to go on a four-day cruise with them to Nevis, St. Kitts, St. Maartens, and St. Barts. I didn't need a second invitation. Leaving Montserrat at noon, we were just easing into our anchorage at Nevis at dusk, and just as we were about to drop the hook, we ran aground! By dint of the crew rocking *Zigzag*, and Bill applying reverse at the correct moment, we freed ourselves and sought a bit deeper anchorage. We sailed to St. Maartens the next day and had a lot of fun shopping for bargains. Then on to St. Barts. So far, with the exception of the grounding, the whole experience had been most enjoyable. The run from St. Maartens to St. Barts was something else. The seas were very high and quite disturbed. Eleanor became quite seasick, couldn't shake it, and spent the whole day draped over the binnacle and hanging on. Just as we were ready to furl sail and motor into the harbour at St. Barts, Bill discovered that his battery was absolutely flat and that he couldn't start the engine. Great! Now we had to sail right up to our anchorage and do it right the first time, as there wouldn't be a second. Bill was at the wheel, Lorna worked the sails, and I was at the bow ready to drop the hook when Bill gave the word. The harbour was full of moored yachts and a couple of old, rusty freighters. Bill selected a spot just past one of these eyesores and told me to anchor, which I did. But the hook didn't hold! We were drifting backwards, in irons, right onto the sharp steel bow of that freighter! Then, as we were about to crash, the dragging anchor got a bite, the boat slewed around the freighter, the anchor let go again momentarily, and just as we were in a perfect spot aft of the freighter, the hook grabbed for sure, and there we were. Although it was a pure accident, I guess it didn't look that way, as we received a real round of applause from the crews of the anchored yachts, a commendation for what they thought was a very fine piece of seamanship. But all of this had been just too much for Eleanor. Over our sundowners she advised that she was jumping ship in the morning, would fly back to Montserrat, and we could bring *Zigzag* back by ourselves.

Next morning, after seeing Eleanor safely off to Montserrat, we went shopping for some necessary boat supplies — a new anchor rope to replace one becoming rather frayed, and a new storage battery. No more dead engines for us. We set sail just after lunch, intending to sail all night and reach Montserrat about noon the next day. Out of the harbour and in the open sea, we found sailing conditions just about as severe as what we had battled the day before. After getting the rhythm of the seas, we felt that although we were running lee rail under, *Zigzag* was still handling the conditions very well, so we elected to continue. By late afternoon, when we had reached the north shore of St. Kitts, long past the point of no return, we realized that conditions were getting worse, and fast! It was pretty tough going, above deck and below. Bill and I had our hands full, and Lorna, in a galley inclined at about a 30-degree angle, was having a wild time trying to make tea and sandwiches for a much-needed supper. Just as we were eating, we had a bit of wild and unwanted excitement. Bill, setting the main sheet, had his finger pulled into the block! At his loud scream, Lorna grabbed the wheel and pulled *Zigzag* up to the wind. We were running very close hauled. I grabbed the boom and, feet braced against the cockpit seat, pulled with all my strength. The combination of our efforts relieved the strain just enough to enable Bill to release his trapped finger. Luckily no major damage resulted.

As darkness fell like a blanket over our heads, we realized that we were in for a real tropical storm. Conditions rapidly deteriorated. The wind increased and it began to pour. And the waves! You wouldn't believe how high a 20-foot wave looks from the cockpit of a puny 35-foot sailboat! About ten o'clock, my turn at the wheel, I noticed that the binnacle light was getting very dim. Then it went out entirely. Advised of this, Bill attempted to start the engine. Dead battery? How could it be? It was brand-new that morning! A couple of checks showed just that, a completely dead battery. A short somewhere, we supposed. But what good was that? Again we had a useless engine, and maybe just when it would be badly needed. So with no light to see the compass, I navigated by the lights along the north shore of Nevis, which we were just passing. This was all right until the storm blew out the generating station ashore! Then, very suddenly, I realized that the monstrous wall of water hanging way up in the air above our bow was a rogue wave! And it was right where the trough that I was sliding into should have been! No way was *Zigzag* going to pass over that rogue wave. I gave a mighty warning shout and threw myself backwards onto the deck with legs wrapped around the binnacle. With its terrible

roar, Lorna, below, said it sounded like an express train overhead. That wave, tons and tons of it, tore the length of our deck
and shot over the transom, almost taking me with it! *Zigzag* staggered like a drunken man, then shook herself, raised her head,
and survived. I told Bill that he knew his boat better than I did,
and that I didn't want the responsibility of handling her in this
storm, so he took over. Then disaster really hit! A wild whirlwind hit us, we spun round an estimated seven times, and the
thrashing boom caught me a clip on the forehead, laying me out
cold for a few seconds. Coming to, I saw Bill looking up at the
mast and muttering, "My God!" The mainsail was split from top
to bottom, the spreader was gone, and so were all the steel cable
stays on the mast. And just over our right shoulders was Nevis
and its terrible rocky shore. Maybe it was just the wind, but for
sure we thought we could hear the roaring surf on the rocky
shoreline. Bill and I struggled frantically, finally managing to rig
a tiny storm jib — the only canvas we dared raise on that
unstayed wooden mast. That up, we set about the task of
working our way to windward and away from that iron shore
that was just waiting to tear *Zigzag* to bits. We were in pretty
desperate circumstances — no lights, no radio, no engine, and
only a scrap of sail — but we were fighting, and seemingly
holding our own. We still had our dinghy streamed well behind
on a long rope. The waves were not getting any smaller even
though we felt that there was some general improvement after
the whirlwind passed. Then, suddenly, along came another of
those monstrous rogues. It lifted our dinghy high into the air.
From that awful elevation, the dinghy plunged over the crest of
the wave and dove headfirst into the trough! The rope parted
with a loud snap and the dinghy went under, never to be seen
again. We worked — oh, how we worked — all night long. By
dawn we found that our efforts had paid off: we had clawed our
way about five miles offshore.

Lorna managed coffee and a sandwich for breakfast. While we
ate and got a badly needed breather, we worked on immediate
plans. Should we head east to the open Atlantic? West? That

way lay the Caribbean, but the next stop, said Bill, was Mexico. We would never last that long! Finally we opted for Mexico and laid *Zigzag* on a course to try to intercept Statia, the last island near at hand before reaching the other side of the Gulf. Because of the very rough seas there was not a boat of any description to be seen anywhere. In the early afternoon we did spot a large white vessel. With no radio, flares or signals of any kind, I grabbed a very large, red shopping bag of Lorna's, got up on the bouncing deck, hung onto the mast with one hand and frantically waved the bag with the other. No luck. Too far off. They couldn't possibly see me. Then, just as I was about to quit, the ship hove to! There was a large inflatable boat being lowered into the water, and sailors going down a rope like monkeys and dropping into the boat. Saved! In just a few minutes the boat was alongside and a young lieutenant came aboard. "What is your problem?" he asked. "Just look around," we replied. After a quick gander at our unsupported mast, the sad condition of our sails, and no dinghy, the lieutenant called the ship on his walkie-talkie, told his commander of our difficulties, and requested that mechanics be sent over with a good 12-volt battery. That done, he promptly got very seasick! After a session over the taffrail, he straightened to attention and said, "Now that the British Navy has disgraced itself, we shall get back to work!" Two minutes later he was over the rail again. But he wasn't alone in his glory: the mechanics arrived with the battery, went below, and promptly got so sick they had to come up for air! The lieutenant said that they could stand all that their ship, H.M.S. *Fawn*, could give them, all day long, but this pitching, heaving sailboat was killing them! Actually, after what we had been through all night, the action of the *Zigzag*, sails down, was like heaven on earth to us.

The lieutenant said that the commander wanted to talk with me on the radio. Me? Why not Bill, he was captain? Well, it seemed that England's Harold Wilson was a favourite of the commander's, and when he heard that there was a Harold Wilson aboard *Zigzag*, he wanted to talk to me. After hearing

207

our story, the commander said that he would lay offshore from St. Kitts and would direct our course by radio through potentially dangerous waters to a secluded but safe anchorage. The *Fawn* was a survey vessel of the Royal Navy and, as such, had just completed a survey of all the waters in this area. The mechanics got our engine started, the lieutenant took the wheel, and, getting his instructions from *Fawn* via his walkie-talkie, did indeed take us to that safe and secluded anchorage.

At anchor there we had two more visits from the ship's boat. The first brought over the ship's doctor, a dour Scot, who checked us all out. Regarding my bump on the head from the boom, he gave my head a healthy tap and said, "Solid ivory. Nothing could hurt that!" The second visit brought us a hot meal, our only food for 24 hours, except for those sandwiches of Lorna's. Finally the commander, on the blower to me, said, "Well, Mr. Wilson, I have put a ship of her Majesty's Navy at your command for three quarters of a day. I believe that you are in reasonable shape, so we shall say goodbye and I'll put my boys back to work. You can leave our battery at the government dock at St. Kitts. Happy sailing!"

The weather having calmed quite a bit, we upped anchor, started the engine, and motored down to Basseterre, the capital. It was dark when we got to the jetty there and found the dock so high (built for large ships not lowly sailboats) that it looked like a very difficult job to climb up. Bill and I were sure that we could make it, but not Lorna, so Bill went up and enlisted the help of a friendly but very drunk dockyard hand, and with me hoisting from below, and Bill and the drunken man pulling from on top, we managed it. All three of us were safely onshore again. Well, not really onshore yet, just on the jetty. And although I had assumed it was a solid jetty, it obviously wasn't. It was bouncing around in the rough seas just like *Zigzag* had. A floating dock this big seemed impossible. When we actually did set foot on good old terra firma, lo and behold, the whole island seemed to be slithering around! We checked in at a small hotel and went right to bed — in beds that were on roller skates and which insisted on drifting all over our bedrooms the whole night long! It wasn't until late the next morning that things settled down and we could walk the streets of Basseterre without looking like drunken sailors.

We flew back to Montserrat that afternoon and were very glad to get there. A lot of our friends had almost given us up for lost. Bill and I went back to St. Kitts two days later with a new mainsail and stays for the mast. When we reached *Zigzag*, tied up at a guarded government dock, we found that she had been completely burglarized. Every foot of decent rope aboard was gone, including that new anchor rope bought the day before the storm. It took almost a day for us to complete repairs. Late in the afternoon, we sailed to Nevis and anchored for the night. Bill, a quiet non-drinker, said, "Harold, after all that we have been through, there is one thing we deserve, and that is a good drink." Turning to fit action to words, Bill shouted, "The damned S-O-B's have stolen all the hootch!" The last straw!

Not really. Safely back in Montserrat, a few days later the anchored *Zigzag* was stolen by three escaping convicts and abandoned just off the coast of Nevis. She was found adrift a month later by a freighter, which took her in tow. Sailboats do not tow easily or safely. After an all-night tow behind the freighter, all that remained of *Zigzag* was the trailing rope! And that was the sad end to a fine boat that had carried Lorna and me safely through one of the most trying experiences of our lives. It was an event that we will never forget, or regret. And if there was a chance that our aging memories might let us down, one day many years later, in 1985 to be exact, we spotted a large white ship doing some strange manoeuvres just out in front of our home, Wilson's Folly. A look with glasses confirmed what we initially thought: it was H.M.S. *Fawn*! When it headed Plymouth-wards, so did we, in our car. At the jetty I requested permission to go aboard, and when granted went looking for the captain. He was a new man, Lieutenant Commander R.K. Jamieson, but he welcomed us aboard, looked up the log and found the entry describing our rescue way back in 1974. The commander and two of his men came out to dinner at Wilson's Folly. It was indeed a pleasure to entertain men from the ship that had saved our lives. The commander told us that Lieutenant Commander Brian Dyde, who had commanded H.M.S. *Fawn* in 1974, had since retired from the navy and was now living in Antigua, where he had set up in business as a cartographer. Later, in 1987, Commander Dyde and his Antiguan wife retired in Montserrat and became good friends of ours.

Chapter 12

Inland Waterways

Having had such an exciting sailing winter, when we got back up to Muskoka in the spring, we began casting around for something a bit more demanding than just day sailing in our own lakes. Remembering how much we had enjoyed our Trent–Severn cruise, we decided to have another go at it. This time, however, not only would we cover the Trent–Severn, but we would also travel the whole length of another similar system, the Rideau. This system starts at Kingston on Lake Ontario and ends up at Ottawa. I acquired detailed charts for the whole Rideau Waterway, and these, added to the pile already on hand for the Trent–Severn, presented evidence of a great deal of intricate navigation ahead of us. We had our Montserrat yard boy, Jimmie Allen, at our cottage for the summer, and we intended taking him with us. One night I laid out the charts for the whole trip end to end. They covered the entire floor and then doubled back. After a long look at the meandering route through countless lakes and rivers and nearly 100 locks, Jimmie said, "Mr. Wilson, if that is the way we are going, then I'm not going! We'll get lost and they'll never find us!"

A few days later, Jimmie's fears allayed, we loaded our stuff in the car and followed the trailer bearing *Lorna* M to Ottawa. (Our old friend Bruce Hamer had sold his marina to Terry Johnson, another very fine person, and it was he who drove the outfit to Ottawa.) There we put the boat into the waters of the Rideau system and went out for a fine dinner with friends. We returned to the marina about midnight and tucked ourselves in below. It seemed pretty cold and damp, but this was summer. Just one of those rare cold nights. When we got up in the morning, the frost was definitely on the pumpkin! It was so cold in the cabin of *Lorna M* that we just couldn't face having to prepare breakfast. So at 6 a.m. we went to a restaurant not yet ready for business and persuaded them to get us coffee and toast. Back at the boat we wondered whether or not we should set out, it was so cold. But this *was* summer, so off we went. I bundled up in everything warm that I could find, started up the kicker and headed off on the Rideau. I was just able to bear it, but I will admit that it didn't help one little bit to look down into the cabin and see Lorna and Jimmie warming themselves in front of our nice little space heater. Squinting though my frost-rimmed glasses, I could see that there was ice on the foredeck. Summer in Canada, the great frozen North!

A few miles south of the marina, we came to the first lock, which was closed. And in spite of the long and insistent blasts from our very loud air horn, it stayed closed. Finally, the lockmaster came out and said, "Sorry, folks, this is as far as you go today. The next lock is out of operation until tomorrow, but come on into my office and thaw out!" Oh what a blessed relief it was to get out of that cold boat. We chatted until noon, then the lockmaster took us to a Colonel Sanders a few miles away. Later we phoned Cathy Veitch, Lorna's niece, who lived nearby. When she heard that we were stranded, she drove over, picked us up and took us to her home for the night. We spent a pleasant afternoon with her and Ed Thibault, had an excellent home-cooked dinner, and wallowed in lovely soft beds in warm bedrooms. The height of luxury!

Next morning the cold front had moved on, the sun was out, and when we reached *Lorna M*, we found that the canal was back in operation. We had arranged for Cathy to meet us at one of the locks later that morning. She would travel all day with us, and at another prearranged lock, Ed would meet us for a ship-board dinner and would then take Cathy home. In mid-afternoon, right on schedule, we came to a place on our chart that showed two possible channels, but neither marked as preferred. Being a right-thinking man, I took the starboard channel.

Easing along slowly, I became aware of a number of very similar, very dead trees off the port side. Looking again, I realized that these trees were really one tree. We were standing still! We had gone aground without even feeling it. Investigation with a long pike-pole showed that we were stuck in soft, very sticky mud. The mud was so deep we couldn't push ourselves free, and the Johnson, putting out its full 9.9 horsepower, couldn't free us either. It looked like a long job of getting a rope ashore and tied to a tree, and then having to winch ourselves off the mud bank by hauling in on that line. But I tried the pike-pole at the stern and luckily found a large rock. A really healthy push on this, combined with the kicker's full output, did the trick. We were a boat again, not a jetty. This knocked our schedule all to pot and, as the canal closed at 7 p.m., we didn't get to our arranged meeting place with Ed Thibault. Cathy fired up my new expensive toy, the ship-to-shore radio, and started calling for "Big Ed." Soon a trucker replied saying, he had seen Ed on the highway just minutes before and that he would raise him. Five minutes later we were talking to Ed. We told him where we were and that soup was on. He was with us in minutes. We had a good fish dinner and saw Cathy and Ed off for home just at dark. Oh, the marvels of this modern civilization!

Ed was a big help to us. He worked at the Royal Military College in Kingston, and Kingston was not only on our route, it was also the place where we hit open water, Lake Ontario and the mighty St. Lawrence River. It was there that we wanted to rig ship. (Yes, we had brought mast, boom, rigging and sails with us.) Reaching Kingston, we motored right up to the private docks at RMC and Ed supplied a couple of strong men to help us raise the mast and rig the ship.

After all those days of constant motoring, it certainly was a welcome relief to go sailing down the St. Lawrence. It is a mighty river. Although we saw quite a number of ocean-going ships, most of the time we had a string of islands between us and them; they kick up quite a wake and it was just fine to be able to avoid that. We entered the Thousand Island area (very beautiful

213

indeed, comes pretty close to Muskoka in that respect) and we sailed right up to the soaring spans of the Ivy Lea bridge to the United States. Then we turned around and sailed west again. We had run before a west wind all of the way from Kingston to Gananoque — easy sailing. But surely going back was going to be a different matter. Waking up at dockside the day after our turnaround, we were happy to find that the gods that smile on sailors had come up with a nice east wind. With sails in wing, on wing position, we ran all the way back to Kingston, and then on to Picton, Prince Edward County.

Lorna and I are life members of the Prince Edward Yacht Club, a privilege presented to us during our motorboat-racing days there. I tied up at their dock, presented my membership card, and we were given all the facilities of the club, including free overnight parking. We contacted our old friends Jack and Margarete LeHeup, spent a pleasant evening with them, and certainly appreciated their help in derigging *Lorna* M the next morning. An early start saw us through the long run to Trenton, where we again entered the waters of the Trent–Severn.

Near the Kirkfield lock, the next day, we found a measured mile laid out on the canal bank and timed *Lorna* M. I was quite pleased to find that our hardworking little Johnson 9.9 was able to push our two-ton boat at a very respectable eight miles per hour, actually almost hull speed for the Grampian.

The rest of the trip was delightful but uneventful. We had no problems with Lake Simcoe this time, or Couchiching. Not wanting to stay at Pier 11 overnight, we pushed on beyond to the next lock, where we could enjoy the free facilities. We also decided that, as this was the last night of the trip, we should celebrate with a dinner ashore. There was a small restaurant at the lock, so, in a sudden rainstorm, we dashed over there. Not open. No dinner! Just for fun we tried the door, and found it unlocked, so in we went to escape the rain and wait for the owners, who couldn't be far off if they left the place open. After waiting a couple of hours, we turned on the lights, got out their menu, and cooked ourselves a good dinner. As no one had turned up by the

214

time we were finished, I wrote a note saying what we had done and what we had eaten. I got the prices from their menu and left the money, and our address in case they felt that things were not right. Never heard a word. Guess they thought all these boat people must be nuts.

Next morning Terry Johnson met us at Pier 11, and *Lorna* M was hauled out and taken back to Hamer Bay on Lake Joseph. A day later she was back in home waters. Thus ended a truly enjoyable cruise of these two beautiful waterways.

The Bromley-Martins came to visit us in Canada the next June. More sailing was the general idea, but this time we were to take them on Ontario waterways in the *Lorna* M. As on our last cruise in these waters, we were motoring entirely, mast, boom and all rigging slung along the port deck and fastened fore and aft to two specially-made steel brackets. Easing out of Pier 11 marina, we entered Lake Couchiching and followed that familiar double line of markers — there to keep you out of the weed patches — all the way to the narrows at Orillia. Through there, we entered big Lake Simcoe, and the most peculiar weather condition imaginable: clear blue sky overhead but the whole lake covered by a 10-foot-thick, dense white-out that cut visibility to less than 20 yards. Remembering the great difficulty that Lorna and I had experienced on our first attempt to find the Gamebridge lock entrance at the southern end of this big body of water, I decided then and there that David should be navigator. When I announced this, he didn't turn a hair, just got out the charts, set up his course, and conned us — by dead reckoning, mind you — all the way down and across Lake Simcoe. When we came out of the pea soup, the *Lorna* M was just about to poke her nose into the tiny entrance to the Gamebridge section! A very nice piece of work, David. Couldn't have done it nearly so well myself.

The good weather that started that day lasted throughout the whole cruise, and all went swimmingly, except for one very unfortunate accident. Remember way back at the start of all this, I quoted the old axiom of the sea: "The captain is always right"? Well, this time he wasn't! Pure captain error. Pulling out of a lock immediately behind one of those horrible square boxes on floats — called houseboats — and feeling that its captain knew where he was going, I went the wrong side of a buoy. In the clear, this shallow draft tub took off at full throttle, so I opened up our trusty 9.9 and took after him. CRASH! *Lorna* M hit a submerged rock with her 4-foot-deep keel and stopped dead. At least she did for about one second. And in that second all hell broke loose! I went headfirst from the helm, landed face-down on top of the compass, then somersaulted down into the cabin. At the same time, Lorna, preparing lunch at the cabin table, did a barrel roll over it, landing bottoms-up on the other seat. Angela, sitting on deck, slid the whole length of the boat and landed sitting on the flukes of the anchor, which was lashed on the foredeck. (She bore the red imprint for days to prove it!) David, old sailor that he was, just grabbed the nearest handhold and held on. After that long second passed, *Lorna* M, pushed on by her own momentum, reared up like a fighting stallion and climbed right over that rock! I climbed back into the cockpit, shut off the engine and, wanting to ascertain the damage as quickly as possible, dove over the side. Underwater I could see practically no damage at all. There was a small area on the leading edge of the keel where the rock had knocked off a goodly hunk of fibreglass, but beyond that, nothing. Back aboard, a thorough check of the hull showed no evidence of leaks, cracks or other damage. We were lucky! So we pushed on for Peterborough. We had arranged to spend the night there with Pat and Eric. Eric met us at the big lift lock and took us to their home for a swim in their pool and dinner. I wasn't feeling too well after dinner, so went to bed early. When I woke up the next morning, I had two of the biggest black eyes ever! In fact my whole face right down to my chin was discoloured from its sudden, hard contact with the compass. I was also feeling pretty groggy — a bit of concussion, I guess. The crew had a council of war and decided that the cruise should be called off and that I should enter hospital for a checkup. But feeling that I would weather this all right, I refused to listen to them and issued the order to push on. With much grumbling from Pat and Lorna, in fact from all, we went back to the canal and pushed off in *Lorna M* for Lake Ontario.

On the run down to Trenton, the constant hot weather made it necessary to stop several times a day to cast anchor and dive into the water to cool off. We visited Picton again, my old racing days stamping ground, made use of the Picton Yacht Club's facilities, and had a delightful dinner with our friends Margarete and Jack LeHeup. They were fine hosts. Not only did they feed us well, they put us up for the night (it is good to be able to really stretch out in bed, impossible aboard) and helped us rig ship the next morning. We had planned on doing the next leg, down the mighty St. Lawrence to the Thousand Islands, under sail, but it was not to be. There was absolutely no wind at all and we ended up doing this section under power also.

At Gananoque, our turnaround point, we headed back to Kingston to begin our trip up the Rideau to Ottawa. Before entering the waterway, we spent a few hours at old Fort Henry watching an interesting military display by the volunteer forces that do this all summer long for the edification of tourists. Then, derigging ship, we headed for the nation's capital. The trip up the Rideau, still in perfect weather, was wonderful. David could not get over the quality of the facilities offered to yachtsmen all along both the Trent–Severn and the Rideau Waterway.

The cruise ended just south of Ottawa at Manotick. Arriving there, we found friends of the Bromley-Martins awaiting them. Quickly we said our goodbyes and separated, the B-M's heading for the U.K. while we hauled ship and loaded her on the trailer that Terry Johnson had brought over from Muskoka.

Arriving at Wawanaissa we found to our surprise and delight that we had been blessed with the almost unexpected arrival of six South American guests. They were Maria and João Villalobos, her sister Ernestina and husband Paulo — all from Sao Paulo — plus Mariatel and Juan Galli from Argentina. The two weeks they spent with us, and our boats, both sail and power, did much to make them believe that Muskoka is one of this world's choice beauty spots.

Chapter 13

Canal Boats

Having enjoyed our previous tastes of canal travel, Lorna and I decided to go farther afield. We had read a travel-magazine account of what sounded like a very interesting cruise of the canal systems in France. This was aboard a canal barge converted from lowly grain carrier to a waterborne hotel for 12 lucky passengers. It toured the Garonne River, the Lateral, and the Canal de Midi in southern France. The *Happy Wanderer*, as it was called, carried its passengers at a snail's pace through the wine country, making many stops for sightseeing, shopping and eating. To assist the passengers in doing these things, the *Happy Wanderer* had a land-based minibus following it all the time. At every stop the bus was there to take the passengers to whatever that stop had to offer. This sounded great to us, but just a little bit binding. Couldn't we do such a cruise on our own? Talking about this canal travel in Montserrat, we learned that a good friend, Tom Watson, from England, knew something about this particular canal area. In fact he owned a small cruiser rental company that operated there! So I twisted his arm, and Tom, who was returning to the U.K. in a couple of days, offered to set something up for us.

A few weeks later we had a phone call from him saying, "Come over to Agen, in southern France, as soon as you can. Your private canal cruiser awaits!" We were on our way in no time, met Tom and his fine wife, Maggie, in the U.K. and they put us aboard a small plane that flew us to Agen on the Garonne River. We were met by a young couple who took us immediately to the cruiser that was to be our floating home for the next two weeks. It was late afternoon and, as the canal ceases operation for the day at 7 p.m., we were told that we should start out right away. The young couple who met us said that they would go with us for a short distance to acquaint us with the boat and canal travel generally. First, they told us that we were the very first people to charter one of these Beaver Fleet boats from the new owner, Mr. Tom Watson. Wait. Tom's outfit was called the Sunshine Fleet; this was the Beaver. It seems Tom decided that his little outfit would not do for us, so he paid a visit to the area and bought out this Beaver Fleet, one of the two largest charter companies operating in these waters! We had the honour of being his first customers.

We slipped our moorings and set out. While the man drove he told me all that he could about the operation of the boat, and the rules and regulations governing canal travel. At the same time the young lady took Lorna in tow and introduced her to the mysteries of cooking and housekeeping on a canal boat. Suddenly the captain (well, he was until I took over) shouted, "Lock coming up!" And there it was, just ahead of us. The captain said, "You will go through 103 of these!" He blew the boat horn and pulled in to the side of the canal. Almost immediately one half of the gate started to swing open. Great service, I thought, just open up the other half and we can slip into the lock. Our captain said, "Someone has to go ashore to operate the other gates." Well, I waited for him to do this, but no sir, opening gates and other menial jobs were definitely not part of the captain's duties. Bowing low, I went ashore, climbed up on top of the lock, grabbed a long handle and cranked for a long time. At least it seemed like that, but actually the gates were opened quite quickly, and the captain drove the boat into the lock. I stayed onshore to finish the other half of the locking-through procedure. When our cruiser was raised to the level of the next stretch of canal, I climbed back aboard and we were off again. A short distance from this first lock, we came to a small cement jetty and we tied up there. Our guide — he had now handed the captain's hat to me — said that we must stay here for the night, as the canal was now closed. He told us a bit more about the boat, said a hasty goodbye and good luck, and the two of them jumped a passing bus and headed back to Agen.

Well, here we were, out in the wilds of France on a boat that was utterly strange to us and that was not as yet stocked with the necessities of life. We were exhausted after our transatlantic flight, we were hungry, and we couldn't speak French! Where was that cafe? We set out down the road, as directed, walked for what seemed literally miles, and found nothing but an International Harvester sign, and it wasn't even lit. Returning home to the boat, we scrounged around and found a few morsels of food — left by the last charterer, I suppose. Out of these we made a rather frugal meal and retired, dead-tired.

What a night that was! I never slept so soundly. The first word we heard the next morning was a cheery "Bonjour!" Climbing out on deck, I found a beaming fisherman, and the saints be praised, he spoke English. He told us that the cafe was just up the road a bit. (We had gone *down* the road.) We climbed a steep hill, found the cafe, and had a wonderful breakfast. The owner told us where to do our shopping for food and ship supplies, which we obtained in spite of the language barrier. Loaded to the hilt with bags and bags of food, we wended our way back to the boat and spent some time getting everything properly stowed, then we had a good look at our floating home and found out a few things of interest. For instance, although the gauge said that our water tank was full, it wasn't. We rectified that. There were two quite nice staterooms, a head, plenty of locker space, a large lounge and attached galley (The roof over this area could be slid back to give us a sort of open-air water taxi), and in a cockpit on the foredeck, there were two bicycles. These were for use on the towpath. Our inspection tour over, we decided that we knew enough about our ship to allow us to set out on our two-week odyssey.

No sooner were we beginning to become accustomed to travelling the straight and narrow in this bulrush-sided canal than we came to our second lock. Pulling over to the dock side and seeing the one gate opening in response to my horn blast, Lorna said, "Let's go, boy. Get that other door open." "Who? Me? Why I am the captain of this ship," I countered. "I must stay with the ship and drive her through the lock. No, my girl, you go ashore and operate those gates!" Popular? That I wasn't! But after a great deal of grumbling, and a great amount of pushing by me, the mate climbed up a slippery, weed-covered, rusty old steel ladder to the top of the lock. Shortly thereafter, there was my pride and joy cranking one of those big iron handles. I then performed the captain's duties in bringing our craft safely through this lock. "One hundred and one more to go," I heard Lorna mutter as she came aboard again.

Canal travel is a dreamy sort of existence. We travelled when we liked, and stopped when and where we wanted. We didn't have to anchor, even at night. All we did was throw two very large meat hooks attached to our bow and stern lines ashore and into the mud of the towpath. We visited many villages, towns and cities with interesting names like Castelsarrasin, Toulouse, Villefranche, Castelnauderay, Carcassone, Aude, Narbonne, Beziers, Agda, and Sete. We explored, saw old ruins, and ate delicious local delicacies in tiny cafes. We shopped, bought fresh wine from the lockmasters' wives for 35 cents a bottle, and searched in vain for peanut butter. (Seems that the French either don't eat this tasty spread, or the French-Canadian name for it, *buerre d'arachide*, meant nothing to them.) One thing we did learn: never buy, or worse yet, drink, French rum! It tastes like a very poor copy of that childhood horror called Fletcher's Castoria.

One might think that canal travel would be boring. Not so. Mostly the scenery was lovely, and the boat's slow speed gave us ample opportunity to enjoy it. There were even moments of excitement, like the time when I attempted to pass a heavily laden commercial barge. As I was alongside it in a very narrow section of the canal, our bow was caught by its very heavy swells and immediately swung directly toward the canal bank. Right into the bulrushes! Luckily they were soft. No harm done, we just came to a rather sudden stop.

The water in the canal is very dirty and there are all sorts of floating debris everywhere. The designer of our boat, aware of this situation, had furnished one piece of marine equipment that was beyond my comprehension. This was a quite large wooden box, amidships and toward the stern — in fact it seemed to be directly over our propeller. One day, I noticed that our speed was dropping off even though our engine seemed to be maintaining its operating speed. Finally we came to a full stop, engine still running, but obviously labouring. What was this? Shutting off the engine, I waited to see if some unexpected current was pushing us backwards. Not so, we just remained stationary. After some thought, a light dawned. Taking the lid off the mysterious box in the stern, I found myself looking down on our propeller. Not that I recognized it as such: what I saw was a huge round blob of quite unmentionable stuff where the prop should have been. Reaching down with fully extended arms, and with Lorna hanging onto my heels like a bulldog, I was just able to get my hands into this mess. After half an hour I had unwrapped about a half mile of baling wire which was doing a great job of holding some 20 plastic cement bags all nicely formed into a ball by the turning propeller!

Carcassone is a very interesting place. We spent half a day exploring the Old City. This is the medieval walled city; the modern Carcassone is built all around it. The Old City has been well restored and is a great tourist attraction. That half-day over, we climbed aboard and prepared to cast off. Not today, we were told by a local fisherman at the lock. It was some sort of a religious holiday, and the whole canal system was shut down. Looking around, we saw crowds of people heading in one direction. Nothing better to do, we followed them, right to the fairgrounds where a local county exposition was being presented.

One night we moored at the top of what is known as The Staircase. This is a series of seven locks, one right after another with no stretches of canal between. I was glad that it was night, quitting time, as I didn't relish doing that downhill run in anything but full daylight. A bronze plaque on the wall of the lockmaster's house said (in French) that the first boat had passed through The Staircase on the 24th of May, and it was exactly 300 years ago that the first ship had slid down this mountainside in The Staircase. So down we went. These are the only locks on this canal system that have been modernized. They are now electrically operated, in sequence, automatically, with no obvious human control. You just blow your horn and the first gates open. Yes, I said gates; the boat's crew does nothing here. But one has to be quite alert because there is just time to enter the lock before the gates snip off your stern. Then there is a rush of water, down goes your boat, the gates ahead of you open, and if you are quick you enter the next lock (and so on for all seven locks). Safely down the mountain, we were just beginning to catch our breath when we came to another prime example of the engineering that had gone into the building of this 300-year-old canal. What had been a bulrush-flanked canal was now a cement conduit. And this was flung across a deep ravine. It carried us safely over to the other side, giving us en route a look at a broad river way down below.

We were to discover that not all of the engineering is so old; some is as modern as tomorrow. We entered one lock that, although it was rectangular instead of oval-shaped like the rest, still appeared to be just another of those 103 locks. The gates closed behind us, and then the whole lock started to move uphill! The lock that we were in was in reality a dry dock, and it was mounted on rails. Two large caterpillars, one on each side, were pulling it, and us, up the hill. Reaching the top, we learned that we had travelled up the height of land once climbed by six ordinary locks. In so doing, we had used no water; the dry dock carried us and the water which floated us from bottom to top. No water was wasted when the gates were opened ahead of us. This experiment, if successful, will save a great amount of the canal water that is always in short supply, particularly in the summer.

At Agde there is an unusual round lock with three openings. One we entered by, one goes directly to the Mediterranean, and the third empties into a further stretch of canal that leads to the Etang de Tau. Although strictly against charter rules — our boat was for canal use only — I decided to take a look at the Med. Fifteen minutes in those rough seas were enough to convince me that the designer was right when he said that the boat should be operated in canal waters only. Back we went through the Agde lock and on to the Etang de Tau. This is an almost landlocked bay of the Mediterranean, and considerably larger than I expected. We travelled miles through a wilderness of tall wooden stakes. These were the supports for several layers of beds which were used for commercial culture of oysters and clams. Eventually we reached the other side, and with the help of local boatmen, we found an overnight mooring at the jetty of the city of Sete. This was the turnaround point of our cruise. The water-front was particularly interesting. We spent the whole evening wandering through the hundreds of stalls selling just about every-thing imaginable, and we had an excellent seafood dinner before calling it a day.

The next morning we retraced our route across the Etang de Tau, through Agde, and down the canal for a bit until we reached the eastern headquarters of the Beaver Fleet. We enjoyed our experience so much that we did the same cruise again a few years later with another of Tom Watson's Beaver boats, a bigger one, crewed by our Montserrat neighbours, Jon and Liz Milligan, and Lorna's brother, Ken, and his wife, Betty.

First it had been our dismasted *Lorna* M in the Trent–Severn system in Ontario; then we had tried two fine canal cruisers in the canals of France; now for something really posh!

In 1985 we did an air, land and sea trip that took us to Moscow, Leningrad and Yalta in the U.S.S.R., then by ocean liner across the Black Sea to the mouth of the Danube River. There we transhipped to a quite luxurious river steamer. It was an unusual-looking vessel, very low in profile, and with no super-structure. It was designed and built this way to allow it to travel the whole length of the navigable Danube, which is crossed in several places by quite low bridges under which the ship must pass. The accommodations were excellent, even if the Russian version of typical American food left much to be desired. Besides bridges, there were also several locks to be negotiated, hence this voyage appearing in the Canal Boat chapter.

Before long we came to the first of the bridges. I was surprised to see just how low they were. As we came up to the first bridge, it certainly did seem to be awfully close to the water. Maybe it would be raised; it certainly was obvious that we couldn't get underneath. We were on the top deck at the time having a swim in the pool. Crew members came up and started folding all the hinge-mounted handrails down to deck level. The bridge followed suit! Then the engine stack was hydraulically lowered until it too was at deck level. And finally the ship's mast, radio antennae and the radar aerial went over the side! We inched forward at a crawl and passed under that immovable bridge with literally only inches to spare. Bridge passed, up everything went again and we proceeded merrily on our way.

The cruise was quite delightful. We visited nine different countries and had excellent shore excursions in all. Life aboard was good too. Our Russian crew all spoke English. We found out that just two such cruises a year have English-speaking crews, and these cruises are reserved for English-speaking travellers. The ship, with a capacity of 250 passengers, was 300 feet long, comfortable, well-handled, and more than satisfactory in every respect.

In ending this chapter on canal boating, let me say that I think anyone would find pleasure in trying such a cruise, whether it be in a privately owned motor- or sailboat, a chartered canal cruiser or barge, or a lordly river/canal liner.

Chapter 14

White Wings

Remember David and Angela Bromley-Martin? David and I did a lot of corresponding. We were both keen to do a cruise together, so we decided to charter a boat from West Indies Yachts, the outfit that chartered the ailing Olsen 38 to Phil Brule and me. We were to sail her in the British Virgins in February. This time, in addition to the four of us, we would have as crew members our old friend Mal Hill and his quite elderly Aunt Helen. Mal's wife, Aline — she sailed in *Kebir* with us — had just recently died as the result of a serious motor accident. We felt that the cruise would be good for Mal, and he assured us that Aunt Helen would hold up her end in spite of her years. Pull her weight? She sure did. Mrs. Coomber — Aunt Helen to everybody — bunked in with Lorna in a sort of shelf berth about 4 feet off the cabin sole. It was comfortable all right, after they were in, but getting in was something different. Aunt Helen stood her trick at the wheel, helped in the galley, and even went ashore on Jos Van Dyke Island with us for a lobster feast cooked on the beach by Abe, a huge native with no other name than Abe, at least as far as I could find out. Returning to our boat, we ran into a bit of a problem in getting Aunt Helen aboard. She had practically no vision downwards, and this made it very difficult for her to climb the boarding ladder. But with one person above pulling, and me below pushing up, we managed it.

It was a still night, absolutely no wind, and as it was still early, David put in an order for rum punch. After he had lowered a copious amount, he announced that he was going to entertain us. In a quiet but perfect dialect, he recited "The Lion Et Albert." He was really good and we applauded — so did the crews of all the other boats anchored in the bay! Shouts of "Louder!" were all that David needed to get him started again. In a voice that could have been heard back in Tortola, he gave us "The Return of Albert." More and louder applause brought on "Joe Muggeridge" and many more gems from the pen of Stanley Halloway. Finally, the rum punch and David's voice both running out, the anchorage settled down for the night. Or so we thought. Suddenly, in the wee small hours, frantic screams of "You hit our boat!" split the air. Dashing on deck we found utter confusion. As is the way with boats at anchor in a confined space on an absolutely windless night, all the craft in the bay had drifted aimlessly from their anchors, and in this confused state our boat had touched another. Ascertaining that absolutely no damage had been suffered by either boat, we pushed clear with the screams of the irate captain — a fellow Canadian, alas — ringing in our ears. Another sloop was almost in the same soup, so we got together with its crew, rafted the two boats alongside, made sure that both of us were well clear of our noisy neighbour, and went back to bed. Next morning, as we were breakfasting in the cockpit, the Canadian charter yacht sailed by, the captain still giving tongue! This kind of sailor I can willingly do without!

It was a very enjoyable cruise but a bit lacking in thrills. David, particularly, missed the excitement of hard sailing; I am content to take anything that comes. So David worked on me during the whole succeeding summer and persuaded me that we should have a go at another cruising ground next winter, one with a bit more challenge, more open water, more wind, and hence more excitement. Now this sort of thinking didn't exactly fit in with the ideas of the distaff side of our crew. It took pretty well all summer to persuade them that it was a sound idea. Our mates won over, we then had to pick another couple to complete the crew. We selected a great pair: Lorna's cousin, Madelyn Morris, and her husband, Ken, both great fun-lovers and good sports.

We decided that the Grenadines, down near the north coast of South America, would be our new cruising ground. The next step was to charter a suitable boat. This we did through Heritage Yacht Charterers in St. Vincent. The boat we selected was a 43-foot Gulfstar sloop. The Bromley-Martins flew over from England in mid-February and the six of us then flew to St. Vincent and went aboard our floating home for the next two weeks. We spent those two weeks exploring the waters and the many beautiful islands between St. Vincent and Petit Martinique, the northern boundary of the Northern Grenadines, those under the control of St. Vincent. The remainder of the Grenadines, the Southern Grenadines, are governed by Grenada. We visited Mustique, the winter home of Princess Margaret, and managed to run afoul of her. There is very little motorized transport available on Mustique, but we managed to rent a jeep before returning to our boat for lunch. Later we went ashore for an afternoon's exploration, only to learn that Margaret had just arrived and commandeered all the wheels on the island, including our jeep! So we hoofed it. Actually there was little to see in Mustique. One sad sight was the wreck of the *Antilles* stuck high on a submerged rock, wracked by fire, and a very rusty, sorry sight indeed. On the shore was one of the *Antilles* lifeboats, an unusual type that I had not seen before. It had rows of seats, each with a vertical pump handle hinged to a gear box in the bilge. Passengers sat on these seats and pumped the handles in front of them. This motion, transmitted by the gear boxes to a central shaft, supplied the motive power to turn a propeller attached to the end of the shaft, and this gave the poor shipwrecked people that it might contain a sure if very slow method of propulsion.

In high seas and quite strong winds, and in the vicinity of Petit St. Vincent and Carriacou Islands, we came across a native fishing sloop in distress. Her sails were in untidy heaps on deck and there appeared to be no rigging on the masts except the stays. The two men aboard, one young and one quite old, were signalling wildly for help. As it is quite difficult for one boat under sail to assist another lying motionless in the water, and as we were within easy radio contact of Petit St. Vincent, I got the marina there on the buzzer and told them the problem. "Right!" they replied. "We will send out the crash boat immediately. What is the name and home port of the boat in distress?" When I replied that it was a native fishing sloop and probably from a nearby island, they just said, "Oh!" And that was all. No crash boat came to the rescue. Because the men were natives, the Petit St. Vincent crowd were quite happy to let these poor souls drift all the way to the Yucatan Peninsula. David and I couldn't stomach that, so off we went, high seas and strong winds be damned, to try to help these shipwrecked fishermen. Not having a proper heaving line, we had to make some very near passes — and as many near misses — under her bows before we were able to get our heavy stern anchor rope aboard the drifting sloop. That accomplished, we towed the disabled craft into still waters in the lea of Carriacou. The younger man climbed the masts and was able to rig jury halyards. He then hauled up their patched, dirty sails. Just as we were turning away, they held up a fine string of fish in payment for our assistance, but we weren't risking a collision with that heavy wooden hull, so with a wave, we sailed off to Petit St. Vincent. And do you know, the people at the marina couldn't have cared less when we asked them why they hadn't gone to the rescue. Sure glad this attitude is not common amongst sailors.

The seas had been pretty high and rough for most of this charter, and the last day turned out to be the worst. We were beating our way back to base and trying to weather the east coast of Bequia about noon. There were two reasons for doing this: first, we needed to make as much progress windward as we could if we were to be able to make a landfall on St. Vincent that night; and second, David and I had noted from the charts that this area has some of the roughest going in the whole Caribbean. The challenge to beat our way through these waters was strong. The waves, some 18 feet high, were tremendous, and the wind was almost frightening. David was handling sail; I was at the wheel; the three ladies were below decks; Ken was doing what he could to help and desperately wiping the almost continuous spray from his face. In his opinion, it was either that or drown. David screamed above the noise of the elements, "Isn't this great? Just as the chart says, this is the roughest!" I told him to take a good look below before gloating too much. He did, and seeing all the first mates lying on the cabin sole with their arms wrapped around the foot of the mast and hanging on for dear life, he shouted, "Better start the iron topsail, Harold, and let's get this boat into some shelter!" We did just that. But this happy state of things was short-lived. In going around the west side of Bequia, besides getting some shelter, we had lost a great deal of our headway against the strong winds. Beating to our anchorage at St. Vincent would now be harder than ever, and to add to this, the Bequia Channel is notoriously rough. The weather had deteriorated. Black line squalls came screaming across the angry seas at us about every half hour. Obviously we were not going to be able to get east enough to reach the tip of St. Vincent with sails alone, so we started up Old Faithful. Sailing as close to the wind as sail and diesel oil would allow, and whipping off all canvas right down to the bare mast every time one of those ugly squalls hit us, we managed to reach our destination just at dusk.

In my charter cruising to date I had always filled the second-in-command position. I had enjoyed the experience and learned much. Now I felt that I was knowledgeable enough to charter a boat and captain it myself. So the next winter, just at Christmas, Lorna and I chartered a 39-foot sloop from West Indies Yachts at Tortola and brought family members Pat and Eric, and Harry and Anne down to the Virgins to spend the two-week Christmas holiday sailing with us. Paul Funkhauser, manager of West Indies Yachts, gave us a mighty good briefing and going over before he let us set sail. After all, it was a pretty green crew. Outside of Lorna and me, the crew was without ocean sailing experience, and this was my first go at being in command. With a certain amount of fear and trepidation we powered out of the tricky entrance to Maia Cove, set sail and away we went.

Christmas Day was something to remember. At anchor at Peter Island and properly dressed for the occasion (in bathing suits) we sat around the Christmas tree. Yes, we had one. Granted it was a wee artificial one, but tied up on top of the binnacle, it served the purpose. We sat around in the cockpit while Santa Claus (Harry) dished out all the presents that had been laboriously and lovingly toted down from Canada. To top everything, we had turkey and plum pudding for dinner. We did well, we thought, but some hardy soul on a nearby yacht put us to shame. Somehow, on Christmas Eve, this athlete climbed the mast and lashed a full-sized real Christmas tree to the peak!

We sailed around and visited most of the British Virgin Islands and did a circumnavigation of St. John's in the American Virgins also. We ate well aboard and had fine meals ashore, like Abe's on Jos Van Dyke Island for lobster and the Bitter End on Virgin Gorda for a more civilized but no tastier dinner. On New Year's Eve we joined 80 other sailors for a rather riotous dinner and New Year's celebration. The owner, a former music hall entertainer from England, put on a very loud, very funny, and very lewd entertainment, and when that was over we all joined in a fancy-dress competition. His establishment, The Last Resort, may have lacked polish in some respects, but when the party broke up in the small hours of the New Year, none of those assembled were in a fit state to notice any shortcomings. Getting into our dinghy, and after hitting only one coral reef, we managed to find our anchored yacht, *Antigone*, and went aboard to call it a night. "Call it a night? Never!" shouted the younger two thirds of the crew. Whipping out a tape of Guy Lombardo doing his New Year's Eve stand at the Waldorf, they stuck it on the boat's tape deck, opened the volume wide and proceeded to help all the other (sleeping) yacht crews bring in the New Year in style. Whith yells of "Pipe down" coming at us from all sides, the kids then gave the assembled guests something to see as well — a whole mess of fireworks brought down from Canada were fired off from *Antigone*'s foredeck. As the last Roman candle sputtered out, *Antigone*'s crew hit the hay.

Antigone's Captain and First mate.

Antigone's (unpaid) crew – Anne Wilson, Eric Warden, Pat Warden (under the boom) & Harry Wilson.

Amongst all these roses there had to be one thorn. Sailing from Jos Van Dyke to Sandy Island one morning, it happened. As I wore ship from port to starboard, Eric, below at the moment, hollered, "We're sinking!" Pandemonium! Everyone shouting! I tossed a couple of buckets down to Eric and ordered the crew to form a bucket brigade. I started the electric bilge pump and started banging away on the Whale hand bilge pump. Half a minute later the pumps sucked air and Eric and the brigade had nothing to toss over the side. What was this? I decided to wait for a few minutes to see if we would take on more water. Immediately, I began getting all sorts of orders: call for help, beach the boat, go to Soper's Hole and get hauled out! I couldn't let this go on. Everyone was frightened, naturally, but in my opinion, as we were not taking on water, I was sure that we were in no imminent danger and decided to get in touch with West Indies Yachts for advice. When I told the crew what action I intended taking, all hell broke out. "You are endangering all our lives and the safety of the boat!" They demanded an immediate beaching, which certainly would have damaged *Antigone* no end. As it appeared that full-scale mutiny was about to take place, I exercised the captain's prerogative and authority, and said, "Listen all, I will say this only once. I have decided to sail around the east end of Tortola and head for our marina. I will contact West Indies Yachts by radio as soon as possible and will get their advice and instruction." I was not popular, but that is what I did. Radio contact with West Indies Yachts a few minutes later soon pinpointed the cause of the apparent leakage: the crew, taking their daily showers, had not used the sump pump correctly to get rid of the shower water. This had allowed a large build-up of water, which, when the boat heeled sharply as she went from one tack to the other, poured out of the shower sump and then ran down the cabin sole and sloshed over Eric's feet, causing great alarm and his wild shout, "We're sinking!" But even though I was proven correct, I have never been able to get that crew's full approval for my actions that day. The captain's lot is not always a happy one.

234

No sooner were we back from that successful family cruise than I got a letter from David Bromley-Martin saying that they would love to sail with us again, this winter if possible. Could we set up a charter? And, if I could, why not make it a flotilla? David and Angela would bring out another Brit couple to round out our crew, and the Bromley-Martins' son Robin would bring out a complete crew for the second boat. I phoned Paul Funkhauser and was able to arrange for the two boats. A few weeks later, all of the Brits arrived — us lowly colonials were definitely in the minority — and we all headed for Tortola and West Indies Yachts. Arriving there we found that our flotilla had increased to three boats. It seems that more English sailors, friends of the Bromley-Martins (and including in the crew their second son), had just completed a transatlantic crossing and had decided to join us for a portion of our cruise at least.

We had another excellent cruise, although the weather was not as good as for our Christmas/New Year effort. We had rough stuff, high seas and brutal winds, like when we were rounding the eastern shore of Mosquito Island on our way to the Virgin Gorda anchorage. At other times there was no wind at all, and under these conditions, boats — particularly at anchor — have a bad habit of misbehaving themselves, like the time we were anchored off Cooper Island (not a recommended anchorage). We wakened quite early and found to our horror that we had apparently drifted anchor and were now in a part of the Virgins that we couldn't recognize. It was quite a few minutes before we realized what had happened. We had turned end for end. Funny, Cooper Island didn't look like the same place at all when it wasn't where it should have been. And worse, our anchor (if we still had one) didn't appear to be out in front on our bow, as it had been when we retired for the night. Now the rope was tucked tightly over the bow and it looked like our anchor was behind us instead of out in front. We were afraid to start the engine in an attempt to get the boat back into proper position, as the anchor rope may have fouled keel, propeller and rudder. Donning fins and mask and trying to forget the warnings of "no swimming between sundown and sunset" and "beware of dangerous fish that come into shallow water," I went overboard to have a look. It was a pretty short one, I can assure you. All appeared in order, but to be on the safe side we took our spare anchor out in the dinghy and dropped it well ahead of our bow. All that could happen now would be a slow circling motion around our front deck cleats where both anchor ropes were secured. So, safe, we went back to bed for a few more hours badly needed sleep. Later, at West Indies Yachts, we learned the answer to this puzzle. After midnight, or really at the turn of the tide, a tide current suddenly appears, and if an anchored boat's bow is pointed away from where this unexpected tide rises, the boat is swung around its anchor — as we found out.

A few days after the start of our cruise, the third boat made its appearance. It wasn't crewed entirely by British as I said; the captain and owner was a retired Australian admiral. For crew he had Michael Bromley-Martin and a very presentable young lady. From then until cruise end the three boats kept close company. All of the Brits then packed up and boarded a plane headed for Old Blighty, the Aussies said, "See you down under," and after doing a really thorough clean-up of our two chartered yachts, Lorna and I turned them over to West Indies Yachts and headed for Beef Island, where we boarded a pre-World War II plane, a trusty DC3, and had a wonderfully relaxing, if somewhat slow, flight back to Montserrat.

Lorna often accused me of doing a lot of off-the-cuff planning with David, planning that she and Angela knew nothing about. Never! I wouldn't hold out on my wife, the best first mate a man ever had. Of course I must admit that David and I talked about the *possibility* of future cruises. David said that he had heard of a new U.K.-based charter company that operated in the Grenadines and had some excellent boats for charter, so why shouldn't he investigate when he returned home? We hadn't laid any plans unknown to our spouses, had we?

Winter over, we went back to Muskoka for another summer. I must admit that David and I kept the mail service of our two

236

countries pretty busy that summer with the steady stream of letters across the Atlantic. None of this was planning — perish the thought — our letters were really just exchanges of ideas and information. "These new F&C 44's are the most! They are beautiful ketches designed by the best naval architect on the job today, German Freres in Argentina. They are fitted out like grand pianos inside and out and they are wonderful sailors." That from David. Me? Well, all that I did was to remember my first-ever captaincy — how great it was, and how little I liked being demoted to mate again when the seniority of the British Navy made itself obvious as David commanded my second cruise of that year. To be captain and to still sail with David meant two boats again, one for him and one for me. Okay, the boats shouldn't be a problem if we ever did reach the planning stage. What about crews? Well, David could get himself a Brit crew, as usual. What about me? To keep things in balance my crew should be all-Canadian. I suggested to Lorna that we have our good friends Ken and Linda Coulson, and Ernie and Glad Whate over for dinner some night — haven't seen them for a dog's age. So we did just that, and wouldn't you know, somehow the table talk got around to sailing. I knew the Whates were sailors; they have a 23-foot sloop very similar to our Grampion 23, *Lorna* M. And it turned out that the Coulsons love sailing too, if on a smaller scale; they have a Muskoka M1.

Well, I guess that right then and there was when thinking turned to planning. Sure, the four of them would love to charter with us in the Caribbean! "What goes on?" shouted the first mate. "Are you planning another cruise? Have you and David been putting your heads together again without telling me?"

When I sent the good news across the Pond, David came right back with the news that if I could raise a crew of six, he could do likewise. And as three are better than two, he would charter three F&C 44's and would bring over two crews from England. Outnumbered again by those darn Brits, but at least there would be one all-Canadian boat and I was to have my second shot at being captain. The date was set for the middle two weeks of February.

A few days prior to the charter date, the rest of my crew came to Montserrat and stayed with us at Wilson's Folly. On the big day the six of us flew to St. Lucia and taxied to Trade Winds Marina. There she was — *Korsar*, our F&C 44 charter. Later in the day the British contingent arrived, or most of it. The third crew had had a very sad experience. One of its male members had died suddenly three days before they were to fly out. His wife naturally opted out. At short notice she was replaced by another woman, but the crew was still one man short. They fixed this by hiring a captain from Trade Winds. Our three boats, peas in a pod, were moored at the jetty. They were *Sea Soldier*, Captain Bromley-Martin; *Ennisharon*, professional captain; and *Korsar*, Captain Wilson. We had a big dinner ashore, then settled down in our respective craft for the night. As captain, I drew the aft cabin, which was quite large and had its own private head and shower. The Whates took the forward cabin, and the Coulsons made do with the main salon. There was a second complete washroom between these last two cabins.

The next morning we were given a thorough introduction to *Korsar* by Ted Bull, the Trade Winds resident manager. She was beautiful beyond belief, and everything worked — all sorts of navigational instruments, deep freeze, refrigerator, propane stove. Instruction period over, we prepared to set sail. As these were unknown waters to all of us, it was decided that a pilot would go with *Korsar* until we were out of Rodney Bay and into the open sea. We would lead the other two boats out. Rodney Bay is a huge man-made yacht basin capable of sheltering hundreds of yachts. It was made by dredging out a large swampy area and connecting this new basin to the sea by cutting a passage through the beach at Gros Islet Bay. Once through this narrow gap, our pilot climbed into his dinghy that we had towed, and left us to our own resources.

This was my first experience at handling a ketch, so for a while there was some fear and trepidation. We hoisted main and jenny, and set off down the leeward side of St. Lucia. As our start had been delayed because of the long indoctrination period, we decided on a relatively short sail to end up at Souffriere Bay, where we hoped to anchor for our first night.

The anchorage in Souffriere Bay is really something. It is right in the shadow of St. Lucia's most impressive landmark, the Pitons, two conical peaks that shoot up almost vertically out of the sea. They are so steep as to be unscalable, and they hang over the bay below looking as if they are ready to drop on any fool mortals who dare shelter at their feet. After an early, hurried breakfast that first morning, we set off on the long run to Bequia. Better learn about sailing these two-masted things, I guess. Up went our mizzen, along with our mighty main and very impressive jenny. All three of our F&C 44's flew out of the bay together and headed south urged on by pretty strong winds. Then, almost from nowhere — actually it came straight down from the top of the Pitons — a vertical down blast hit us, drove the bow almost underwater, and set us spinning around on our keel like a sea-going top. Well, that sure scared the hell out of at least one F&C 44 captain that day: me! Enough of this ketch bit; let's get back to something that I know, like a good old sloop. Down came the mizzen. It was furled and flaked down, to stay that way for almost all the rest of the cruise. The other captains were more courageous than me; they stuck with their three sails. With over 60 miles to go to our anchorage at Bequia that night, it would appear that I would be bringing my lightly clothed *Korsar* in a very poor third. But I had read in the ship's instruction book that the F&C 44 sailed best when the angle of heel was kept low and that it handled equally well as a sloop or a ketch, so we would see. Certainly under much lighter press of canvas, *Korsar* was markedly easier than the hard-worked *Sea Soldier* and *Ennisharon*, who were running with lee rail under most of the time. Much to our surprise, and my delight, we not only kept pace with our hard-pressed mates, we actually drew ahead of them quite often!

It is a long run from St. Lucia to St. Vincent, quite a bit of it real open-sea sailing completely out of sight of land, and in this section the weather took a foul turn. Black line squalls with heavy winds and rain appeared about every half hour. The only way to handle these was to roller furl the jenny just before the squall hit us, and turn into the wind under the main only and ride it out. One time, as the blackest of the squalls was roaring up on us, the jenny furling line jammed! Something had to be done, and smartly. Donning a safety harness and putting strongman Ken at the wheel, I worked my way to the foredeck to tackle the nasty job of hand-stowing that wildly flapping genoa jib. The waves were like mountains. I was on my hands and knees trying to hang on. For pure safety sake, I snapped my safety harness to the handrail right at the bow. Bang! The squall hit, the bow plunged underwater and I flew over the port bow like a tether ball at the end of my safety harness. The part of my body with the greatest amount of padding hit the side of the boat with a bone-jarring crack, the bow took another plunge, I did another man-on-the-flying-trapeze act, hit the starboard side another good crack, and at the end of the third wild plunge of the bow, found myself back on deck and struggling again with that wild mountain of flapping canvas! This time I was lucky. I got it all gathered in and tied up, somehow, so that it no longer presented such a challenge, and then got back at the wheel and on course for Bequia once again. A bit later, the weather condition improved a lot, we cleared the fouled furling line, got our jenny back in use, pulled into Admiralty Bay in the middle of the afternoon, and dropped anchor there at the same moment as the other two boats. We had had a relatively easy sail; the other two had beaten their brains out! I guess German Freres knew whereof he spoke when he said, "Remember, the F&C 44 was designed to sail best when the angle of heel is kept low." It had been a day to make me realize just how good was our crew. As first mate, Lorna was a constant source of help and sound advice, and as head of the galley slaves, very useful in keeping the crew's bodies and souls together. Ernie, with years of Power

Squadron behind him, was an excellent navigator. Glad, his wife, a good sailor, was always ready with a helping hand. And the youngsters, Ken and Linda, supplied all the pep and vinegar sometimes lacking in the older members of the crew. Ken's knowledge of engines also made him a most useful engineer.

At Bequia we saw a very unusual-looking ship come to anchor in the outer harbour. It was British from its flag, but what type it was we hadn't the faintest idea. A few minutes later a landing barge put off from the ship headed for the town. As it drew abreast of our flotilla, it suddenly veered toward *Sea Soldier*, David's boat. A voice over a loud bullhorn aboard the barge demanded, "By what right do you fly the white ensign?" David's reply that he was a Royal Navy captain and a member of the Royal Yacht Squadron settled that question. The captain then invited the crew of the *Sea Soldier* to come aboard his ship, HMS *Fearless*. On his return, David gave us a full description of this rather unusual war ship. It was known as a harbour attack vessel. It carried four fully armed tanks, and these were carried two apiece in two tank-landing craft which were housed in dry dock below the stern deck. When these were to be deployed, seacocks were opened and the stern of the *Fearless* allowed to sink some 14 feet. The transom of the ship, actually two huge steel doors, swung open, and the two landing craft, now afloat in the belly of the ship, would start up their own engines. Leaving *Fearless*, they would dash for the shore, or harbour, drop their bow landing ramps, and away would go the four tanks to the attack. Even in her half-sunken condition, *Fearless* was capable of full operation. When the tank-landing craft returned, they entered their quarters in the bowels of *Fearless*, the ship was pumped out, and it was then ready for whatever action was required. Of interest to us, particularly, was the fact that David had acted in an advisory capacity in the design of this unusual ship. Later, at a beach party and barbeque on Princess Margaret beach, we met a lot of the crew. They were all young lads, and very happy ones, as they were just at the end of a six-month tour of duty, next stop home. That is what they thought. A week later they were down in the very deep south as *Fearless* did her part in the Falkland Islands war between England and Argentina.

On the whole, ours was a leisurely, fun cruise, but it had its moments, like when we were coming back north from Petit St. Vincent and we were hit by a violent squall just as we were trying to locate Grand de Col, a very shallow and dangerous reef somewhere between Palm Island and Union. Visibility was decreasing rapidly and we had to find the marker on that reef — we had to! If we didn't we would end up on the reef for sure. Luckily, just as the heavy mist brought on by the squall was obliterating everything, we found the marker. We already had the sails down and the engine running, so I just headed into the squall and brought *Korsar*'s bow as close as I dared to that marker and rode out the squall right there.

That over, we went into Union Island, but not liking the appearance of the anchorage, we decided against staying there for the night, and went on to the next island, Mayero. The wind had died away completely and there was not a ripple on the waters of the bay. This will be a really quiet night, we thought, no need for an anchor watch, everyone can turn in and have a good sleep. Which we all did. With all six of us sawing it off, snores echoing from bow to stern, CRASH, something hit the boat and she quivered from end to end. Everyone was on deck in seconds. What could have caused that noise? Had another boat hit us? We had been alone in Saltwhistle Bay when night fell. There wasn't a boat in sight. Had we hit bottom? The depth sounder showed 20 feet; we only drew six! We did a thorough search, but no answer. Nothing else to do, back we went to bed. We were just nicely asleep when CRASH, there it was again. Well, there had to be an answer, and as captain I decided that it was my duty to find it. Sending all the others back to their slumbers, I stayed on deck, determined to find out what had caused that crash, even if I had to spend the whole night doing it. Just as I was about to despair of learning anything, CRASH! Looking hastily around I could see no explanation for the noise. But wait a minute. We weren't facing as we had been when we anchored;

our anchor was no longer out ahead of us. Rushing up to the bow, I quickly discovered the reason for the unexplained midnight crashes. There was absolutely not a breath of wind, so what had moved us from our anchorage? Well, it seemed that a slight current, finding its way into circular Saltwhistle Bay, had swung us around and away from our anchor. No problem, until a further swing of *Korsar* had brought her bow up short on the heavy anchor chain and this, slapping hard against the iron pipe which carried it through the steel hawse hole, made the loud crash that had pretty nearly ruined the night for the crew. Mystery explained, we went back to sleep and let it crash all night.

Back at Bequia, and cruise end only two days off, we decided to stage a race between *Sea Soldier*, *Ennisharon* and *Korsar*. It was to be a long beat, about 60 miles, up to Marigot Bay in St. Lucia. And this was to be a no-holds-barred contest between boats, crews and captains. Rules? Well, we would start together at 6:30 the next morning, would take whatever course we liked, use our engines only in case of a dead calm, and the first boat into Marigot Bay was the winner. We were off on time and all headed out into the choppy Bequia channel. Knowing these islands and the peculiar habit of the easterly trade winds to whip around the end of an island and cling to it, I elected to sail quite close to St. Vincent while the other two went miles to the west to get better winds — which they didn't because St. Vincent's high mountains cause the wind to go sky high as it passes over the island and it is a long way offshore before the wind gets back to water level. While *Sea Soldier* and *Ennisharon* were starving for wind, *Korsar* was sliding up the lee shore of St. Vincent at a great rate. Of course this couldn't last forever. When we were about a third of the way past St. Vincent, we ran out of wind. Flat calm. So start the iron topsail! After using our engine for another third of the length of the island, we picked up the breeze sweeping around the north point of the island, set sail, shut off the engine, and proceeded merrily across the channel between St. Vincent and St. Lucia. Needless to say, the other two boats were out of sight. Or were they? Way back, and well out to sea, we spotted a sail that might belong to one of our flotilla. But we had a great lead and we held it all the way to Marigot Bay. We were first in, the winners! About two hours later, just at sundown, in came *Ennisharon*, second. Where was David Bromley-Martin in *Sea Soldier*? When he finally sailed in, the next day at noon, I had my whole crew standing rigidly at attention in salute to the pride of the British Navy. All he could say was "Damn colonials!"

All good things come to an end. Later that day we pulled into Rodney Bay, said goodbye to all our Brit friends, and to the three fine ships, *Korsar*, *Sea Soldier* and *Ennisharon*, certainly, as David stated, the best charter vessels afloat.

In the years following, we did more cruises with the Bromley-Martins. The four of us, plus another Brit couple, Jonnie and Gordon Strang, set out in another fine F&C 44 on a hard sail to Grenada and back to St. Lucia. All went well, but we did have one experience that was almost a disaster. Flying down the coast of Grenada, pushed by a 35-knot wind, we were suddenly hit by a wild gust that laid our ship on her beam's end and tossed all six of us onto the low side of the cockpit, then underwater! With the cockpit full, we had only seconds to do something. But what? David and Gordon furled the jenny — oh so carefully — while I let go all sheet ropes and brought the ship as much to wind as possible. This did the trick, freeing all the weight of the water in the three sails. The F&C staggered, shook herself, and came upright! Knockdown — bad word in any sailor's vocabulary, but a much worse thing to experience!

In 1986, this time with a crew of eight, we tried out a new French boat, the Beneteau First 456. It, like our F&Cs, had been designed by German Freres of Argentina, both were excellent boats. We anchored one day at Union Island, which has a rather poor anchorage, protected from the sea only by an underwater reef which afforded no wind protection at all. It was dead calm when we went to bed. Then crash! At 5:30 a.m. we rushed up on deck to find that we had just crashed into another moored yacht! I got the engine going, said "Sorry" to the other boat's irate captain, and moved back into safe waters. Examination showed that our plow anchor had been fouled by a very large plastic bucket. When the morning wind rose, we dragged, and if it hadn't been for that conveniently moored yacht, we would have been on a rocky shore in minutes. Right there and then David and I decided that our bare-boating days were over. If we sailed again we would have a captain. "And a cook too!" screamed our two first mates.

And that is the way it went. Just a month ago, February 1990, we completed a most enjoyable two-week cruise from Antigua to Guadelupe, the Saintes, and Dominica. Now the cautious sailor, I had a very safe 67-foot sloop with a crew of eight and a paid crew of three — one of them a cute three-year-old blonde, the daughter of our boat's owners. Push-on-regardless David had a very sleek-looking ocean racer, a Mystic 60. Our ship, *Elise*, rode as if it were an ocean liner, but the 45-knot winds one day caused David's *Sassenach* to ship a green roller that filled the cockpit, thus supplying them with an unlisted and totally unde- sired on-board swimming pool!

Where will our next exciting cruise take us?

Chapter 15

Tall Ships

Throughout my boating life, right up to my retirement from racing, I had had little time for or interest in craft other than motorboats. I was a true stinkboater. Oh, sure, there were others, sailboats, for instance. I had had a few and had enjoyed using them, but my only real love had been fast racing craft. I knew of and admired the fine wind-powered racers that competed for the coveted America's Cup, and I knew of the great attraction that the largest of the tall ships had for the sail-conscious part of the boating fraternity, but that was not my cup of tea.

My insurance company changed everything. No more racing, no more race boats. So what would I do on the water? I readjusted my sights and began to look around. One day, while cruising in the *Island Princess* through the Panama Canal, I came across one of the saddest sights imaginable for a boat buff. It was the already rotting remains of what must have been one of the world's most beautiful sailboats, a large four-master, and it lay there very poorly moored to the canal side with its rigging drooping and only half supporting the tatters of its sails, which dropped down onto the filthy, littered decks. As we slid past this sad sight I noticed her name on the stern plate, *ANTARNA*. The name didn't mean anything to me, but I decided I'd look into it later. It might be interesting to learn the history of this once proud beauty now in the last stages of decay.

This encounter also jogged my memory. I remembered an early meeting with Captain Bromley-Martin and mention of "his" schooners. Schooners were definitely tall ships, as were the sloops and ketches, large and small, that had taught me the joys of sailing such craft on lake and ocean. Maybe this was the time to grow up a bit and expand my new-found enjoyment of sailing to the much bigger tall ships. So I wrote to Captain Bromley-Martin, reminded him of our conversation at Hope Platt's home in Montserrat, and asked for information about his schooners. It seems that he was head of the Sail Training Association of the United Kingdom, STA for short, a body which owned and operated the two 153-foot schooners *Sir Winston Churchill* and *Malcolm Miller*. Starting every March and finishing in December these two ships did cruises every two weeks. The purpose of this service was to train young men, and sometimes young ladies, to become sailors, to learn how to live with fellow humans, and to become well-adjusted people. The crews were always in the age bracket 16 to 21 years. That seemed to wash me out, but I asked David if they ever took old fuddy-duddies out. "Certainly," he said, "if they know enough to be able to take a berth as officers." I found out immediately what qualifications I needed, boned up on them, and made my application to become an officer of one of the STA schooners, as soon as possible. Almost by return post I was advised that I had been assigned a berth on the *Malcolm Miller* and that I should report aboard on a given date. I was also told that I would be an officer occupying a position bearing the unusual title of "Supernumerary." What was I to be? Little did I suspect that this title, "Supra" as I would be known to the crew, was the lowest of the low in the officer category, and that the word supernumerary was really an archaic Old English expression meaning. "general handyman"!

I crossed "the Pond" via Air Canada, got myself to Southampton, and found the *Malcolm Miller* moored alongside at one of the many jetties. As I stepped aboard, I was amazed and confused by the apparently haphazard appearance of the standing rigging — hundreds of ropes, furled sails in a most hopeless mess! Had I bitten off more than I could chew? I'd never learn the uses of this tangle of cordage. But right away, the bosun, a very tough character, took the officers in hand and made certain that we knew the purpose and proper use of every "bit of string," as he called the heavy ropes of the rigging.

248

The crew of 39 was to arrive the next day, so this, my first day aboard, was spent learning all about my duties as supernumerary. First, I found that I was the purser's assistant and could also claim the title of assistant purser. That sounded more impressive than supernumerary, which somehow suggested to me the end of the line, but I was to learn that titles didn't make a bit of difference, Old Supra was still the joe-boy. My first job was to sign on all 39 new crew members the next day. At that time I was to collect from them all of their credentials, passports, travel papers, tickets, money and valuables, store them safely away, dole them out as required by the owners, and to be responsible for crew entertainment aboard and ashore. I was to hold myself in readiness to perform any sailing task that was assigned to me. I was to help the purser run an every-evening tuck shop that purveyed sweets of all kinds to the ever-hungry crew. I had to stand in as watch officer if necessary, stand my trick at the wheel, and even polish brass on the daily "Happy Hour" house-cleaning of the whole ship. And, in the absence of a qualified surgeon aboard, I was to act as the ship's doctor. God help the crew!

The next day came all too soon. The signing on of the 39 green-as-grass youngsters was some job. And there were 11 part-time officers like myself, plus a permanent crew of five: the captain, chief officer, engineer, bosun, the cook and his assistant. The crew signed on, I just had a very short period to become acquainted with the rest of the 16-strong "top brass" section before the order came to cast off.

I was very surprised to see one of the new crew members — he had never been aboard a ship before — put at the wheel for the difficult task of getting the *Malcolm Miller* away from quayside, through the muddle of traffic in Southampton Harbour, and out to the open sea. But that was the way it was. A crew member had his assigned duty to do, so let's get on with it. Actually, the lad at the wheel was backed up by the watch officer to whose watch he had been assigned, and this man very quietly gave him minute-by-minute orders that, followed out correctly, got the

Malcolm Miller under full sail.

The *Miller*'s Captain, Mark Kemmis-Betty and the mizzen watch crew.

Malcolm Miller through this initial, very trying part of the two-week voyage.

When we hit the open sea, we hit wild weather. Strong winds, very choppy seas. Inside of minutes every person aboard (except the purser and his lowly assistant) was sick as a dog. We didn't have time to get sick, especially me. As the new ship's doctor I was handing out seasick pills like they were going out of style. The going got so bad that when we came across the British Aircraft Carrier *Ark Royal*, lying-to in the shelter of nearby land, Tony Butcher, our captain, ordered us to anchor in her lee, and there we rode out the storm. As the crew members were still in pretty tough shape, we made an unscheduled overnight stop at a nearby jetty and the men were allowed to go ashore to recover their land legs.

What a cruise this turned out to be! We had wild gales, flat calms, rain, fog, bone-chilling cold, and hot, burning sun. We visited out-of-the-way places. In France we visited Roscoff and St. Malo, where we were privileged to see the world's first, and only, tidal-power electrical generating set-up. In the Channel we stopped at the islands of Guernsey, Aldernay and Sark. We also stopped at the small island of Lundy, made famous, to stamp collectors (like myself) by the actions of the former owner of this small bit of the U.K. Mistakenly feeling that as owner of the island, he was its rightful ruler, he had proclaimed himself King of Lundy and issued his own currency and postage stamps! The monetary unit he named "Puffin" after the funny-looking sea birds that inhabited the island. Unfortunately for this self-named king, when some of his postage stamps appeared in the mainland U.K. post offices, questions were asked in the British Parliament, and very shortly the King of Lundy was dethroned. On the U.K. mainland we visited Weymouth and Milford Haven.

For thrills we had plenty of wild sailing with lee rail under. I was at the wheel during Happy Hour one day when the water roaring along our underwater lee deck shot over the transom like the tailrace from a huge hydro-power generator and the log in

251

front of me wavered just on the 14-knot mark — an astounding speed for a 153-footer! We felt our way up the fog-bound English Channel with our radar and all 55 pairs of eyes aboard "watching out" for the heavy boat traffic that was all around us, and too darn close for comfort. There were climbs to the dizzying 102-foot crow's-nest, swims in the Channel's ice-cold waters, and we were forever polishing brass. Our ship's bell, mounted on the bridge, and on which the time was tolled every half hour, seemed to be always dull in spite of its daily polish. But, work or play, enjoyment or drudgery, these things were all parts of the thrill of a lifetime. My first taste of the real tall ships made me hungry for more.

Over the next few years I did nine more cruises with STA, four more in the *Malcolm Miller* and five with her sister ship, *Sir Winston Churchill*. We covered different areas, such as the Irish Sea, Bay of Biscay, the South Coast, the English Channel and the North Sea. Not all were as exciting as the first one, but they all had their high points, and I wouldn't have missed any of them.

As one cruise came to an end at Southampton, we learned that it was Cook's birthday. The officers got together and planned a party for him. In a weak moment I offered to make West Indian rum punch for the party of 16. A big job, but I felt that I could handle it. Then the Captain said, "The cruise is over, so the boys are also free to drink if they so wish. Let's have the party in the half deck (crew's living, eating and sleeping quarters) and, Harold, can you make punch for all? I think we should have about three rounds." With 55 souls aboard, that meant 165 rum punches! I commandeered all the canned fruit juices I could find in the ship's stores, also four large bottles of Old Navy Rum, and two huge 10-gallon cooking pots from the galley, then I sallied ashore and raided the local stores for Angostura Bitters and the final necessity, nutmeg. I spent the rest of the afternoon in my tiny cabin mixing all of this hell's brew in those two big pots. The party went well, as did the punch. Then, in just reasonable shape, all but the three of us who had volunteered as a harbour crew went ashore for further festivities. In the still of the wardroom and at a late hour, I produced a pitcher of punch that I had hidden away at the party, and the three of us were about to toast each other when, down came Mark Kemmis-Betty, our captain. "Ah ha!" he said. "I thought as much! I'll have a nightcap also." That was quite a party to end what had been quite a cruise.

My last STA cruise, in the *Churchill*, was made in 1986. On that occasion I took my grandson, Steven Elliott, along with me. He was a lowly trainee and I a lordly officer who had to be addressed as "Sir" at all times. A sailor's life can be hard at times, especially if he is a raw trainee and his grandfather is one of the afterguard, but I must say that I was very pleased with Steven's performance; he became the best upper-rigging man in the crew.

That cruise ended my STA adventures, at least up until the present, and I think that there is little likelihood of my being offered another berth in the future, as in 1986 I was told that I was already four years over the allowable age limit! All ten of my STA cruises were high points in my sailing career. Probably my best memory of this experience was the realization of what these two-week cruises did for the crews of trainees. These lads came from all walks of life and from many countries. There were polished products of public schools, toughs from London, and farmer's and miner's sons. In every case, at the end of the cruise, all these lads had become not only excellent sailors, but also fine, self-reliant, well-mannered young gentlemen. This is what sail-training is all about. I hope that the tall ships remain with us forever!

The story of one of these fine ships, the *Sea Cloud*, is worth the telling. In the mid-twenties, Edward Hutton married Marjorie Post (of Post Toasties fame) and gave her, as a wedding present, a beautiful four-masted barque called *Hussar*. When their marriage broke up, Marjorie kept the boat and renamed it *Sea Cloud*. During WWII the ship served as a sub-chaser with the U.S. Navy, where her surprising turn of speed — thanks to her 30,000 square feet of canvas and her 6000 h.p. diesels —

must have caused consternation to some U-boat captains. After the war she was sold to dictator Trujillo of the Dominican Republic. He called her *Angelita*. When Trujillo died, the *Angelita* was bought by an American and renamed *Patria*. Not liking her $200,000 a year maintenance costs, he in turn sold her to Panamanian interests, and she became *Antarna*.

Remember what I said about that rotting hulk in the Panama Canal? Remember the name *Antarna*? There she was, and just about at the end of her tether. But luckily some wealthy German enthusiasts saw her, bought her, and took her home to the land of her birth, Germany. There, in the shipyard where she was built, she was lovingly restored to mint condition, even to the fireplace in the master's bedroom suite and the gold-plated fixtures in his bathroom. They then renamed her *Sea Cloud*.

Today she sails Caribbean waters as the most expensive charter yacht afloat. And why shouldn't she be just that? After all, she was the largest, fastest, and costliest private sailing yacht ever built. Long life to you *Sea Cloud*!

Chapter 16

The Dripping Tap

Ever had a tap that kept dripping? Well, having finished writing virtually everything I know about my hobby, I find that, like that dripping tap, my mind just won't turn off. It has kept up a constant dribble of places, names, things, and events, all connected with boats.

Remember Count Rossi? While getting ready for our race in Detroit with him, a boatbuilder friend of mine, Bryson Shields, badly in need of an electric drill and a certain size of bit, approached the big, burly Italian in charge of Rossi's fabulous spares, parts, and tool set-up. Knowing that this dumb guard would have no knowledge of English, Bryson made all sorts of extravagant and meaningful motions, to which Luigi replied by motioning for Bryson to help himself. Returning later to replace the borrowed tools, Bryson decided to give Luigi a language lesson. Summoning his very best Italian accent and vocabulary, he said "Gracias senor!" Luigi simply said, "That's all right, Bud. Anytime you want anything, just ask Luigi!"

Count Rossi had two boats in that Detroit race, *Alagi* and *Aradam*. He drove one and had another Italian as driver of the second. The old Indy maestro Ralph DePalma was on hand to see that his compatriots got full measure while in the States, and as he knew Charlie Volker well, Lorna and I were taken into Rossi's pits to meet the competition. DePalma, introducing Rossi's number two, said, "This is Guido Cataneo. He doesn't understand or speak English, but fair warning Mr. Wilson, he knows all about blonds. Keep a close watch on your lovely mechanic!"

Still at Detroit, but years later, after Lorna had temporarily given up her mechanic's seat to Charlie Volker, Charlie and I headed for the start of our first race as a team. Charlie's first job was to watch his stopwatch and the 10-foot-diameter starting clock, and give me the word when to turn and race back at top speed for the starting line. He hadn't given me the signal yet, but a glance over my shoulder showed that big clock indicating just two seconds to go! Well, we made the best recovery that we could from that spot down near the Belle Isle Bridge, and finished last. Of course there were other reasons for our last-place finish that day, and other reasons why my face was red. After a couple of laps our engine had begun to overheat badly, so we stopped. Feeling that something must have plugged the water inlet, I tore off my racing jumpsuit and dove into the river, pulled out the offending garbage, and hauled myself back into *Miss Canada*. We were right at the Belle Isle Bridge when this mid-race swim occurred, and as I made my appearance a wild roar of laughter went up! I had forgotten that I had nothing on under that jumpsuit.

Walter Harvey, my Harmsworth racing mechanic, was a small man. He could squeeze into the tiniest places. One day he was in the very cramped place where the two large batteries used to start the huge Griffon were located. He was flat on his stomach in the bilge and crammed under the port exhaust manifold. Hearing a distant siren, and knowing that it was a friend named Sparks coming to see us, I said, "Walter, there's Sparks!" Like a snake with the jitters, Walter shot backwards out of his cramped position, flew out onto the dock and ran! When he had calmed down and realized that there would be no explosion, Walter yelled, "Next time say MR. SPARKS!"

That brings back a memory of another *real* explosion that we had. Charlie and I had acquired a used Merlin out of a Spitfire which was still in running condition. As you never can tell how good an engine is until you try it, Charlie and I decided to run this one on our dynamometer. Ready to run, we started up this war-weary Merlin and let it run no-load for several minutes. As all seemed fair, we wound up the dynamometer to full capacity and opened the throttle wide. And it was good, that old engine. It peaked out just a bit over the 1,600-horsepower mark. Not bad. Maybe with a bit of careful tuning? Then all hell broke loose! Bits and pieces of tortured metal flew all over our basement test cell. And the crazy engine, although it was trying to jump right off its mountings, still continued roaring. Finally, Charlie got to the control panel and switched off the ignition. Silence, and what a relief. It was a wonder we were not hit by those flying hunks of metal. Days later we found the reason for this terrible explosion that almost cut that Merlin in two: a broken connecting rod. The break area showed that it had been cracked for some time. The Spitfire pilot who set that plane down for the last time certainly did it at exactly the *right* time!

After WWII, my company, Ingersoll Machine & Tool Company, got into the manufacture of a few interesting, novel, and not too successful bits of marine equipment. One was a small water-jet propulsion unit to be used in small fishing boats and which would allow operation in very shallow or rocky waters. To publicize this, we developed one with a special high-powered go-kart engine. This unit was mounted on an aquaplane, on which the operator stood, hung onto the handlebars, and with them and a lot of body English, directed this thing we called WHAT ZIT. It would do about 30 mph and was quite a thrill, but also quite a handful. John Loveridge, my general manager at Ingersoll Machine, driving it into the bay at our Muskoka island one day, did the wrong thing and ended up on the beach, running!

Another was the Fly-Lo, a two-place hovercraft that we built for sport and special purposes like flying over thin ice on a lake, over soft heavy snow, or any handy golf course. It had a twin-hulled frame and a Volkswagen engine which drove it about 40 mph on land and 30 on water. It could go forward, backwards, and even sideways if you didn't watch out. It could hover motionless, and it could do 180-degree turns that would have put my *Little Miss Canada I* to shame. It was fun to drive but quite unpredictable, as I found out when I broke a rib giving it its first sea trials. Unfortunately both the water jet unit and Fly-Lo were ahead of their time, and both died a natural death after a relatively short production period.

The third venture, a free-piston engine, we hoped would be a real profit-maker. Over a period of three years we worked with the inventor, a young German engineer named Tom Braun, and with Queens University in Kingston, where Tom was on the Engineering staff. In the simplest of terms, a free-piston engine is an air compressor. It has one cylinder, sealed at both ends, and in this cylinder are two pistons, free of all such things as connecting rods, flywheels and any other moving parts except the pistons themselves. By means of a diesel explosion between the two pistons, they are forced outwards and then bounce back for another explosion. All the air compressed, plus all the products of combustion, are piped to an external turbine which turns the power from the engine into useful rotary motion. There is a lot more to it, but that will give you an idea. Our big objective with these engines was to sell them to the Canadian government for installation in fishing craft all across Canada. Besides being much more efficient than an ordinary diesel, these units could be tucked into any otherwise useless corner of the fishing boat, thus leaving the useful centre of the boat unencumbered for fishing purposes. The government claimed that with our engines — if they worked — a 40-foot vessel would have as much usable space as a 60-footer fitted with standard diesels. The big day came when all the brass arrived from Ottawa to see our engine prove itself in our fine test cell at Queens University.

258

Already it had run over 1,000 hours at full throttle, no problems, and we were very confident that, tests over, the government would give us the long-desired order. So we started it up, and after a few minutes warm up, opened up to full power. It ran perfectly for half an hour, and then, with a horribly loud and very expensive noise, our engine blew itself to pieces! Horrified, I was looking at the mess in wonder, when the top brass came over, put his hand on my shoulder and said, "Don't take it too hard, Mr. Wilson. We have seen things like this happen before." And he left, forever.

Besides the tragic experience that Lorna had with the *Sarah Maude*, she also had some lighter moments. Backing out from Greavette's dock one day, the wind caught the *Sarah Maude*, and fearing that she would hit the tracks of the underwater marine railway used for launching boats, I yelled to Lorna to grab our 15-foot pike-pole and push us off. She did just that, but the pike slipped on the dock and Lorna did a most masterful swan dive into Lake Muskoka to the edification of about 50 onlookers!

Then there was the day when the *Sarah Maude* rested at the jetty at my father's Florida home. The boat was dirty — Dad hadn't used it for weeks — so Lorna and I, armed with two new buckets, mops, soap and wipers, set out to give her a bath. The tide had pushed the boat 3 feet away from the jetty, so I picked up a short two-by-four, and laying it between dock and the boat's gunwale, I walked over carrying all the stuff except the two brand-new buckets. Safely aboard, I told Lorna to come aboard with the buckets. Just then the tide gave another nudge, and that slender two-by-four bridge, and Lorna, dropped into the briny! Seconds later, after a healthy push up from the bottom, 10 feet down, Lorna surfaced and tried to hand me one of the buckets. The second one pulled her to the bottom. Again she pushed up and tried to give me the other bucket, and down she went again. After repeating this jack-in-the-box stunt several times, she came to the surface to find my father and me about to expire from laughter. With a shouted "You and your damn buckets!" she let them both go. An Irish temper is a terrible thing, isn't it?

Aboard the *Malcolm Miller* for my first experience of tall ship sailing, a cocky young trainee said to me, "Sir, I haven't seen you up in the crow's-nest yet." "Get me a safety harness," I replied, "and let's go." At the top of the ratlines, with my head pushed against the platform of the crow's-nest, I came to a sudden stop. No place to go! The trainee said, "Let go, and when you are falling backwards, reach through this hole in the floor, grab this bar and chin yourself." Easy? Well, I managed it and soon was standing with the trainee, both of us looking down on the *Malcolm Miller* 100 feet below. "Didn't think you'd have the nerve," he said. Young punk! Looking up I saw the topmost yardarm, about 20 feet up the mast. The only way to get to it was by a series of short spikes sticking out either side from the mast. "I wonder what it is like out on the end of that arm," I said. "Don't know," he replied, "and you're not going to find out." Without a word I started up. When I reached the yardarm, there was my tormentor, right behind me. Getting our heels well caught on the flapping foot rope that hung just below the yardarm, lying on our bellies on the arm itself, we edged our way out to the extreme end. Boy, was that scary! Safely down on deck a few minutes later, we found that we had developed a quite healthy respect for each other.

Remember Phil Brulé, the man who bawled me out for half-hitching the main sheet on his boat? Well, he and another old friend, Dr. Mal Hill, one of Canada's foremost radiologists, did another cruise with me in the STA schooners, this time aboard the *Sir Winston Churchill*. One day I persuaded the captain to let me go out in the ship's boat to get some good pictures under sail. While I was doing this, and the captain completely oblivious, Phil ran the Canadian flag to the peak. My pictures were excellent — so good in fact that STA used them in advertising litera-

Supra – (the author) accepts a dare to climb to the crow's nest.

ture. Not till after printing was it discovered that the *Churchill* was flying Canadian colours instead of British!

This same ship gave me one of my greatest sailing thrills. During Happy Hour every day the crew cleaned ship and the officers sailed it. One time, in very heavy winds, I was at the wheel with two lads detailed to help me hold it, otherwise it would have sent me flying. The lee rail was under and water was roaring the whole length of the deck. With the log in front of me wavering on 14 knots (very fast for a 153-footer), the captain yelled in my ear, "How do you like this?" Silly question! Before I could give a better answer than an ear-to-ear grin, Mark Kemmis-Betty, the skipper, said, "I thought so. Well, I guess I had better get some sail off this ship before I sink it."

And I'll never forget this one. On one of the *Malcolm Miller* cruises, as Supra I had been assigned the upper bunk in the tiny stateroom that I shared with the purser. He always wondered how I managed to get out of my bunk without falling. The last morning of the cruise, I managed to do just that. I fell the 6 feet backwards, and landed in a heap, jammed between the bunks and the cabin bulkhead. My mate managed to get me out just in time to help him with his last task of paying off the crew. That over, I grabbed a bus for Heathrow airport, where I was to catch my plane for Canada. Arriving at the airport, I found that I had grown quite stiff. I had quite a bit of trouble walking and carrying my duffel bag. When I reached Toronto, it was something else again. I couldn't walk at all, as one leg was useless. I solved this at the luggage reclaim by using a cart to carry my duffel bag *and* me! Lorna, outside the glass barrier between customs and freedom, got quite a shock when she saw me shuffling along with my left leg riding the luggage cart while my right pushed us slowly across the floor. It had been a great cruise, and even though handicapped at its end, I had enjoyed every minute.

Handicapped? Well, that makes me think about a very special ship that I saw, again at the Southampton dockside. She was England's newest and largest tall ship. Lorna and I watched her sails being stowed at the end of her successful sea trials and were immediately invited aboard by her captain, my old STA friend Mark Kemmis-Betty. We were her very first invited visitors. This beautiful 173-foot, three-masted, ship-rigged schooner had been built by her owners, Jubilee Trust, for one particular reason: to be able to take handicapped persons to sea as active sailors, not just as passengers. Mark showed us, with obvious pride, all the special arrangements that had been made to make this possible, such things as electric hoists between decks and to the crow's-nest, ramps and deck tracks for use of wheelchairs, special eating, sleeping and living facilities, and electric winches operable by wheelchair occupants. It was even possible for a blind person to properly man the wheel by steering with the aid of an audio compass. The *Lord Nelson*, as this new ship was called, was now ready for the first of her scheduled cruises, and already there were people on the waiting list trying to obtain berths. Besides the eight permanent crew members, there would be 40 new crew members signed on for every cruise, 20 of them able-bodied and 20 handicapped.

Later on, at the end of that summer, Mark told me that the effect on the morale of crippled, lame and blind crew members was unbelievable when they found out to their delight that they could handle their appointed duties just as well as their able-bodied buddies. I hope that the *Lord Nelson* has a long, happy, and successful life.

Then there was the night that I startled the hell out of all the inhabitants of Keewaydin Island when I dribbled gasoline on the water behind my canoe and then set it alight. That quarter-mile-long flickering flame sure raised a lot of commotion and got me into a lot of trouble!

I said earlier that I got all my love of speed from my father, but many were the quiet, slow cruises I had with mother in *Little Miss Canada II* when she would shout — as a passing boat driver sneered at us — "Okay, Harold, give it to him!" Hell, Mom loved speed too!

Can't shut that tap off. Still dripping! I have mentioned lots of boats, races, episodes and people. There are hordes more, but I'll stop right here and leave the unwritten ones as just what they are, honoured and cherished memories.

And so, as I write "The End" to this record of my boating life, let me say that I hope it has been of interest to my family and to the others who have read it.

To all of my readers, a fair wind and GOOD SAILING!

The Originals – still at it, and still afloat after 57 years at sea together.

Index